Microsoft®
SharePoint®

for
dummies®
A Wiley Brand

Microsoft®
SharePoint®

2nd Edition

by Rosemarie Withee and Ken Withee

A Wiley Brand

Microsoft® SharePoint® For Dummies,® 2nd Edition

Contents at a Glance

Table of Contents

Introduction

Microsoft has started another transition. Previously, SharePoint was a product designed for only the largest enterprises. Then, Microsoft shifted SharePoint to the cloud and made it available to any size organization for as little as $5 per month. Now, Microsoft is transitioning SharePoint once again to simplify it and make it more accessible to smaller organizations. What does this mean? It means that getting started with SharePoint is easier than ever. And when you are ready to dig deeper into the more advanced features of SharePoint, they are still available, too.

This book covers SharePoint Online as of the calendar year 2021 and also touches on the SharePoint Server product. You can think of SharePoint Server as a snapshot of SharePoint Online that is designed to be installed by large IT departments at your organization. SharePoint Online, on the other hand, is the online service-based version of SharePoint that Microsoft delivers to you over the Internet. SharePoint Online is constantly changing. SharePoint Server is a glimpse of SharePoint Online at a specific point in time.

It is important to note that if your organization uses an on-premises version of SharePoint, you need to check what version you are running. *On-premises* means your IT team members have installed the software and they are the ones who manage it for you. It's common for an organization to be running an older version of SharePoint when it is installed on-premises. So be sure to check what version you are running. Past versions of SharePoint On-Premises include SharePoint Server 2013, SharePoint Server 2016, and SharePoint Server 2019.

TIP

If your organization is running SharePoint Online, then you automatically have the latest version of SharePoint and this book is for you. If your organization is running, or planning to run, SharePoint Server, then this book is for you, too. The main difference between SharePoint Online and SharePoint Server is with backend setup, configuration, maintenance. With SharePoint Online, Microsoft covers all of these things for you. With SharePoint Server, your local IT team covers it.

Microsoft understands that people are attached to their smartphones, and as such, they created a SharePoint Mobile App to accommodate everyone. The SharePoint Mobile App is covered throughout the book. In addition to the SharePoint Mobile App, you will also find new service integration for creating workflows using Microsoft Power Automate (Chapter 15), building forms with Microsoft Forms

(Chapter 16), building your own mobile-based apps with Power Apps (Chapter 17), and creating data dashboards with Power BI (Chapter 24). All of these are new since the last edition of this book. Don't let the complexity of these types of features fool you. SharePoint is intended to be a self-service environment, and this book helps you get the most out of the platform without the need for years of experience.

We're not saying that SharePoint is easy; in fact, like any enterprise software system, you can expect to have a bit of a learning curve. Microsoft is on a mission to make the curve as easy as possible. However, if your organization uses SharePoint, you have a wealth of solutions to solve your particular needs, and you don't need a degree in computers to do it.

About This Book

This book is intended for anyone who encounters SharePoint or is curious about using the product. SharePoint is a vast software application with many nooks and crannies, and no single book can cover everything. This book is designed to provide an introduction and an overview of the platform. It shows you how to get the most out of the product, whether you have never used SharePoint before or are deeply familiar with specific aspects it.

Others who may benefit from this book include

>> **Developers:** This isn't a development book, but the best SharePoint developers are those who understand the product. The exciting aspect of SharePoint development is that you don't need to write programming code to develop business solutions in SharePoint. If you can work with a web browser to develop a web presence in a site like Facebook or LinkedIn, then you can develop and administer your own SharePoint site.

>> **IT professionals:** This isn't a book that explains how to set up SharePoint Server for your organization. However, this book helps you understand what features your end users may want to see in SharePoint and how you can make it happen.

>> **Managers:** If you manage a department or business unit, you need to understand how to get the most out of SharePoint. If your company has made significant investments in SharePoint deployment, it'd be a shame if you didn't know how to leverage that investment.

Foolish Assumptions

Because SharePoint is such a huge topic, we have to make some assumptions about your configuration and starting knowledge, such as

>> **You have access to some version of SharePoint Online or SharePoint Server.** If you don't have access to SharePoint, then sign up for SharePoint Online. After the free trial period, it costs as little as $5 a month. If you want to try to install SharePoint yourself for on-premises environments, a trial license is available for 30 days. Just download it from the Microsoft download center and get started.

>> **You're a contributor or administrator.** Of course, many of the scenarios in this book require only that you be a contributor. So long as you know who your administrator is, you can ask that person for elevated permissions. And if you want to be master of your own SharePoint universe as an administrator, you can sign up for SharePoint Online and control all aspects of your SharePoint environment in a fairly intuitive interface.

>> **Ideally, you have a sandbox or test environment where you can try different scenarios.** It isn't the best strategy to lock down security on your human resources site only to find out nobody in your entire organization can get to their pay stubs. You need a test environment or test site where you can play around with SharePoint, and then take that knowledge to your department site. Luckily, if you have access to SharePoint, you have your own personal site that you can explore. Another alternative is to use SharePoint Online. (Yes, you can buy a single license.)

Icons Used in This Book

A handful of icons are used in this book. Here's what they mean:

Tips point out a handy shortcut, or they help you understand something important to SharePoint.

This icon marks something to remember, such as how you handle a particularly tricky part of SharePoint configuration.

TECHNICAL STUFF

This icon is our chance to share with you details about the inner workings of SharePoint. Most of the information you find here pertains to some aspect of SharePoint that requires configuration at the server. That means you can point out the stuff beside this icon to IT and ask IT to make SharePoint do that.

WARNING

Although the Warning icon appears rarely, when you need to be wary of a problem or common pitfall, this icon lets you know.

Beyond the Book

In addition to what you're reading right now, this product also comes with a free access-anywhere Cheat Sheet that describes some common SharePoint site templates, apps, and Web Parts, among other things. To get this Cheat Sheet, simply go to www.dummies.com and enter **SharePoint For Dummies Cheat Sheet** in the Search box.

Where to Go from Here

All right, you're all set and ready to jump into the book. You can jump in anywhere you like — the book was written to allow you to do just that. But if you want to get the full story from the beginning, turn to Chapter 1 — that's where all the action starts. (If you are already familiar with SharePoint, you might want to flip ahead to Chapter 2, where you can get your hands dirty with creating a site and developing it to fit your needs.)

1

Getting Started with SharePoint

IN THIS PART . . .

Get familiar with SharePoint as a product and platform. SharePoint is a complicated beast, and most people use only a smidgen of its functionality.

See how SharePoint Online has changed the game and what it means to use a cloud-based solution, and learn when you should use SharePoint Online or SharePoint On-Premises.

Figure out what it means to develop a SharePoint site and how SharePoint works at a fundamental level.

Get your head around the vastness of SharePoint by exploring some of its functionality at a high level.

Chapter **1**

Getting to Know SharePoint

When we first heard about SharePoint, we just didn't get it. What the heck was this thing called SharePoint? We knew it was a Microsoft product that was supposed to do lots of things, but we just couldn't figure out exactly what it was or how to get started working with it.

Well, after years of working with SharePoint, we have finally figured a few things out. SharePoint is a web-based software platform that is definitely capable of doing lots of things — more than you could ever imagine. And therein lies the problem. If you ask ten people what SharePoint does, you're very likely to get ten different answers. SharePoint has such a depth to it that it's hard to get your head around it.

In this chapter, we help you see the SharePoint big picture. You discover how SharePoint works and gain understanding on exactly what the term *SharePoint* means. This chapter peels away the mystery and shows you SharePoint at a basic level. After all, you need to understand SharePoint at a basic level before you can dive into its advanced functionality.

Up and Running with SharePoint in Three Minutes Flat

It is human nature to learn things by exploring and it is no different with software. You could read a hundred books about SharePoint and still barely understand what exactly it is and what it does. Our thinking is that there is no better way to get to know SharePoint than to get up and running with it, clicking buttons to see what they do.

With SharePoint Online you can get up and running with a trial in minutes. SharePoint Online comes bundled with Microsoft 365. The easiest way to get started is to sign up for a free trial of Microsoft 365. Here's how:

1. **Open your favorite web browser and go to www.office.com.**

   The Office home page appears, as shown in Figure 1-1.

2. **Click the Get Office button.**

   To get SharePoint, you will need a business plan subscription.

3. **Click the For Business tab to see the available business plans.**

   In the table that appears, you will see that the Microsoft 365 Business Basic plan comes with the SharePoint service and is currently $5 per month (see Figure 1-2). We prefer using the latest Office clients like Word, Excel, Outlook, and PowerPoint, so we will choose the Microsoft 365 Business Standard plan.

4. **Once you've chosen the plan you want, click the "Try for free for 1 month" link.**

   A welcome screen appears that asks for your information.

5. **Walk through the wizard, providing your information as needed, in order to get up and running with Microsoft 365 and SharePoint Online.**

TIP

Note that as a business name you can just use your own name and choose that your business size is one person. You will then choose a domain name, which is ⟨your choice⟩.onmicrosoft.com. This is your Microsoft 365 domain. In our example, we chose sharepointfordummies.onmicrosoft.com for our domain. You can always add a custom domain later if you prefer. For example, we might connect sharepointfordummies.com to our Microsoft 365 account and get emails there, too.

Once you have filled out the information, your free trial will be created, as shown in Figure 1-3. This can take a few minutes. Once it is created, you will be given a link to go to your Microsoft 365 dashboard.

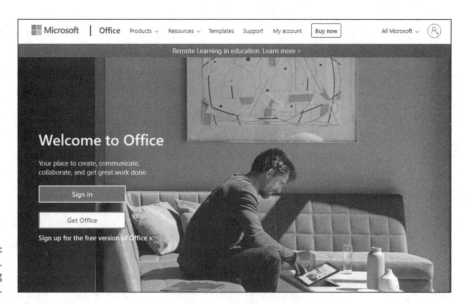

FIGURE 1-1:
The main office. com landing page.

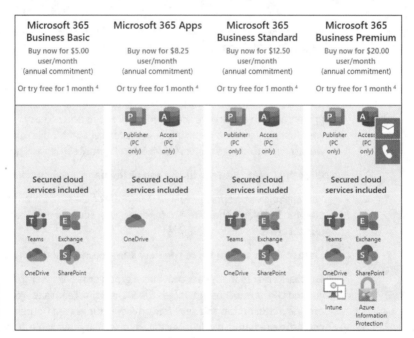

FIGURE 1-2:
Choosing a Microsoft 365 business plan.

When you first land on your Microsoft 365 dashboard, you will see a quick tutorial and then be presented with the Microsoft 365 main landing page. In this case we are focused on SharePoint, so let's crack it open and get started.

Thank you for choosing Microsoft 365 Business Standard

1. Signup started

2. Nice to meet you, Rosemarie

3. Thanks for creating an account with us, Rosemarie

4. Quantity and payment First 30 days are free

5. You're all set

Thanks for signing up for a Microsoft 365 Business Standard trial.

Your username is
info@sharepointfordummies.onmicrosoft.com.

We've sent a confirmation email to
info@portalintegrators.com.

Get Started   Manage your subscription

Highlights of what you can do

- Get started quickly with **documents, spreadsheets, presentations,** and **email**

- **Work from anywhere,** on any device

- Securely meet online and chat with **Microsoft Teams**

- Back up and share files with a terabyte of **cloud storage**

- Free **24/7 support** included

Word   E   Live chat   t   Feedback

FIGURE 1-3:
Completing the sign-up process for the free trial.

1. **Click the Microsoft 365 app launcher icon in the top-left corner of the page and select SharePoint in the drop-down menu that appears, as shown in Figure 1-4.**

   Because this is the first time you are opening SharePoint Online, you will be presented with a quick tutorial. After you finish the tutorial, you will be presented with a welcome screen for SharePoint and an easy way to create your first site, create a post, or install the SharePoint Mobile App. Right now, we just want to create our very own SharePoint site.

2. **Click the Create Site tab at the top of the page, as shown in Figure 1-5.**

   You will be given a choice: create a Team site or create a Communication site. Chapter 5 explores the different types of sites. For now, the Team site will suit our purpose.

3. **Choose Team site and give the new site a name and description.**

   The dialog box that appears provides a group email alias for the site and shows you the URL you will use to access the SharePoint Team site. You can also provide a description and set basic privacy settings (see Figure 1-6). Once you enter the site name, it will be validated to see if it is available. If the site is available, more fields will appear including Group Email address, Site Address (which are pre-filled), Privacy Settings, and Language. In the Privacy Settings field, you can choose for the site to either be private where only members of the site can access it, or public where anyone in the organization can have access to it.

4. Click Next and then click Finish in the next dialog box that appears.

In this dialog box, you are able to add any additional owners or members of the Team site. In our case, we are the only user of our new Microsoft 365 subscription right now.

App launcher

FIGURE 1-4:
The main
Microsoft 365
landing page.

Select SharePoint

Congratulations! Just like that you are up and running with your very own Share-Point site (see Figure 1-7). Feel free to start clicking around and exploring it, or wait until you read about various functionality through the book. Notice Share-Point helps you out by showing some common tasks in a pane along the right side of the page. You can close the page or click around and explore the suggestions.

TIP

You can always get back to your Microsoft 365 dashboard and your SharePoint site by opening your web browser and going to www.office.com and logging in with the user you created. Note that the new site can take up to 2 hours to appear in your frequent sites list. Alternatively, you can type in the full web address of your new SharePoint site. In our case the web address is https://sharepointfordummies. sharepoint.com/sites/myfirstsharepointsite.

Click to create a SharePoint site

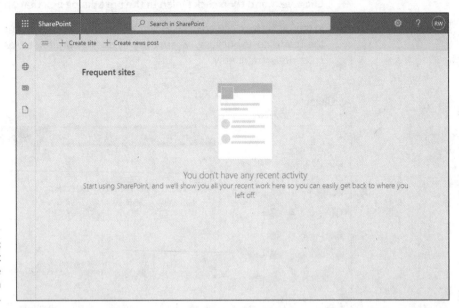

FIGURE 1-5:
The SharePoint landing page where you can create a new site.

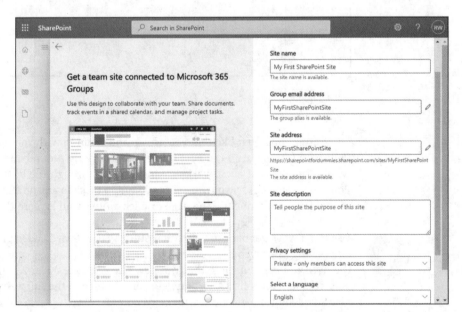

FIGURE 1-6:
Creating a new SharePoint site.

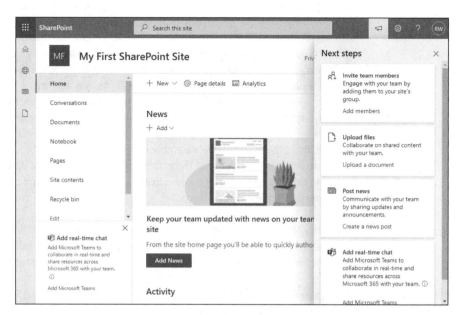

FIGURE 1-7:
A new SharePoint
Team site.

TIP

If you are using SharePoint Server, your IT team has likely installed SharePoint at your office location. Since the installation is at your local company premises instead of in a Microsoft data center somewhere, the term for this version is aptly called *on-premises.* If your organization is using SharePoint on-premises, your IT team will have likely created your SharePoint site for you and sent you a link to access it. (You find out more about the differences between SharePoint Online and SharePoint On-Premises in Chapter 2.)

Wrapping Your Head around SharePoint

At a basic level, SharePoint is a *web-based software platform*, meaning that SharePoint is software designed for you to interact with using a web browser.

TIP

In past versions of SharePoint, you really needed to use Microsoft's web browser (previously Internet Explorer) to work with SharePoint. Times have changed though, and you can now use most any web browser to work with SharePoint. Best yet, Microsoft supports the browsers and doesn't care what operating system you are using. Prefer to use a Mac? No problem. Is Linux your thing? SharePoint is supported.

No, really, what is SharePoint?

Maybe you're a whiz at Microsoft Word or a spreadsheet jockey with Excel. Going forward, you're going to have to be just as good at SharePoint to get the most out of your desktop Office client applications. Microsoft continues to integrate functionality that used to be locked up in client applications, or not available at all, with SharePoint. For example, using SharePoint with Office, you can create your own mobile apps with PowerApps, create an online gallery of PowerPoint slides, display interactive spreadsheets in web pages, create rich forms with Microsoft Forms, integrate data from all over the Internet into dashboards using Power BI (one of the latest business intelligence services from Microsoft), and reuse information from your company's databases in Word documents just to name a few. You can even use SharePoint right from Microsoft Teams without ever realizing you are using SharePoint. To learn more about Teams, check out *Microsoft Teams For Dummies* (Wiley, 2021). We cover all of these scenarios throughout the book.

Officially, Microsoft represents SharePoint as a "business collaboration platform for the enterprise and web." *SharePoint* is a platform from Microsoft that allows businesses to meet their diverse needs in the following domains:

- » **Collaboration:** Use SharePoint's collaboration sites for activities, such as managing projects or coordinating a request for proposal.
- » **Social networking:** If you work in a large company, you can use SharePoint as a social network for the Enterprise experience to help you track coworkers and locate people in expertise networks.
- » **Information portals and internal websites:** With SharePoint's web content management features, you can create useful self-service internal portals and intranets.
- » **Enterprise content management:** SharePoint offers excellent document- and record-management capabilities, including extensive support for metadata and customized search experiences.
- » **Business intelligence:** SharePoint is an ideal platform for providing entrée into your organization's business analysis assets. It integrates with Power BI and lets you create insightful dashboards from data all over your organization and the Internet (not just SharePoint).
- » **Business applications:** Use SharePoint to host sophisticated business applications, integrate business processes' backend databases and your SharePoint content, or simply use SharePoint as the means to present access to your applications.

You can approach SharePoint with the following model in mind:

- » **Product:** SharePoint is a product with a lot of features. Explore how SharePoint works without any customization when you're deciding how to approach a solution, and then decide if you want to customize it for your specific needs.

>> **Platform:** SharePoint provides everything you need to deliver a robust business solution. It provides the infrastructure (the "plumbing") required to deliver web-based solutions and has many prepackaged solutions you can use right out of the box without any customizations at all.

>> **Toolkit:** Finally, SharePoint is a set of components and controls that you can mix and match to provide a solution. You can create sites, pages, and apps, all without leaving the comfort of your web browser. You can bring this same concept to mobile devices with the SharePoint Mobile App and PowerApps.

A Microsoft product

SharePoint is a software product that Microsoft develops and sells to customers. If you followed along and created a Microsoft 365 Business Standard account, you will eventually have to pay Microsoft $12.50 per month in order to continue using it. If you choose the Microsoft 365 Business Basic plan, you will get SharePoint, but not the Office clients, and will pay $5 per month. Regardless of how you purchase and use SharePoint, you can rest assured that your organization is paying Microsoft a licensing fee. In other words, SharePoint isn't free.

In the past, SharePoint was a considerable cost for an organization wanting to adopt it. In addition to buying all of the licenses for your organization, you would also need an IT team to install and manage it. For this reason, SharePoint used to be considered enterprise-class software, as only large organizations could afford it. This has all changed. In the first few minutes of reading this book you have already gotten up and running with SharePoint. In the past, it would have taken months for a giant IT project to get SharePoint up and running. You just did it in minutes!

Many different SharePoint definitions

SharePoint has many different types of users, and depending on where your role fits in, you might have a very different experience from a fellow SharePoint user. For example, you might be assigned to create and administer a SharePoint website for your team. In this case, you might see first-hand the vast functionality of SharePoint websites. On the other hand, you might be a user of a SharePoint site. In this case, your SharePoint world might be only the site that someone has already created for you. To confuse matters even further, many organizations will roll out SharePoint and give it a spiffy internal name; for example, "Connect." So even though the cool new web tool called Connect is actually SharePoint, most users don't even realize it!

On the more technical side, if you're an infrastructure administrator, you see SharePoint as a platform capable of offloading the difficult job of website administration. If you're a software developer, you see SharePoint as a web platform for developing programs for users.

The vastness of SharePoint creates areas of specialization. The result is that a person's view of SharePoint is greatly affected by how that person uses the product. It's important to keep this in mind when talking with people about SharePoint. If you ask ten people to define SharePoint, you're likely to get ten different answers, as illustrated in Figure 1-8.

FIGURE 1-8:
There are many different ways to define SharePoint.

TIP

SharePoint has many different administration levels, and each requires a different level of technical ability. For example, if you're comfortable working with software like Microsoft Word and Excel, then you won't have any problem administering a SharePoint site. At a deeper level, there are also SharePoint infrastructure administrators. To administer SharePoint at the infrastructure level is a role that falls squarely into the realm of the IT geeks.

SharePoint is a platform, so the user roles an organization defines depend on the organization itself. Here are some examples of the possible roles of users in SharePoint:

» **Anonymous visitors:** People who browse to a website that just happens to be using the SharePoint platform. Anonymous visitors just see SharePoint as a website and nothing else.

» **SharePoint visitors:** People who browse to the site and authenticate so that SharePoint knows who they are. Visitors might still just see a SharePoint site as any other website, except they notice their name in the top-right corner of the screen and know they must log in to reach the site. Visitors might not use any of the features of SharePoint, however, and just browse the information posted to the website.

» **SharePoint casual users:** People who know all the company documents are posted to SharePoint and know they can upload their own documents to their personal SharePoint site. Casual users might realize that they are using SharePoint, or they might just think of the platform as the name the organization has given to SharePoint. For example, we have seen organizations give their web platform tool names such as Source or Smart or Knowledge Center. SharePoint is the name of the web platform product from Microsoft, which is often unknown by users of a tool built on the SharePoint platform.

» **SharePoint users:** People who are familiar with SharePoint and its main features. SharePoint users often perform various administrator functions even if they don't realize it. For example, they might be responsible for an app that stores all the company policies and procedures. Thus, they are an app administrator. Users might also be responsible for a site for a small team, in which case they are site administrators. As you can see, a user can play many different roles.

» **SharePoint power users:** Power users are not only familiar with the main SharePoint features and functionality but also dive deeper. Power users might be familiar with the functionality differences of different features, routing documents using workflows, and building site hierarchies. Power users might also be a site collection administrator and thus responsible for a collection of sites.

» **SharePoint technical administrators:** Technical administrators are people from the IT department who are responsible for SharePoint. Technical administrators are less concerned with using SharePoint for business and more concerned about making sure the platform is available and responsive. An administrator might play many different roles. For example, farm administrators are responsible for all the servers that make up SharePoint, such as web front end servers, applications servers, and database servers. Specialized database administrators focus just on the database components. There are even administrative roles for specific services, such as the search service or user profile service. Depending on the size of the SharePoint implementation, these technical administrator roles might be filled by a single overworked individual or a team with highly specialized skills.

More than a website

SharePoint is called a *web platform,* as opposed to just a website, because of the sheer amount of functionality and capabilities it includes. In fact, if you already administer a SharePoint website, you can easily create a new website right within the existing website. You can also develop websites with an extraordinary amount of functionality without writing a single line of code. The result is a platform for websites instead of just a single website. The multitude of features and the complexity of the product are what lead to confusion.

TIP

The terms *SharePoint website* and *SharePoint site* can be used interchangeably. Both terms mean a website that is powered by SharePoint. Because this book is all about SharePoint, we sometimes abbreviate these terms to just *site*.

One thing that makes SharePoint so special is that you don't need to be a computer genius or even a power user to be a website developer and administrator in SharePoint. You just need to be comfortable using a computer.

TECHNICAL
STUFF

The terms *website* and *web application* are often used interchangeably. In the deep, dark technical world of SharePoint administration, the term *web application* has a very specific meaning. A web application is a technical construct, and each web application has its own databases associated with it. If you create two SharePoint web applications, they store their content and configuration information in different databases. As with technology these days, a simple word can have different meanings, depending on the context of the conversation.

THE DIFFERENCE BETWEEN SOCIAL MEDIA AND SHAREPOINT

SharePoint has some similarities with social media services such as Facebook, LinkedIn, and Twitter, but differs from them in its intended use. Facebook, LinkedIn, and Twitter are designed for consumers as a whole, whereas SharePoint is designed for individual organizations.

SharePoint has many of the social and profile features of Facebook, LinkedIn, and Twitter, but these features are only available to people within your organization. In other words, only the people in your organization can use the features of SharePoint. Although SharePoint includes social and profile features, it also includes much, much more. Think of SharePoint as a product for business and productivity that also happens to have the social and profile features of sites such as Facebook, LinkedIn, and Twitter.

Taking a Peek at a SharePoint Site

The primary purpose of SharePoint is to provide websites to members of an organization or employees of a company. When you create a website, you select which type of template you want to use to create the site. The dialog box shown in Figure 1-9 shows the different templates available.

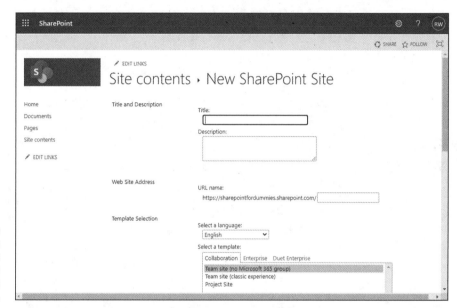

FIGURE 1-9:
The dialog box used to select a website template when creating a SharePoint site.

TIP

The templates you have available depend on where you are creating your SharePoint site and what features have been activated for your SharePoint environment. For example, in SharePoint Online, a tab for Duet Enterprise appears, and if the publishing feature is active, you will see Publishing. If you are looking for a template that doesn't appear in the list of templates, you will need to figure out which SharePoint feature makes the template available. SharePoint features are explored in more detail in Chapter 18. In general, Microsoft is moving to simplify SharePoint. One way it is doing this is by making it easy to create a Team or Communication site, which means you would need to hunt a bit to find the other templates. (We cover this in Chapter 18.)

The template tells SharePoint which features and functionality should be included on the site. Keep in mind that you can always add more features and add and remove features as you decide to make your site more specific for your needs.

One of the most common SharePoint site templates is called the Team site template (the template you used at the beginning of this chapter). The Team site template includes features such as a discussion board, a library to store documents, and a calendar. In fact, many books simply talk about the Team site template and call that SharePoint. As you learn in this book, the Team site template is very important, but it is just another SharePoint website template. Part 3 explores building and customizing a site based on the Team site template.

TECHNICAL DIVE INTO THE SHAREPOINT BUILDING BLOCKS

To obtain a perspective on SharePoint, it is important to understand how SharePoint is put together. As mentioned in this chapter, SharePoint is a web-based platform. A number of technologies are required in order to make the platform available. Each technology builds on the one below it. In this manner, it is common to call the whole ball of wax a *technology stack*.

The SharePoint technology stack begins with server computers running the Microsoft Windows Server operating system. On top of Windows Server are some additional technologies required by SharePoint. In particular, SharePoint needs a database and a web server — Microsoft SQL Server and Microsoft Internet Information Services (IIS), respectively. In addition, SharePoint also needs Active Directory, which manages the servers in the domain. Only when this entire stack of technology is available can you install SharePoint, as shown in the figure.

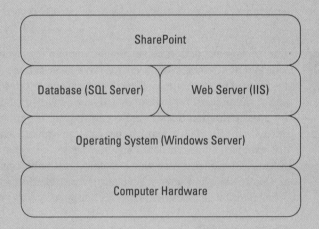

SharePoint will only work with the Microsoft stack of supporting technologies. For example, you cannot swap in an Oracle database or the open source Apache web server. SharePoint would simply refuse to install and might ask you what the heck you are trying to do using a non-Microsoft product to install SharePoint.

Getting Familiar with SharePoint Terminology

You should add a number of terms to your SharePoint vocabulary. Some terms are made up by Microsoft marketing, some are industry standards, and others are buzzwords that have grown to have various meanings depending on the context of the conversation. In the following sections, I describe the various components of SharePoint, how the terms that define functionality fit together, and what they mean.

Branding

The term *branding* refers to the way a SharePoint site looks and behaves to users. Branding includes things like the colors, fonts, images, logos, and layout of the various components on a site. Branding your SharePoint site is covered in Chapter 18.

The term *branding* is not specific to SharePoint; it is borrowed from the marketing industry in which an organization will brand its product. For example, Coca-Cola has a very strong brand. In the software world, *branding* refers to the look and feel of a piece of software or website.

Business intelligence (BI)

The term *business intelligence* is definitely not new. An article was published in the October 1958 edition of the *IBM Journal* by H. P. Luhn called "A Business Intelligence System." The article describes how an organization can process documents in order to make business decisions. Business intelligence has continued to evolve over the years and has morphed into something of a catch-all phrase for using data to drive business.

In the Microsoft realm, business intelligence (BI, pronounced *bee-eye*) consists of a number of different technologies. In fact, we wrote an entire sister book on the subject — *Microsoft Business Intelligence For Dummies* by Ken Withee. As SharePoint has become a central and nearly ubiquitous application, it has also become a prime place to show the data that decision makers need to make decisions. In other words, SharePoint is a perfect display case for all those fancy charts, graphs, performance indicators, and other data.

Unfortunately, business intelligence has a fairly steep learning curve in SharePoint. Tools such as Report Builder, Dashboard Designer, and PowerPivot unleash endless possibilities, but figuring out how to use them all takes time. One thing you will find with business intelligence in SharePoint is that there are often many ways to achieve the same result. And therein lies the learning curve.

At the basic level, if you can create a chart in Excel, you can plunk it into a SharePoint library and embed it on a page using a Web Part (which is a component that shows data on the page). Ta-da! You just achieved business intelligence in SharePoint. The consumers of the data might never even know how easy it was to put that data in Excel and embed it in a SharePoint web page. And that is the point. These things shouldn't be difficult to get started.

At the other end of the spectrum, however, you might need to create a data cube (a specialized database in the big data world) with millions or billions of records, and then use a specialized tool such as Dashboard Designer to create an interactive graph with clickthrough capabilities. Whew! That sounds complicated, and trust me, it is.

You need serious expertise when diving into the depths of business intelligence, but that doesn't mean you can't understand it at a high level. Many different tools and features make up business intelligence in SharePoint, and Chapter 24 covers one of the latest business intelligence services from Microsoft called Power BI. In that chapter, we discuss Power BI and also walk you through the other SharePoint business intelligence features at a high level. We try to provide you with insights into techniques you can use to get started right away.

eDiscovery

The term *eDiscovery* relates to the legal world of business. In particular, the word derives from *electronic discovery* in litigation. If you have ever watched the TV program *Law & Order,* you understand that critical evidence can make or break a case. In the high-tech world of digital information, it's a rather tricky endeavor to discover and hold electronic documents.

SharePoint has a number of features specifically designed for eDiscovery. This is great news if you're a decision maker looking to comply with legal requirements, or you're a lawyer. If neither applies to you, then just knowing SharePoint handles eDiscovery is good enough.

Identity management

Frankly, modern technology can often be a real pain. It seems that there are gazillions of systems in any organization, and each requires its own username and password. I have so many usernames and passwords on various websites across the Internet that my mind just tries to block it out. Of course, then I forget my password and have to go through the tiring process of resetting it each time I want to log in to a particular system. On the other side, when a user logs in to a system, that system also needs to know what the user can access.

TIP

Identity management refers to the functionality of a software system that manages users and what they can access. Identity management isn't specific to SharePoint and is used by any system that requires you to enter a username and password.

Microsoft has made great strides in simplifying identity management. SharePoint uses claims-based authentication in conjunction with an open authentication standard called Open Authorization (OAuth for short) in order to play nicely with other systems. What this means for you is that you shouldn't have to remember yet another username and password when working with SharePoint. If only the rest of the Internet could be so thoughtful!

Mobile

The computing world has become mobile. People are more likely to have their computing device be their phone and tablet than any other type of computer. Microsoft recognized this and created the SharePoint Mobile App and also created a tool called PowerApps that allows you to create mobile SharePoint apps without needing to be a programmer. We cover the SharePoint Mobile App throughout the book and we cover PowerApps in Chapter 17.

Records management and compliance

In the world of information work, you often hear about *records management* and *compliance.* Depending on how much of a rebel you are, you might think of these terms as keeping people and processes in line or as an invitation to break some rules.

Every organization has a different set of rules around managing records and keeping processes compliant with company policy. This line of thinking is not specific to SharePoint, and, depending on your organization and industry, could be buttoned-up strict, as in the banking industry, or open to the world and free loving, as in many technology startup companies.

In SharePoint, a number of features are specifically designed to keep records organized and easily managed. In addition, SharePoint has compliance features that even the stodgiest of stodgy big banks will adore. And as someone who has done consulting work for the banking industry, let me tell you, there are some really strict compliance rules out there. (Considering that they're keeping track of our money, that's a good thing.)

Search

If you have ever used Google, Bing, or Duckduckgo.com, then you're familiar with search engines. These search engines for the Internet are amazingly powerful and eerily comprehensive. SharePoint does a bang-up job of managing content, and the next logical step in managing content is finding content when you need it. As an organization grows, the need for search grows too. Search is covered in more detail in Chapter 23.

TIP

Search is one of those topics that spans from simple to mind-numbingly complex. At a base level, you have search capabilities for every SharePoint site right out of the box. The tech geeks can go deeper and optimize search for your organization. For example, your search query can be aware of your role in the organization and display results specifically for you. So, for example, if you're in sales and searching for a product, your search results will be sales materials. If you're an engineer and searching for a product, your results will include specifications. SharePoint search can make this happen, but configuring it is best left to the IT department.

Social

In recent years, computers and the Internet have been connecting people like never before. This new way of interacting through computers is called social computing. The biggest public social network of all is Facebook. Not every organization wants to be in such a public space though.

SharePoint is designed for organizations, and the social aspects of SharePoint share a common goal with Facebook — connecting people. The difference is that SharePoint connections are limited to people within a particular organization. The social aspects of SharePoint are covered in Chapter 10.

Web content management

Content is a fairly simple concept. When you create a Word document or an Excel spreadsheet, you generate content. If you develop a web page for your colleagues to admire, you generate content. Even if you just pull out a pencil and paper and start writing, that's content. If you scanned that paper, you could then let SharePoint work its content management wonders on the scanned image file.

SharePoint is especially powerful in handling content, as described in Part 5. One particularly tricky piece of content, however, is the content you develop for websites. You know, all of those web pages that contain policies and procedures and documentation and all of that? If the content is created for a web page, then it's web content and it holds a special place in the heart of SharePoint. The web content management features of SharePoint are legendary, and many organizations first started using SharePoint for just this reason.

Content management often goes by the name Enterprise Content Management (ECM). Don't be fooled by the terminology though. The *Enterprise* portion of ECM just means the system manages content at a large scale, as found in a large company or enterprise.

SharePoint and web content have a special relationship that all comes down to delegation and control. SharePoint provides the ability for many people to generate content and for a few people to approve content. This maintains order because a select group of people control what goes out to the world. SharePoint streamlines this process by allowing approved content to be published automatically.

You might be wondering what makes the relationship between SharePoint and web content so special. Well, it all comes down to delegation and control. SharePoint provides the ability for many people to generate content and for a few to approve content. After it's approved, content can be published automatically to be consumed by the world or those in your organization.

Workflow

Workflow is one of those things in business that happens whether anyone wants it or not. If more than one person is required to achieve a goal, then a workflow is involved. SharePoint has been good in the past at handling workflow within SharePoint, but it lacked integration with other products. To address this deficiency, Microsoft created a new product called Microsoft Flow. Microsoft Flow is not part of SharePoint, but it integrates with SharePoint as well as with many, many other products (both Microsoft and others).

Using Microsoft Flow you can finally build a workflow that mimics the way you work. If you use products such as Survey Monkey, GitHub, Twitter, or many others, you can use Microsoft Flow to build workflows that integrate with SharePoint. We cover using Microsoft Flow with SharePoint in Chapter 15.

IN THIS CHAPTER

» **Exploring SharePoint Online**

» **Determining why SharePoint Online has become so popular**

» **Finding out what version of SharePoint you are using**

» **Understanding the benefits to a service-based offering**

Chapter **2**

Introducing SharePoint in Microsoft 365

J ust a handful of years ago, it wasn't easy to adopt SharePoint. SharePoint fell squarely into the realm of enterprise-class software. *Enterprise-class software* is powerful, expensive, and resource-intensive. In order to adopt SharePoint, you needed to be a large organization with big bucks and a large IT support team.

The rapid rise of super-fast and ubiquitous Internet connectivity caused a paradigm shift in the software world. Microsoft and other companies quickly came out with new applications that offered enterprise-class software, including Share-Point, over the Internet. Microsoft branded its SharePoint offering as SharePoint Online and packaged it with products such as Exchange (email), Teams (instant communication), and Office (productivity).

TIP

Microsoft called the various combinations of services (SharePoint, Exchange, Teams, and Office) as Office 365. Recently, Microsoft has added Windows licensing and management to the existing Office 365 bundles and changed the name to Microsoft 365. We still use the terms Office 365 and Microsoft 365 interchangeably. Though we expect Microsoft will continue to ditch the Office 365 branding in the future.

In this chapter, you see how SharePoint Online has changed the game and what it means to use a cloud-based solution. You will read about the differences between SharePoint Online and SharePoint On-Premises and find out which you should use and when. Finally, you explore some of the benefits of using SharePoint Online.

Accessing and Using SharePoint

At its heart, SharePoint is a website. To use it, you open up your web browser and navigate to the location of your SharePoint site. With that said, Microsoft has recognized that the world has moved to a mobile-first environment. Many people do all of their computing with a mobile phone or tablet. To accommodate this, Microsoft created the SharePoint Mobile App. The SharePoint Mobile App can be installed on your iOS or Android device and used to interact with SharePoint.

TIP

Many people who are brand new to SharePoint might only access and work with SharePoint through a mobile app on their smartphones or tablet devices. Even if you only use a mobile device, you should be aware that you can always open a web browser on a good old-fashioned desktop or laptop computer and access SharePoint.

We cover signing up for SharePoint with Microsoft 365 and opening it with a web browser in Chapter 1, and we cover installing the SharePoint Mobile App in Chapter 4.

Getting Familiar with SharePoint Online

Microsoft offers SharePoint over the Internet in a product called SharePoint Online. With SharePoint Online, Microsoft takes care of all the heavy lifting. To get SharePoint going, someone has to procure and set up the servers, and install the operating system, databases, web server, and SharePoint server. This all has to be done in a special climate-controlled facility called a data center. The data center has to be secure and redundant. After all, what if a disaster happened and the data center computers in the data center — or worse, the data center itself — were destroyed? Finally, the whole setup must be scalable so that as more users begin using SharePoint for mission-critical business processes, the servers and sites can keep up with the added load. And that isn't the end — after everything is up and running, someone still needs to manage all the updates and keep the servers humming smoothly. Whew! What a lot of work.

With a hosted solution, you or your organization pay someone else to do all this for you — you simply use the final product, SharePoint. With SharePoint Online, Microsoft sells its SharePoint platform as a service, so the actual servers and software are run in its data centers, managed and maintained by its employees. You, being a customer of Microsoft, connect to this managed version of SharePoint over a secure channel of the Internet and use it to develop business solutions on the SharePoint platform. (Maybe a better name would be "SharePoint Infrastructure Hosted and Managed by Microsoft," though it's too cumbersome for marketing.) Figure 2-1 illustrates this point.

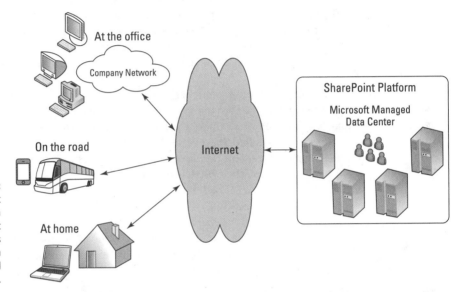

FIGURE 2-1:
The SharePoint platform runs in the Microsoft data center and is accessed in a secure channel over the Internet.

TIP

Microsoft is not the only company that offers SharePoint over the Internet. Other companies also offer SharePoint hosting, though Microsoft seems to have cornered the market recently because they also offer so many other things for the same price as SharePoint. In our view, one of the biggest competitors to SharePoint has become WordPress. WordPress is another web platform that includes endless plugins to extend it. Another competitor to SharePoint Online is an internal SharePoint site hosted by your local IT department.

REMEMBER

SharePoint Online is when Microsoft manages SharePoint in its data centers and you access it over the Internet. SharePoint On-Premises is when your local IT gurus manage SharePoint in your company data center.

Determining What Version of SharePoint You Are Using

A key aspect of understanding SharePoint is first determining what version of SharePoint you are using. The main thing you need to determine is if you are using SharePoint Online, SharePoint On-Premises, or a hybrid of both. If you signed up for SharePoint with Microsoft 365 in Chapter 1, you are using SharePoint Online. If your organization has provided you access to SharePoint, then it is a little trickier to determine which version you have. Since SharePoint Online is part of Microsoft 365, you can usually just look for the app launcher in the upper-left corner of your browser. The app launcher is where you can switch to other apps like Outlook or Teams. If you see the app launcher (*hint:* it looks like a waffle and is sometimes called the waffle icon), then you are using SharePoint Online.

If you don't see the app launcher, you are probably using a version of SharePoint that is being managed by your organization. This is called SharePoint On-Premises. Updated versions of SharePoint On-Premises are released every few years. The latest version is called SharePoint Server 2019. Prior versions include SharePoint Server 2016, SharePoint Server 2013, and SharePoint Server 2010. Microsoft has put together a nice article on determining the version of SharePoint you are using. To find it, search for "Which version of SharePoint am I using?" on the `https://support.office.com` site.

TIP

Microsoft usually releases On-Premises versions of SharePoint every three years. If the trend holds, then the next On-Premises version will be SharePoint Server 2022.

Understanding Why SharePoint Online Has Become So Popular

Putting a complex computer platform in place is difficult. Organizations discovered this when they implemented enterprise resource planning (ERP) software in the 1990s and 2000s, and it still holds true today. Putting the SharePoint platform in place is not an easy endeavor. Larger organizations usually require a more complex implementation. As the complexity of the implementation increases, so do the costs, time, and risk. The current best practice is to use an experienced consulting firm with expertise in implementing a SharePoint platform. As in dealing with any services company, sometimes you pick a winner, and sometimes it's a complete disaster.

SharePoint Online takes the implementation of the infrastructure out of the equation with a known variable in cost and resources. This is music to a bean counter's ears! Predictability! The predictability of cost and time to implement are why SharePoint Online and other cloud solutions are becoming so popular. They reduce complexity and provide a fixed and certain cost on a SharePoint platform that is guaranteed to follow best practices. Having a known variable in place for the infrastructure frees up resources to focus on the actual business problems. Which, by the way, are your main reasons for implementing SharePoint in the first place, right?

TIP

Microsoft has introduced the SharePoint Online offering to cater to everyone from small businesses to large multinationals. In fact, you can even purchase just one license if you're a solo entrepreneur. Because Microsoft has already built out the offering, it can offer it's just as easy to offer the same reliability and security to small companies as it does to large companies. It is, after all, the same product — the only difference is the scale.

Differences between SharePoint Online and SharePoint On-Premises

In the past, there have been some major differences between SharePoint Online and SharePoint On-Premises. For one, SharePoint Online used to trail the version of SharePoint that was available on-premises. For example, when SharePoint 2016 came out, it took SharePoint Online a painfully long time before it became comparable to SharePoint 2016.

REMEMBER

The current on-premises version is SharePoint 2019. The previous version was SharePoint 2016, and the version before that was SharePoint 2013. SharePoint Online doesn't have a version number.

Times have changed, however. Microsoft has moved to focus on SharePoint Online instead of the on-premises versions. It rolls out new features in SharePoint Online, and then grabs a snapshot of the online version and makes it available for organizations that choose to deploy it themselves on-premises.

TIP

You can think of SharePoint Server 2019 as a snapshot of the features available in SharePoint Online around the year 2019. One thing is certain, though: If you want the latest and greatest features, SharePoint Online is your best bet.

In fact, one of the major development areas with SharePoint Server 2019 is its integration with SharePoint Online. This is to accommodate organizations that want to keep some of their data on their local premises and in their own control, but want to leverage some of the benefits of having Microsoft manage SharePoint for them. This concept of using some SharePoint Online and some SharePoint On-Premises is called a *hybrid approach*.

With that said, there are still integration points with other local server products and advanced functionality that are only available with SharePoint On-Premises. This is an ever-changing landscape, so the best way to stay on top of the available features is on the frequently updated SharePoint Online feature matrix located on Microsoft's docs.microsoft.com site. The best way to find the features is to search for "SharePoint service description."

SharePoint Online is when Microsoft manages SharePoint in its data centers and you access it over the Internet. SharePoint On-Premises is when your local IT gurus manage SharePoint in your company data center.

GETTING TO THE BOTTOM OF THE CLOUD

Network diagrams often show a network as a cloud, as shown in the following figure, because it would be too complex to diagram all the components that make up the network (such as routers, switches, hubs, and cables).

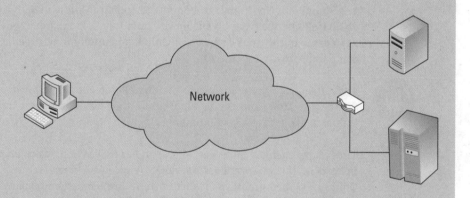

The biggest network, and cloud, of all is the Internet. When a diagram shows communication over the Internet, a big cloud is used because it would be impossible to try to show all the network hardware that might be encountered between two computers communicating via the Internet. The cloud simply becomes an abstraction for a network with the assumption that communication can occur over that cloud.

If a company sells access to software that lives in their data centers and that is connected to by customers over the Internet, that solution is said to live "in the cloud." The term comes from the perspective of the customer, who may have no idea where the actual servers that serve up the software are located. From the customers' perspective, they just access the software using an Internet domain name. This cloud concept and technology is nothing new. Whenever you surf the web, you use a service in the cloud. You just know that when you type in the web address, the site appears in your web browser. This concept is catching on with business applications; you hear more and more about cloud solutions.

Exploring the Benefits of SharePoint Online

If you use SharePoint in your day-to-day operations, the good news is that it doesn't really matter whether you are using SharePoint On-Premises or SharePoint Online. They are both SharePoint, and you can focus on your job. With that said, it's nice to at least have a high-level understanding of some of the infrastructure benefits to SharePoint Online. If nothing else, you can impress your IT friends.

Using SharePoint Online instead of trying to build and manage the platform with your own organization's resources gives you a number of benefits. You simply sign up, pay a monthly licensing fee, and access SharePoint over the Internet. The following sections take a look at some of the things that Microsoft does behind the scenes with SharePoint Online.

Data center and hardware

If you have ever toured a data center, you have some idea of the amount of effort and resources it takes to keep everything running. Data centers have rows and rows of computers with flashing lights, humming fans, and coils of cables running ceiling to floor. Control rooms that resemble something NASA would use to run space missions monitor all these servers. The control rooms contain computers and monitors that report on everything in the data center, from temperature and humidity to individual fans in particular servers and everything in between. These control rooms are often called a network operation center (NOC) and are the nerve center for a modern data center.

Most organizations that have the need for servers find a data center that can be used to host their gear. Hosting your computers in a data center can cost a fortune, but paying to host your own gear in an inferior environment can cost even more in the long run.

Microsoft invested a tremendous amount of money in building its own state-of-the-art data centers that house the servers that make up SharePoint Online. The nice thing about SharePoint Online is that you don't have to worry about the various costs of hosting and managing your own gear. The price you pay for SharePoint Online covers everything, including the data center.

The servers that run SharePoint Online are state of the art and come from the leading industry manufacturers. In fact, Microsoft has modularized the setup, and the computers come in massive containers that look very similar to the containers you see on cargo ships. These container pods are sealed by the manufacturer and never opened at the data center. This is a security mechanism to keep humans away from the computers. When a single piece of hardware fails, the workload of that server is simply shifted automatically to other servers (possibly in other pods). When enough servers fail, the pod is taken offline and the workload of that pod is shifted to another pod without service interruption. A new pod with the latest hardware is then shipped to replace it, and the old pod is decommissioned, with the data being wiped to security standards, and sent back to the manufacturer.

Microsoft has developed this system of data centers and pods throughout the country with built-in redundancy. If a data center goes down, the workload is shifted to another data center. If a pod goes down, the workload of that pod is shifted to another pod. If a server within a pod goes down, the workload of that server is shifted to another server. This system of redundancy is included in the price of SharePoint Online. You might care about how it works or you might just care that Microsoft has guaranteed uptime of 99.9 percent. In the end, you're free to focus on your business and solving business problems using the SharePoint platform without having to worry about what it takes to make that platform consistently available.

Software platform

The physical computers required to run the SharePoint platform are one thing, but you also have to take into account the operating systems and associated software such as the web servers, databases, and SharePoint itself that run on the server computers. The Microsoft platform uses the Windows Server operating system, the Internet Information Service (IIS) web server, and the SQL Server database. All these software systems are just the supporting actors for the SharePoint software itself. The amount of time and resources it takes to get all these software components installed, updated, and configured can be daunting. Administrators are valuable resources, and their time is often better spent dealing with the desktop computers of the users.

When you sign up for SharePoint Online, you don't have to worry about installing and managing the software components that make up the SharePoint platform. Microsoft takes care of all of that for you, and it's all included in the price. In addition, when new versions of the software stack are released, Microsoft upgrades everything automatically without additional cost for the service. Microsoft also monitors the servers and logs 24 hours a day in order to make sure nothing goes awry. The monitoring takes place in network operation centers described in the previous section.

Backup, redundancy, and security

You might think that with the hardware and software in place, the rest would be easy. However, the SharePoint platform itself needs to have a backup and disaster recovery plan, in addition to being available, redundant, and secure. With SharePoint Online, the Microsoft teams take care of all this for you, and it's guaranteed in the contract.

With the hardware, software, and plans in place, you as a customer are free to focus on developing business solutions on the platform instead of working through the process of setting everything up yourself.

Chapter **3**

Wrangling SharePoint Functionality

The reason SharePoint is so difficult to define is that it's a product that has a tremendous amount of functionality. SharePoint has functionality for administrators, business users, report developers, analysts, programmers, and just about anyone else in any organization. You name it, and SharePoint provides functionality designed for that particular user. Coming to terms with the vastness of SharePoint is a key concept in learning about the product.

In this chapter, you discover some of the main functionality that makes up SharePoint. You find out about SharePoint templates and how they're used to create websites. You discover the importance of the Team site template, but find out it isn't the only game in town. You explore apps and see that almost everything in SharePoint is an app. Finally, you take a high-level fly-over of some of the most common functionality in SharePoint. The whole smorgasbord of functionality is really the definition of SharePoint, and you get a bird's-eye view in this chapter.

Coming to Terms with Website Templates

If you haven't experienced SharePoint before, you might think that creating a new website is difficult. Before SharePoint, you would need to gather up the right files and write HTML code to create a website. Tweaking the code and building the website were burdensome tasks. To make matters worse, you had to fiddle with the web server and the security and get everything just right. In short, you needed an advanced level of technical expertise. Some would have argued you needed an advanced degree in computer science! Making changes to the website after it was completed required the same advanced skillset. One of the main reasons SharePoint took off was that it allowed people to create and manage websites with advanced functionality, such as content management and workflow, without needing an advanced technical skillset.

Creating a SharePoint website is as easy as a few clicks of the mouse (assuming you have the right permissions). The primary decision you need to make when you create a SharePoint site is which template to use. Choosing a template is accomplished on the New SharePoint Site screen, shown in Figure 3-1. Instructions for creating a new site are briefly outlined in Chapter 1 and further detailed in Chapter 5.

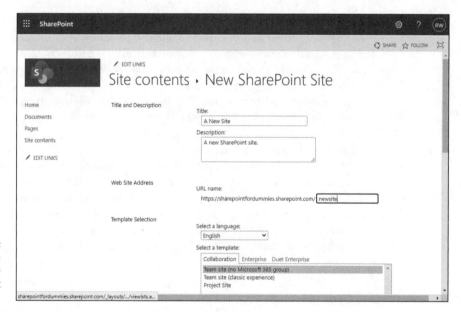

FIGURE 3-1:
Choosing a template on the New SharePoint Site screen.

TIP

A SharePoint site template outlines what functionality the site will include after it's created. You can always add or remove functionality as you see fit. Keep in mind that the templates you see depend on a number of factors including the edition of SharePoint you are using, whether you are using SharePoint Online or SharePoint On-Premises, and which features are activated.

TIP

The most popular SharePoint site template is called Team site. The Team site template is so popular that many books forget to mention that there are other templates available as well. Working with a SharePoint site built using the Team site template is what we usually cover throughout the book, unless otherwise noted, but keep in mind that other templates are available, too.

Show Me the Apps

SharePoint extends the way you think about adding functionality to a site. In previous versions of SharePoint, all containers were considered a type of list. What a list meant was fairly generic. You might have a list that provides calendar functionality, or you might have a list that provides discussion board functionality. The concept of a special list with some functionality was one of the hardest things to get our minds around when we started working with SharePoint. SharePoint now removes the confusion by calling everything an app. Instead of a specialized calendar list, you now have a Calendar app. Need a discussion board? You now add the Discussion Board app.

Microsoft has also expanded the ability to develop custom solutions for SharePoint called *add-ins*. The result is that third parties or in-house developers can create add-ins for any purpose you can conceive. Imagine you're in Accounts Payable and you use SharePoint to manage your invoice documents. You might request an add-in from your IT department to route documents through the various approvals before finally being submitted to the payment system.

If you use SharePoint Online, you can browse, purchase, and install apps and add-ins from the SharePoint Store without leaving SharePoint. It's similar to using the App Store on an iPhone or the Google Play store on an Android phone to buy and download an app.

SharePoint has the ability to use apps on your mobile device as well. Since so many things are called "apps," this can lead to some confusion. Just remember that an app can live inside a web browser or on your mobile phone. And on your mobile phone you can use the main SharePoint Mobile App or you can create your own SharePoint apps using PowerApps, which we cover in detail in Chapter 16. For example, now you can take your Accounts Payable app that you built using a

SharePoint list and turn it into a real live iOS or Android app that people install directly on their devices. The backend is still using SharePoint, but you have expanded your regular SharePoint web-based app into the mobile realm.

TIP

Many SharePoint power users are comfortable with the concept of a data container called a list. You can still start with a blank list and add functionality as required. Nothing has changed in this ability. You are now just creating your own custom app by starting with the Custom List app. After you give your new app a name, it appears alongside all the other apps.

Working with Web Pages

A SharePoint site wouldn't be very interesting without content. A SharePoint site is a container for pages. Pages in turn are containers for actual content; developing pages allows you to add content to your SharePoint sites.

Under the covers there are different types of pages you can create but Microsoft has removed a lot of the complexity and makes getting started with create a generic page much easier.

To create a simple page:

1. **Open a web browser and navigate to your SharePoint site.**

2. **Click the gear icon in the upper-right corner and select Add a Page.**

    A Create page appears, as shown in Figure 3-2. (We selected "I've done this before" and clicked the Let's Go button so that we could get straight to the Create page screen.) If you are adding a page for the first time, an option to work through a tutorial also appears. Feel free to work through the tutorial.

3. **Choose the Blank template and select Create page.**

    The other templates available in addition to the Blank template are the Visual template and the Basic Text template. These templates provide additional ways to build a page. You can play around with them to see what you like best. We recommend starting from scratch so we can learn how things work before we let Microsoft help us automate things. So we chose the Blank template.

4. **Develop the page by clicking the plus (+) icons and adding components.**

    The new page opens in editing mode and you can click around and add content, as shown in Figure 3-3. You add components by clicking the + icon. If you are familiar with WordPress or other content management systems, you will notice a trend. Web-based content systems are trending toward a standard way of adding content and SharePoint is no exception. We spend a lot of time building WordPress pages as well as SharePoint pages, and the feel of both has trended together. If you are familiar with one you will be familiar with the other.

5. **When you are ready to publish your page, click the Publish button that appears in the upper-right corner.**

    Your page will be published and you will be offered some common tasks such as adding the page to your SharePoint site's navigation, posting the new page as News on the site, emailing the page, sending the page to Yammer, saving the page as a template to create additional pages, and copying a direct link to the page.

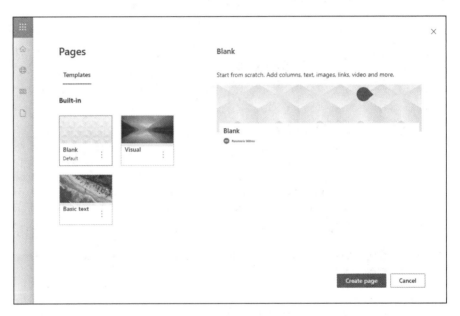

FIGURE 3-2:
Creating a new SharePoint page.

You learn how to create different types of pages in Chapter 6.

The four primary types of pages that can be created and developed from the browser in SharePoint are:

>> Site page

>> Wiki page

>> Web Part page

>> Publishing page

Following is a brief overview of the four types of SharePoint pages.

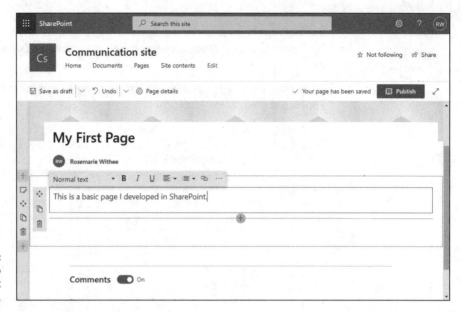

FIGURE 3-3:
Adding content to
a new SharePoint
page.

Site page

A *Site page*, which is the page you created in the earlier exercise, is a standard page that allows you to add components and content without needing much up-front planning. Using a Site page, you can quickly get content onto a page and shared with others around your organization. The Site page is new and was designed to make the onramp to using SharePoint less of a burden for newcomers.

TIP

The default page that is created when you select Add a Page from the Site Settings gear icon is a Site page.

Wiki page

A *Wiki page*, also known as a content page, is the Swiss Army knife of pages and allows for easy development and customization using a rich text editor built right into the browser. A Wiki page is easy to develop and is an extremely powerful and intuitive collaboration, data capture, and documentation tool.

Web Part page

A *Web Part page* provides Web Part zones where you can drag and drop various Web Parts from the gallery. A *Web Part* is a reusable piece of functionality that can be dragged and dropped right onto your pages. A number of Web Parts are available right out of the box, and Web Parts can also be custom developed to meet your specific needs. Imagine a Web Part developed specifically for your organization. After the Web Part is deployed, you could add that custom Web Part to any page you work with on any site in your organization.

Web Parts are discussed later in this chapter and in more detail in Chapter 6.

Publishing page

The *Publishing page* is designed to separate the functionality between managing content and managing the look and feel of the page. A Publishing page is only available when certain features are turned on by site administrators. All Publishing pages live in a special library called Pages. The Pages library is created automatically when the publishing features are turned on for the site. These pages use a special library because the Pages library already has preconfigured functionality such as versioning and workflow that is designed for the management and distribution of content, or in other words, publishing content.

TIP

The Publishing page is only available when the publishing feature has been activated at the site collection and site level.

Chapter 6 covers creating and developing pages.

Understanding Web Parts

A Web Part is one of those fairly rare things in technology that has a descriptive name: A Web Part is a part of a web page. You can think of a Web Part as a bundled piece of web functionality that can be added to a SharePoint page. For example, you will find web parts to add the list and library apps you have created on your site.

SharePoint has a number of Web Parts available that you can add to your pages. You add a Web Part using the Web Part Gallery, shown in Figure 3-4.

TIP

The Web Parts that are available out of the box depend on how your SharePoint implementation was set up and which features are activated.

In addition to the Web Parts that ship with SharePoint, you can also add custom Web Parts to the Web Part Gallery. A number of third-party developers create Web Parts that can be purchased; Web Parts can also be developed by in-house SharePoint developers.

Web Parts are covered in more detail in Chapter 6.

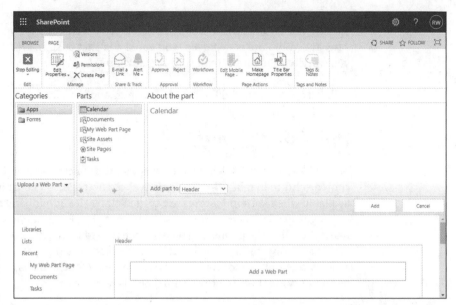

FIGURE 3-4:
The Web Part
Gallery in
SharePoint.

Digging into SharePoint Features

Terminology is often a central point of confusion in most technology. SharePoint is no different. For example, the term *feature* means some sort of functionality or grouping of functionality. In SharePoint, the word *feature* has a very technical meaning: a collection of SharePoint functionality that can be activated and deactivated. When SharePoint programmers hear the term feature, they immediately think of a particular technical part of SharePoint. SharePoint programmers can bundle together a grouping of functionality they have developed for SharePoint into a single feature. Programmers might develop a bundle of functionality and package the entire thing into a single feature that users can activate or deactivate. For example, if you work in financial services, you might need a number of workflows, pages, images, and custom Web Parts on your SharePoint site. A programmer could build all of this functionality for you and package it all into a feature. When you're ready to use the functionality, you activate the financial services feature.

Microsoft developed a number of features that ship with the SharePoint product. You can view these features on any SharePoint site as long as you're an administrator. For example, the Mobile Browser View feature ships with SharePoint; it provides a view of SharePoint data specifically designed for smartphone browsers (see Figure 3-5).

Features are covered in detail in Chapter 18.

FIGURE 3-5:
The Mobile Browser View feature in SharePoint.

Integrating with Office

One aspect of SharePoint that fails to get as much attention as it deserves is its integration with Microsoft Office. If you use Office products such as Teams, Word, Excel, PowerPoint, OneNote, and Outlook, then you're already primed to leverage SharePoint. In fact, you might be working with SharePoint from within Office and not even realize it!

Working with SharePoint from within Microsoft Office products is covered in Chapter 9.

2

Diving Headfirst into SharePoint

Explore the SharePoint Mobile App — get it installed and learn how to access some of the most common elements of SharePoint right on your smartphone.

Take a deep dive into SharePoint sites. Learn how to create your own site using one of SharePoint's many site templates and how to link sites together with Hub Sites.

Work with Web Parts to display content on web pages.

Learn how to create, upload, and view content in SharePoint and take advantage of SharePoint as a content management system to get a handle on all your digital data.

Explore how SharePoint can be used with the Office productivity apps on desktop computers and laptops as well as on mobile devices.

Take a look at SharePoint's social networking features that let individuals and groups communicate, collaborate, share, and connect.

Chapter **4**

Discovering SharePoint in Your Pocket

O ver the years, SharePoint has become the dominant product for company intranet sites. Remember, an intranet site is a website for only your organization and includes things like human resources information, company policies, time entry, and so on. Microsoft recognized that more and more people are using mobile devices; thus, it created a SharePoint Mobile App. Think of the SharePoint Mobile App as SharePoint running on your mobile phone. Microsoft likes to claim that the app provides your organization's intranet right in your pocket.

In this chapter, you get the SharePoint Mobile App installed and learn how to use the app, including how to navigate and access some of the most common elements of SharePoint.

Installing the SharePoint Mobile App

Before diving into the functionality of the SharePoint Mobile App, you first need to install it on your smartphone and/or device.

Installing on iOS

To install the SharePoint Mobile App on your iPhone or iPad:

1. **Open the Apple App Store on your iOS device.**

2. **Tap Search at the bottom of the screen to display the Search bar.**

3. **Search for "sharepoint" in the search bar.**

   Make sure you choose the Microsoft app, as shown in Figure 4-1.

4. **Tap the Get button to install the app on your device.**

5. **Once the app has finished installing, tap the Open button.**

FIGURE 4-1:
Installing the
SharePoint app in
the Apple App
Store.

Installing on Android

To install the SharePoint Mobile App on your Android phone or tablet:

1. **Open the Google Play store on your Android device.**

2. **Search for "sharepoint" in the search bar.**

   Make sure you choose the Microsoft app, as shown in Figure 4-2.

3. **Tap the Install button to install the app on your device.**

4. **Once the app has finished downloading and installing, tap the Open button.**

FIGURE 4-2:
Installing the SharePoint app in the Google Play store.

Signing into the SharePoint Mobile App

When you first open the SharePoint Mobile App after installing it, you are presented with a sign-in screen where you can choose to sign into SharePoint Online or SharePoint Server (the on-premises version of SharePoint run by your local IT team), as shown in Figure 4-3.

TIP

To keep things simple, we will sign into SharePoint Online using the trial account we created in Chapter 1. If your organization is using SharePoint Server On-Premises, then you will need to get the sign-in information from your IT department.

FIGURE 4-3:
The SharePoint
Mobile App
sign-in screen.

To sign into SharePoint Online:

1. **Tap the Sign in to SharePoint Online button.**

2. **Enter your username.**

   In Chapter 1, we created our account and chose the account name share-pointfordummies.This gives us the domain: sharepointfordummies. onmicrosoft.com. We also chose the username as info. So our sign in username is info@sharepointfordummies.onmicrosoft.com.

3. **Enter your password and tap Sign In.**

   You will be asked if you want to let the app give you notifications. For our example, we do.

4. **Tap Yes.**

   The first-run experience for the SharePoint Mobile App appears and provides you guidance on the Find tab at the bottom of the screen, as shown in Figure 4-4.

Congratulations! You are up and running with SharePoint on your mobile device.

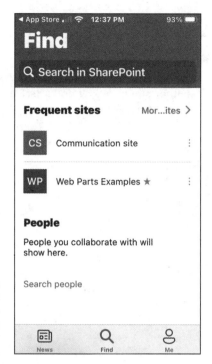

Finding Your SharePoint Stuff with the Find Tab

When you first sign into the SharePoint Mobile App, the screen opens with the Find tab already selected, as shown earlier in Figure 4-4. The other tabs you will notice at the bottom of the screen include a News tab and a Me tab. The Find tab is critical to the SharePoint Mobile App for a number of reasons. The most obvious is that SharePoint has a lot of stuff, and your mobile device has a small screen. Finding the stuff you need can be a challenge.

The Find tab includes sections for your Frequent SharePoint sites, People, Recent files, and Featured links. Under the Frequent sites, People, and Recent files sections, you can expand the search even further beyond your frequently visited sites. For example, you can browse for more files or search for a file in the Recent files section, and search for more people in the People section.

Exploring a SharePoint site

Because we have only created one SharePoint site (in Chapter 1) at this point, that site is prominently displayed as our frequent site on the Find tab, as shown in Figure 4-5. We also created another site called "Web Parts Examples" that you will see in the screenshot, but won't use it for now.

FIGURE 4-5:
The Frequent sites section of the Find screen.

To open the site, called "Communication site" in this example, just tap the site name. The app opens the site and we are in the same SharePoint site we would be in if we opened the site in a web browser. Figure 4-6 shows our SharePoint site open in the mobile app.

We can swipe the screen with our thumb and move down the screen. The first section we see is called News. The next section is called Events, which is followed by a Documents section.

The reason we are seeing these sections is because we created the site using the Team site template. It may not have been obvious in Chapter 1 that we created a Team site because the process of getting started with this template is very straightforward. We cover creating sites using other templates in Chapter 5, and in those cases, you will see different sections as you open those sites in the SharePoint Mobile App.

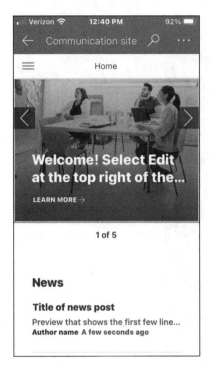

FIGURE 4-6:
The SharePoint site.

TIP

You can customize the sections that show up on the default page of a SharePoint site. For example, if you want to add a particular SharePoint Library or List app you have created, you are free to do so. We cover how to do this in Chapter 6.

Opening navigation

The site navigation menu is located in the upper-left corner of the screen in the form of three horizontal lines. This is often called a "hamburger menu" because some have said it looks similar to a hamburger. If you tap the hamburger menu the navigation for the SharePoint site slides out from the left side of the screen, as shown in Figure 4-7.

REMEMBER

The SharePoint site you view in the SharePoint Mobile App is the exact same SharePoint site you can view in your web browser on a desktop or laptop computer. If you change a SharePoint site, you are changing the site for both the users of the SharePoint Mobile App and for those who access the site through a traditional web browser. As you develop your SharePoint sites, it is a good idea to keep in mind the experience users will have on the site when they are using their web browsers or their phones or tablets.

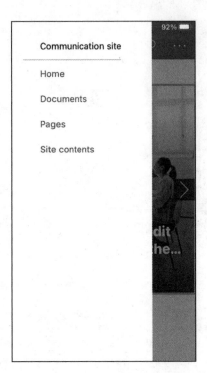

FIGURE 4-7:
The navigation
menu on the
SharePoint
Mobile App.

You can open a SharePoint component from the navigation menu by tapping that item. If you don't want to navigate away from the screen you are currently on, you can slide the navigation back to the left and it will close for you.

Getting the Latest News with the News Tab

The News tab is a one-stop location for all the news coming in from across the various parts of SharePoint that you have access to. This includes news from different sites as well as announcements and other social news posts.

The News tab is shown in Figure 4-8, and we posted a news page about the new book. We posted the news page on our laptop and then on our smartphone, we swiped down to refresh the page and the news appeared right away. We cover the social aspects of SharePoint in Chapter 10.

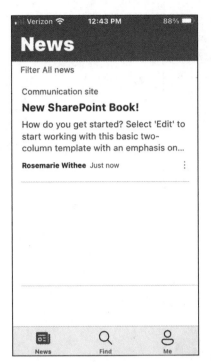

FIGURE 4-8:
The News tab on
the SharePoint
Mobile App.

All About You with the Me Tab

The Me tab shows you your profile, lets you edit your profile, and shows a listing of all of your recent and saved content. The Me tab is shown in Figure 4-9.

You will notice a listing of a couple of pages we recently worked on: "My First Page" and "first-webpart-page." These pages show up because SharePoint thinks that since we recently worked on these, we might want to view our latest work. This is a recurring theme throughout SharePoint.

TIP

One of the recurring complaints of SharePoint in the past was that there was just too much content "stuff" everywhere, and it was hard to find anything. This problem becomes bigger when you are working on a small smartphone screen or tablet because you don't have as much screen real estate to view things. The solution Microsoft came up with is to show your recent content first, since it is likely that what you were recently working on, say before lunch, you will want to continue working on after lunch. We cover working with content in greater detail in Chapter 7.

Also on the Me tab is the Settings icon that looks like a gear. It is located in the top-right corner of the screen. When you tap the gear icon, the Settings screen appears, as shown in Figure 4-10.

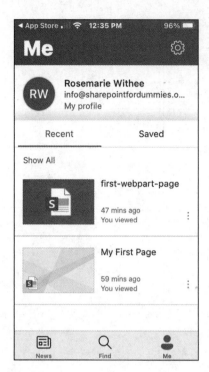

FIGURE 4-9:
The Me tab on
the SharePoint
Mobile App.

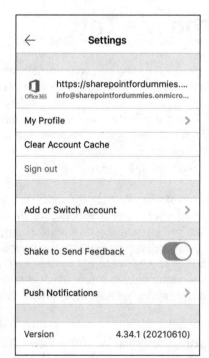

FIGURE 4-10:
The Settings
screen of the
SharePoint
Mobile App.

From the Settings screen you can edit your profile, clear your account cache on this device, switch the account you are using, sign out, send feedback, toggle push notifications, learn about what's new in the app, see the version of the app you are currently using, send feedback, view help, set privacy and cookies, and review third-party notices. We cover working with your Microsoft 365 Profile page in Chapter 13.

Chapter **5**

Understanding SharePoint Sites

I n Chapter 1, you get up and running with Microsoft 365 and SharePoint Online in a matter of minutes by creating a SharePoint site using the Team site template. In this chapter, you take a deeper dive into SharePoint sites. You learn how to create your own site using SharePoint's various site templates and how to access it in Microsoft 365. You explore some of the basic components of a site such as its navigation and pages. You also learn how SharePoint sites can be linked together using a new feature called *hub sites*.

Accessing SharePoint Sites in Microsoft 365

If you are following along with the book, you created a Team site in Chapter 1. You then learned how to open that site using the SharePoint Mobile App in Chapter 4. You can also open the same Team site using your favorite web browser such as Microsoft Edge, Google Chrome, Mozilla Firefox, or Apple Safari. (And if you haven't yet taken a peek at Chapters 1 and 4, do not despair — keep reading. You can get caught up along the way.)

To access the SharePoint Team site you create in Chapter 1, you must first sign into Microsoft 365 and then choose SharePoint from the available apps. Here's how:

1. Open your web browser and navigate to www.office.com.

If you have signed in before, your dashboard will load. If you have not yet signed in, you will need to sign in here with the credentials you create in Chapter 1.

2. Click the waffle icon in the top-left corner of the screen and then select SharePoint, as shown in Figure 5-1.

The Frequent Sites page appears, which lists your frequently visited SharePoint sites (see Figure 5-2). In this case we have some of the sites we frequent including the Team site we created in Chapter 1.

TIP

You can also click SharePoint from the left side of the main dashboard to access the Frequent Sites page. However, if you are in another app, such as Outlook, you can always get to SharePoint using the waffle icon in the top-left corner.

Select SharePoint

Waffle icon

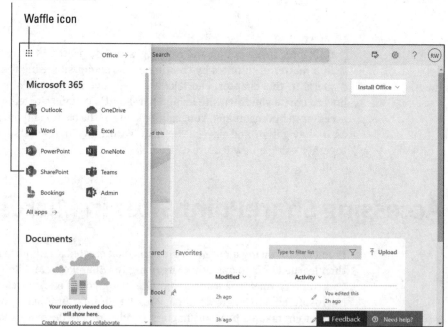

FIGURE 5-1:
Selecting SharePoint from the main office. com landing page.

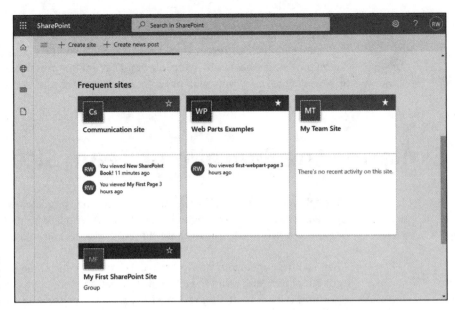

FIGURE 5-2:
The Frequent
Sites page in
SharePoint.

3. **Click the SharePoint site you want to open.**

Presto! Your SharePoint site opens and you are ready to begin exploring it, as shown in Figure 5-3.

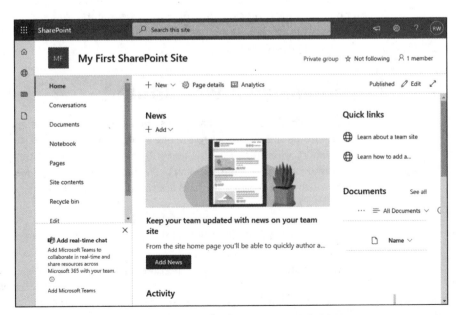

FIGURE 5-3:
The main page of
a SharePoint
Team site.

TIP

Accessing a site that is hosted in SharePoint Online, which is part of Microsoft 365, may be a little different than sites that are hosted on your network. If your SharePoint site is hosted by your internal IT team on-premises, instead of going to www.office.com, you will need to ask them for the web address of your SharePoint site.

Exploring the SharePoint Team Site

Although you can choose from many different site templates when you create a SharePoint site, the most popular is the Team site template, as it contains a number of useful features for teams to share content and apps and collaborate on projects.

When you first open your newly created Team site, you can do a number of things right out of the gate. From the left-side navigation menu, you can partake in Conversations (which is an integration with Outlook), you can store your digital documents in the prebuilt Document Library app (Documents), you can open OneNote to keep shared notes (Notebook), and you can create new web pages (Pages).

The default page that appears when you first open your Team site is the Home page, which is also always accessible by selecting Home from the navigation menu. The Team site Home page has lots of useful functionality. It includes sections for News, Quick Links, Activity, Documents, and site Comments. You can also customize the Home page sections to fit your own needs, which you learn how to do in Chapter 6.

Finding your way around

All SharePoint Team sites have the same features. If you're using a new Team site, your site should be similar to the one shown earlier in Figure 5-3. If you are using a default Communication site, you will see a site using that template designed for communications. If your site has been customized, it may look slightly different. Never fear: All the same features are there. You may just have to hunt a little bit to find them.

Almost every SharePoint site contains the following major sections:

>> **Header:** The header spans the entire top of the page. The header in a SharePoint page acts much like the menu in a traditional Windows application, such as Microsoft Word. SharePoint even features the ribbon in the page header, similar to how the ribbon appears in the top of many Office applications. You expand it by clicking one of the tabs such as Files or Library. After

you click a tab, the ribbon expands in a way that looks very similar to the rest of the Office products. We take a closer look at the ribbon in Chapter 6.

>> **Left navigation pane:** The navigation pane provides quick access to the site's document libraries, lists, and discussion boards. You can even add links to content you create, such as documents and web pages. The navigation is fully customizable and you can add any links you want. You can even add links to websites outside of SharePoint, such as a link to your partner website or any other favorite website.

>> **Page content:** The content displays in the body of the page. Microsoft has done a nice job of provide a good default page for the Team site. You can add your own pages and also customize the default page. Web pages are explored in Chapter 6.

Generally speaking, the header and left navigation pane stay fairly consistent, whereas the body of the page changes to display the content of the web page. This is very similar to how most websites work. However, some sites have different layouts. For example, the Communication site includes navigation across the top and then large tiles and sections that are geared toward distributing information to an organization.

Microsoft has spent a lot of money on usability research to determine how best to lay out the pages in SharePoint. We highly encourage you to use the layouts provided by Microsoft instead of creating your own custom layouts. We have seen more than one site turn into a never ending journey of changes and edits that end up causing confusion for people that land on the site.

Uploading documents

On a default Team site (see Figure 5-3), you see a section in the lower-right part of the page called Documents. This seemingly innocuous little section is actually an example of SharePoint at its finest.

A link to the Documents section also appears in the navigation menu. This is a common theme in SharePoint. There are seemingly endless ways to do any one task in SharePoint, which can make for some interesting breakroom chatter. One person might insist on how to do something in SharePoint while another person might insist on a different way. In SharePoint both ways can be correct!

In a nutshell, Documents is a digital repository to store your files. Under the covers, however, Documents is a combination of pages, apps, and Web Parts. (You discover how it all comes together in the next few chapters.) Adding a new file, such as a Microsoft Word document, to Documents is as simple as clicking the ellipses link in the Documents header and then selecting New, as shown in

Figure 5-4. After a document is located in SharePoint, you have all the content management functionality right at your fingertips, such as check-in/check-out, versioning, security, and workflow.

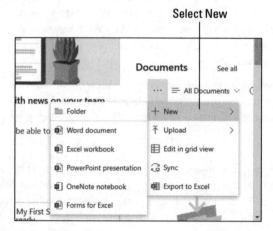

FIGURE 5-4: Adding a new document to a SharePoint Team site.

Sharing your Team site

A site without any users is a bit pointless. You can share your SharePoint Team site in a number of different ways. The easiest way to share is to invite users to the site. When you share a site, the people you are sharing with will receive an email with all the information they need to access the site.

Share your site from your web browser

To share your SharePoint site using your web browser, follow these steps:

1. **Open your web browser and navigate to the SharePoint Team site you want to share.**

2. **Click the gear icon in the upper-right corner and select Site Permissions.**

    The Permissions pane opens.

3. **Click the Invite People button and choose to add members to the group of users who can access the site or choose to share the site only.**

    In this example, we will choose to share the site only, as shown in Figure 5-5, which opens the Share Site window shown in Figure 5-6.

     If you choose to add members to the group you will be presented with a list of users who are already part of your Microsoft 365 subscription. If you are following along with the book, you will only see a single user (unless you have added more along the way).

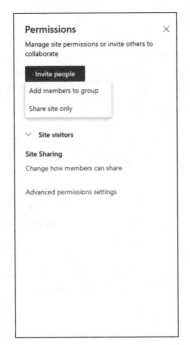

FIGURE 5-5:
Inviting people to
a SharePoint site.

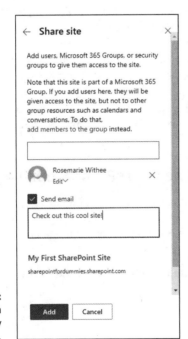

FIGURE 5-6:
Sharing a
SharePoint site by
sending an email.

4. **Enter the email address of the person with whom you want to share the site.**

WARNING

If the person is outside of your organization, a message that alerts you to that fact appears. This notice is important, as you want to be careful not to share information outside of your organization if it shouldn't be shared. If you are an administrator, you can turn off the ability to share with people outside of the organization completely.

5. **Type a message to the person with whom you are sharing the site, confirm that the check box for Send Email is selected, and then click Add (see Figure 5-6).**

TIP

If you are using the classic SharePoint experience, your interface will be different than we describe here. For example, in the past, a Share button would be displayed at the top of a site. However, there could be a number of reasons why you may not see this button. We have seen where it doesn't appear in the Chrome browser but appears in others. We outlined the procedure to share a site via the Permissions window since this method works regardless of whether you see a Share button at the top of your screen or not.

REMEMBER

If you don't have permission to share access to the site, you won't see the Site Permissions link when you click the gear icon — SharePoint automatically removes it. In general with SharePoint, if you read about something and it doesn't match what you see on your site, it is probably due to one of two issues: First, you might not have the right permissions for that particular feature; or second, the feature might not be activated or configured for your site. For example, if email is not configured for your SharePoint instance, you won't see the Share button.

To find out more about activating and deactivating features, check out Chapter 18. And of course, you must also have the right permissions to activate the feature you're looking for.

Share your site from the SharePoint Mobile App

To share your SharePoint site using the SharePoint Mobile App, follow these steps:

1. **Open the SharePoint Mobile App on your smartphone or tablet and navigate to the site you want to share.**

2. **Tap the ellipsis icon in the upper-right corner of the screen.**

The site options shown in Figure 5-7 appear.

3. **Select Share This Site.**

From this point the process is the same as you would use for sharing anything else from your mobile device. For example, on iOS you see the familiar sharing mechanism displays, as shown in Figure 5-8.

4. **Choose how you want to share the site.**

FIGURE 5-7:
The options for a
SharePoint site
on an iPhone.

FIGURE 5-8:
Sharing a
SharePoint site
from an iPhone
using the
SharePoint
Mobile App.

Creating a SharePoint Site

You can create a new SharePoint site using your web browser or the SharePoint Mobile App. When you create a SharePoint site, you first must select the site template you want to use. Each site template includes all the preconfigured elements you need, such as specific features, default pages, and navigation. The most popular site template is still the Team site template since it contains a broad set of features designed for team interaction and collaboration. But it is important to understand the other templates that are available so you can use them when you need them.

You can create a new SharePoint subsite using your web browser or the SharePoint Mobile App. The following sections show you how.

TIP

Microsoft is making a push to simplify SharePoint. One way they are doing this is by moving away from subsites. Subsites are still valuable in our opinion and can still be used when needed. However, be aware that Microsoft would rather you just create top-level sites.

Create a subsite from your web browser

To create a new site using your web browser, follow these steps:

1. **Open your web browser and navigate to your existing SharePoint site.**

2. **Click the gear icon in the upper-right corner of the screen and choose Site Contents.**

   The Contents screen for the site appears.

3. **Click the New drop-down menu and select Subsite, as shown in Figure 5-9.**

   The New SharePoint Site screen appears, as shown in Figure 5-10.

4. **In the Title and Description section, enter a title and description for the new site.**

5. **In the Web Site Address section, enter how you want the site to appear in the URL of the web browser.**

6. **In the Template Selection section select a site template for the site.**

   The Team site template is the default, but there are several other site templates to choose from as well. We recommend creating one of each and exploring them to understand how the templates work. This is important so you can create the right site for your particular situation. In this example we will choose to create a Document Center site.

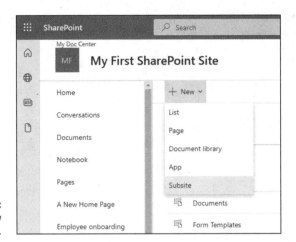

FIGURE 5-9:
The New
drop-down menu.

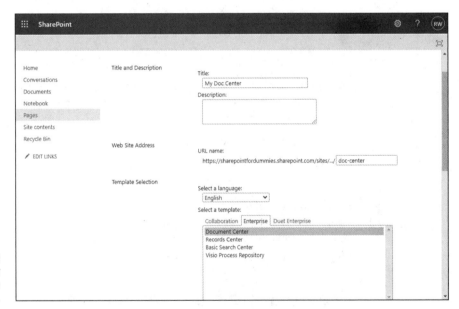

FIGURE 5-10:
The New
SharePoint Site
screen.

TIP

Microsoft recently retired the Blog site template from SharePoint Online. If you are using SharePoint On-Premises, you might still see it. Microsoft is constantly changing SharePoint Online, so if you don't see something exactly as we describe it then things might have recently changed.

TIP

If you are ever in doubt about which template to use, you are usually safe with the Team site template.

7. **In the Permissions section, choose whether you want the new site to have the same permissions as the parent site or if you want to create new permissions, as shown in Figure 5-11.**

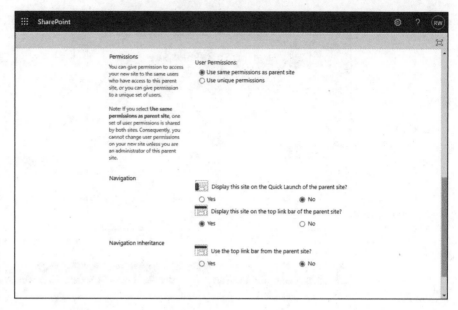

FIGURE 5-11:
Setting
permssions in the
New SharePoint
Site screen.

8. **In the Navigation section, decide how you want the navigation displayed on the parent site and if you want the new site to show the parent site's navigation too.**

9. **Click Create to create the new SharePoint site.**

   After a few moments your new site will be created and opened in your browser, as shown in Figure 5-12.

TIP

In addition to creating a subsite you can create a parent site called a Site Collection. To do that, you need to go into the administrative interface of Microsoft 365. We cover how to create a Site Collection you can use as a client portal in Chapter 20.

Create a site from the SharePoint Mobile App

To create a new site using the SharePoint Mobile App, follow these steps:

1. **Open the SharePoint Mobile App on your smartphone or tablet.**

2. **Tap the hamburger menu in the top-left corner to open the navigation window and tap Site Contents.**

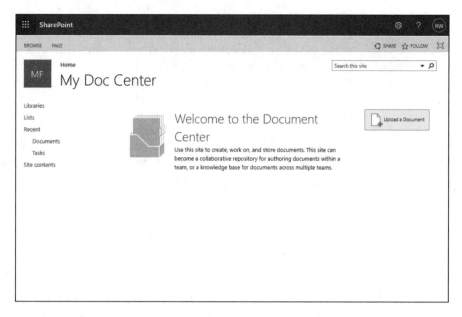

FIGURE 5-12:
A new SharePoint
site based on the
Document Center
template.

3. **On the Site Contents screen, tap the plus (+) icon, as shown in Figure 5-13, and choose Subsite.**

4. **Fill in the title, URL, permissions, and navigation information for your new site (as described in the previous section for creating a site using your web browser) and click Create.**

FIGURE 5-13:
Creating a site in
the SharePoint
Mobile App on an
iPhone.

Every SharePoint site is contained within another SharePoint site in a hierarchy. At the top of the hierarchy is a special type of site called a *site collection*. Creating and administering a site collection takes special permissions. Every site within the site collection is called a *subsite*. Both types of websites are often just referred to as a *website* or *site*. The site you just created is a subsite of whatever site you were in when you created it. There are really no differences between using a site that is a site collection and a site that is a subsite. To users, both types of sites look and act the same. The differences lie in the navigation, security settings, and features. (The differences between administering a subsite and a site collection are discussed in Chapters 19 and 20.)

Requesting a SharePoint Site

If you aren't a site administrator, you won't have permissions to create a new SharePoint site. In this case, you need to request one. Most organizations have a process for requesting a Team site. For example, you might send an email request to the SharePoint administrator or fill out a form.

Whatever you have to do to get your own SharePoint Team site in your organization, get one. At a minimum, you need to provide your SharePoint administrator with the following information to get a Team site:

>> **The site name:** This is the friendly caption that appears in the header of your site and in any site directory where your site may be listed.

>> **The site template:** The template determines what kind of site SharePoint makes for you. SharePoint includes dozens of predefined site templates. Your company may even create custom site templates. Tell your administrator you want a Team site, which is the most popular of all the site templates.

>> **The web address or URL:** This address is the unique location where your Team site is hosted. In most organizations, all Team sites are located off the same root web address. Some examples we've seen include

```
http://intranet.company.com/sites
http://portal/projectsites
http://sharepoint/sites
```

Your organization may also ask who has permission to access the site. By default, all SharePoint Team sites have three basic kinds of users, which are called SharePoint *groups:*

- » **Visitors** have Read Only permission. They can view your site without making any contributions.

- » **Members** can participate in your Team site by uploading and editing documents or adding tasks or other items.

- » **Owners** have Full Control permission to customize the site. SharePoint administrators likely assume that if you're requesting the site, you're also the proud owner of the site unless you specifically tell them otherwise.

You need to decide which users fit into these three SharePoint groups. SharePoint offers more than just these three groups, and you can create your own groups to meet your needs.

Your site's users must be connected locally to your network or have permission from your network administrator to access your network remotely. Some companies set up a special kind of deployment for SharePoint, called an *extranet*, that provides a secure way for non-employees to log in to their SharePoint Team sites without actually being on the internal company network.

Setting up SharePoint in an extranet environment can be done in lots of ways. Configuring a SharePoint extranet in your company's network can be complex and is outside the scope of this book. However, the good news is that SharePoint Online, which is part of the Microsoft 365 suite, eliminates many of the technical barriers to creating an extranet.

Grouping Sites with Hub Sites

SharePoint includes a feature that enables you to group SharePoint sites together in a single unit called a *hub site.* In particular, with a hub site you can group navigation together to make sites easier to navigate as a group and create simple content rollups and search areas. If you have the need for more than one SharePoint site, and you need to group them together and have a single entry into all of the sites, a hub site is the way to go.

If you are a SharePoint administrator, you can create hub sites using the new SharePoint Admin Center or with PowerShell. (We cover SharePoint administration in Chapter 18.) To create a hub site, select Active Sites from the Admin Center and then select a site. You will find Hub as an option in the top menu. In the Hub drop-down menu, you can register a site as a hub site or associate a site with a hub site.

Microsoft provides detailed guidance on creating a hub site using PowerShell, but be warned. PowerShell is a command-line interface and is not for the faint of heart. If you want to read about creating a hub site using PowerShell, check out the Microsoft article "Set up your SharePoint hub site" on the Microsoft Office support site. The easiest way to find it is to go to support.office.com and search for the exact title.

CHOOSING AMONG EDGE, CHROME, FIREFOX, AND SAFARI

Which browser should you use with SharePoint? Firefox, Chrome, Edge, and Safari browsers have some differences; for instance, some pages look better in Firefox or Chrome than in Edge. Because Chrome and Firefox were designed to be OS-agnostic, they support Mac and Linux users as well as Windows users and Microsoft Edge supports Windows, macOS and soon Linux. Microsoft has worked hard to make the SharePoint experience the same in all mainstream browsers; however, you might find a scenario where something doesn't work as expected in all browsers. The bottom line is that if you think something should work and it isn't currently working, try the same thing in a different browser, then choose the browser that works the best and is speedy.

Chapter **6**

Working with Web Pages and Web Parts

H ow many times have you heard, "We need the team to get on the same page?" Well, that's not a problem if you're using SharePoint. If you're a facilitator, communicator, and/or have a creative streak, you need this chapter. Although SharePoint gives you a lot of helpful tools to work with content, the ability to communicate effectively with your team, starting with a customiz-able home page, pulls everything together.

Web pages and the components you can add to those pages called Web Parts let you arrange and present information in a collaboration site. Pages can display freeform text, tables, hyperlinks, and images, as well as Web Parts that show app content from your site (or other sites!) arranged as you want. Web Parts can be closed temporarily or moved. You can also modify Web Parts to show only the data you want from an app. You can inform, organize, and focus your team with your pages, something that otherwise would take a lot of effort with email and network shares. In this chapter, we show you how to work with web pages and Web Parts to collaborate effectively with your team using SharePoint.

Understanding SharePoint Web Pages

The SharePoint site you create in Chapter 1 is based on the Team site template. The default home page for this site is called the *Site page.* In addition to the Site page, you can create more pages for your site and choose the type of page you want it to be. The types of pages you can choose are:

» Site page

» Web Part page

» Wiki page

» Publishing page

Sometimes giving users too many choices is worse than just having a really nice default choice. So what Microsoft has done is make it really easy to create a Site page. A Site page is a very flexible and easy-to-use page type, so it makes sense that it would be easy to create one.

TIP

While the default home page for the Team site template is the Site page, you can change the home page of your site to any Wiki page or Web Part page. Simply click the Make Homepage button in the Page Actions area of the Page tab on the ribbon while editing the preferred page. Or to change the home page to a different Site page, navigate to the library where your Site pages live, select the ellipsis next to a page and select Make Homepage from the drop-down options.

Creating a Site page

You have a couple of options to create a Site page. When you first land on your SharePoint site, you can click the New drop-down menu at the top of the page and then select Page, as shown in Figure 6-1. You can also click the Gear icon located in the top-right corner of the screen and choose Add a Page, as shown in Figure 6-2.

In addition to the default Site page, you can create other types of pages for your SharePoint site, such as Web Part pages and Wiki pages. Creating other pages takes a little bit more work than creating a Site page, but once you get a grasp on the basics of how SharePoint works, you won't have any problem.

Select Page   Click New

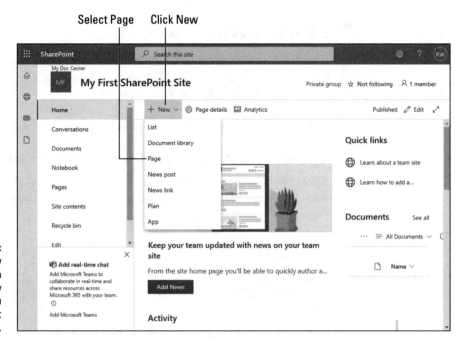

FIGURE 6-1:
Creating a new
Site page from
the New
drop-down menu
on a SharePoint
site.

Select to add a page   Gear icon

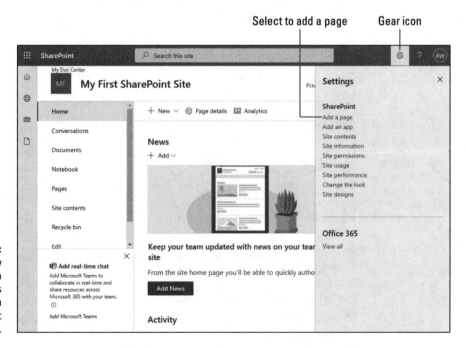

FIGURE 6-2:
Creating a new
Site page from
the Settings
drop-down menu
on a SharePoint
site.

Creating a Web Part page

To create a new Web Part page or Wiki page, you need to first navigate to the location where the page will be stored. In this example, we will create a new Web Part page in the Team site we created in Chapter 1.

To create a new Web Part page for your SharePoint site, follow these steps:

1. **Open your web browser and navigate to your SharePoint site.**

2. **Select Pages from the navigation menu on the left side of the screen to open the location where your web pages are stored, as shown in Figure 6-3.**

Select Pages

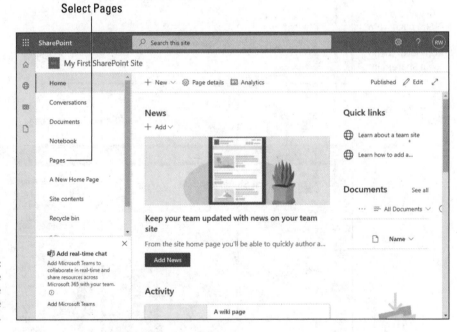

FIGURE 6-3: Opening the location where your page will be stored.

3. **Click the New drop-down menu at the top of the screen and choose Web Part Page.**

The New Web Part Page appears.

4. **Provide a name for your new page in the Name text box and then select a layout template.**

The layout is how the Web Parts will be organized as you add them to the page.

5. Select the location where you want to save the new page.

In this example, we will choose to save it in the Site Pages location. Figure 6-4 shows the completed form.

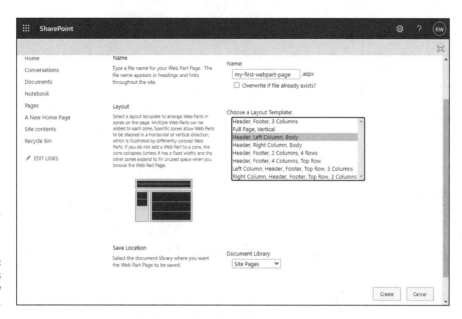

FIGURE 6-4:
Fill in the details to create a new Web Part page.

6. Click Create to create your new Web Part page.

The new page is created and opens up for us to edit in Edit mode, as shown in Figure 6-5. You can now add Web Parts to the page, which we will do shortly.

A Web Part page contains various Web Part zones in which you can place Web Parts; it doesn't have the same editing experience as the Wiki page (which you learn about next). The Web Part page, however, provides for a consistent layout of Web Parts in order to create ordered pages with Web Part functionality. For example, you can drag and drop Web Parts between zones without reconfiguring the Web Parts. A Wiki page, on the other hand, is more freeform. You could insert a table on a Wiki page and then insert Web Parts into different cells of the table, but that's a lot of work. With a Web Part page, you choose the Web Part zone layout when you create the page and add Web Parts to the available zones.

TIP

Building a page using the Site page in SharePoint is similar to building a page using the visual builder in WordPress, as in both programs it is very easy to get started quickly building pages. You can add Web Parts to a Site page, too, but you don't have as much control over the layout. The Web Part page is designed specifically for Web Part layouts and takes a little more time to get your brain around. However, it provides a more structured layout environment.

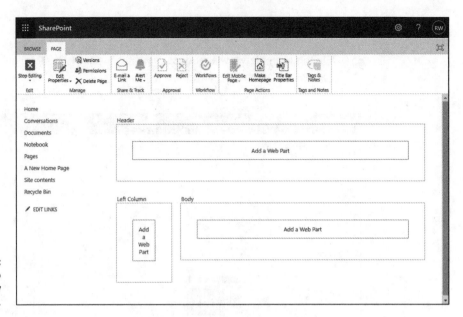

FIGURE 6-5:
The new Web Part page, ready for editing.

Creating a Wiki page

A Wiki page is designed to be intuitive and easy to get up and running with SharePoint pages. A *Wiki page* is similar to a Microsoft Word document. You place the page in Edit mode and start adding content. Just like a Word document, you have the ribbon at the top to format text and insert items. And when you want to get advanced and modify the HTML, all you need to do is click a button to edit the source code.

Only members of your Team site's default Members group have permission to modify Wiki pages. If you want some people to be able to read your Wiki pages but not edit them, add those users to your site's default Visitors group. See Chapter 21 for more details on managing site access.

A Wiki page consists of an editable region where you place your content. In this editable region, you can place almost any kind of content imaginable — freeform text, tables, hyperlinks, images, even Web Parts. A Wiki page combines the best aspects of a typical Wiki page with a Web Part page.

You can create new Wiki pages for your site the same way you created a Web Part page earlier in this chapter. Just choose Wiki Page instead of Web Part Page in the New drop-down menu.

You can create additional Wiki page libraries if you want to manage a specific wiki topic in your site.

Introducing the Ribbon

Whenever you edit a web page in SharePoint, a ribbon appears at the top of the page with items you can use for whatever you happen to be editing. The ribbon is usually tucked away in the header of the SharePoint site until you open a page in Edit mode. And for Site pages, Microsoft has removed it all together in an effort to streamline the content-creation process.

One thing to keep in mind when using SharePoint Online is that Microsoft is constantly tweaking the user interface. More than once we have been surprised to find the user interface different from what we are used to and were expecting. After poking around a little bit, we figure it out and get used to the new user interface because the features and functionality don't change all that much. On the other hand, SharePoint On-Premises has a locked-down user interface that can be valuable for companies that don't like change. However, On-Premises comes with a massive management and maintenance cost and is usually only seen in the largest of companies these days.

The ribbon in SharePoint features menu items that are relevant to the kind of page you're viewing, arranged in tabs. For example, the home page of a Team site displays two tabs: Browse and Page. You find most of the menu commands you need to use on the ribbon, and some ribbon buttons contain drop-down lists.

Figure 6-6 shows the ribbon with the Page tab active. Notice that this is a blank page. It is the Web Part page we created earlier in the chapter. We simply clicked the Stop Editing button to exit Edit mode, and then clicked the Page tab to see the ribbon for the page. If we were to select Edit Page in the top-left corner, we would return to Edit mode and the screen shown earlier in Figure 6-5.

The ribbon displays commands based on what you are working on in SharePoint. These commands are *contextual* because the commands that appear depend on the context of where you are in the site. For example, if you are working on a Document Library, you will see Files and Library tabs on the ribbon, in addition to the standard Browse tab. If you are working with a Microsoft Word document, you will see items related to Word.

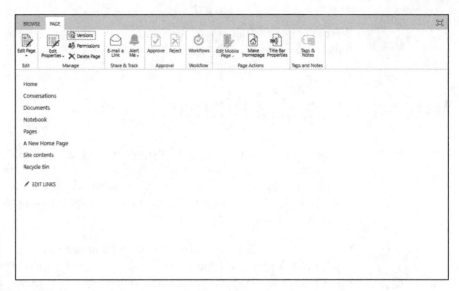

FIGURE 6-6:
Use the ribbon to access menu commands.

Deciding What Type of Page to Create

For some who have lived through different versions of SharePoint over the years, it may simply be familiarity that keeps you using a Web Part page. Converting previous sites to the new version may be a factor as well. However, the need for creating rich content pages in a collaboration site is now better served by the Site page. The Site page tries to combine both the flexibility of a Wiki page and the structure of the Web Part page.

TIP

If you are in doubt about what type of page to create, start with a Site page. If you want to go deeper, choose between a Web Part page and a Wiki page, depending on your needs:

» **Web Part page:** Use when you need mostly Web Parts with little text content. Examples include pages with multiple List View Web Parts, Office application Web Parts, custom search and site directories, and pages that use connected Web Parts. Web Part pages are simple to create without the editor needing skills in rich content editing. Although versioning may be turned on in the library in which you store your Web Part pages, the Web Parts themselves don't retain history.

» **Wiki page:** Use when you have mostly a need for rich text content, such as text, tables, links, and images. You can still insert Web Parts or use no Web Parts at all. The HTML content in Wiki pages is also subject to versioning if versioning is turned on in the library.

TIP

There is also a special type of page called a Publishing page, which is part of a SharePoint Publishing *site.* Publishing sites let you control at a very granular level how content is published to your SharePoint website pages. You can lock down a Publishing page and allow people to enter or edit content but not change the look and feel or the location of the content. This is important for broadly consumed websites in order to maintain a consistent look and feel of content throughout the site. We touch on Publishing pages in Chapter 22, but Publishing sites require significant resources to implement and manage and are beyond the scope of this book.

Digging into Web Parts

Web Parts are reusable components that display content on web pages in SharePoint. Just as the name implies, a Web Part is a part of a web page that is all packaged together nicely and easy to work with. Web Parts are a fundamental part of the Team site experience, so make it a point to get comfortable with them and know what your options are.

REMEMBER

The Team site template is just one option when creating a new SharePoint website. There are other templates you can choose to create a new website (as you learn in Chapter 5), and Web Parts are critical to all of them in SharePoint.

Adding a Web Part to Your Page

A Web Part is an individual component of content that can be placed on a SharePoint page, in either a zone in a Web Part page or in Rich Content areas of the Site page or Wiki page. Web Parts can be moved, added, and deleted, framed by borders and titles, and closed and reopened, depending on your need. In other words, they are a little piece of web functionality all wrapped up in a nice package for you.

In a Team site, you may place Web Parts on your home page for your users to read and access items from your apps, such as announcements, documents, links, calendars, and contacts. You can add text for additional instructions and images to enhance the collaboration experience.

To add a Web Part to the Site page that was added by default to your Team site, follow these steps:

1. **Open your web browser and navigate to your Team site.**

2. **Click the Edit button that appears in the upper-right corner of the page.**

   The page opens in Edit mode.

   With a Site page you can add Web Parts in nearly any location. Look for the plus (+) signs. Some plus signs let you add new sections and some let you add Web Parts, as shown in Figure 6-7.

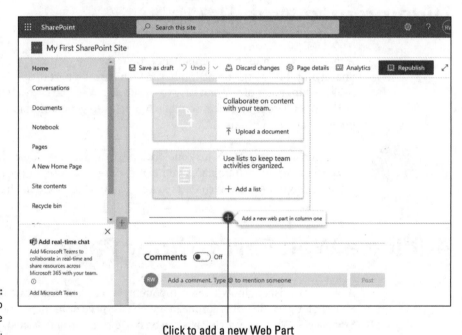

FIGURE 6-7:
Adding a Web Part to a Site page.

Click to add a new Web Part

3. **Click a plus (+) sign to add a new Web Part.**

   If you are using a Web Part page, you just click the Add a Web Part link in any location as shown earlier in Figure 6-5.

TIP

4. **Select the Web Part you wish to add.**

   In this example, we will add a YouTube video to the page, as shown in Figure 6-8. Once the Web Part is added, you can configure it using the dialog box that opens.

5. **When you are finished adding the Web Part, click the Publish button to update the page.**

The YouTube Web Part

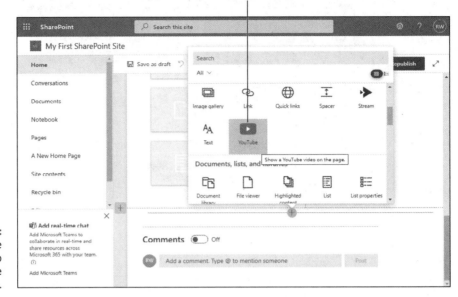

TIP

Some Web Parts can be used only if certain functionality is enabled in your site. For example, to use Business Data Web Parts, Business Data Sources must be enabled. Other categories of Web Parts, such as Content Rollup Web Parts, provide the ability to feed data from lower-level sites to a site higher in the hierarchy, such as the home page of an intranet. In addition, connector Web Parts, such as GitHub, Twitter, Salesforce, and Trello, require you to log in to those services so that they can appear on the SharePoint page.

If you add a Web Part to a Site page, the interface shown earlier in Figure 6-8 appears. If you are adding a Web Part on a Web Part page, you will see the traditional Web Part Gallery that has been a part of SharePoint for some time (see Figure 6-9). The Web Part Gallery first shows a list of Web Part categories, and when you click a category, you see all the Web Parts contained in that category. When the Web Part name is highlighted, you see a description as well as an example of each in the About the Part section before inserting it.

Follow these steps to insert a Web Part on a Web Part page or Wiki page:

1. **From the Web Part page, click the Page tab, then select Edit Page to enter Edit mode.**

   In a Wiki page, you insert Web Parts into one of the Rich Content areas in the layout. In a Web Part page, you insert Web Parts into one of the zones on the page. Note that the Page tab only appears in the classic experience which a Web Part page uses. A Wiki page, on the other hand, uses the new experience and you go straight to the edit button at the top of the page.

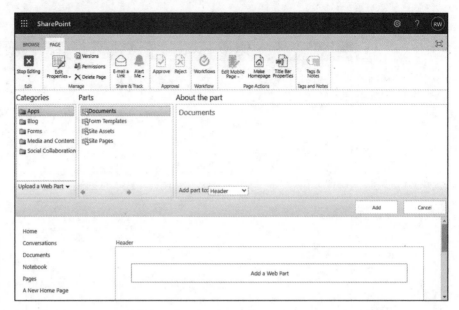

FIGURE 6-9:
The Web Part
Gallery on the
Web Part page in
SharePoint.

2. **In a Web Part page, click inside a zone.**

    The Web Part Gallery, shown earlier in Figure 6-9, appears. The About the Part section contains a drop-down list containing the names of all the zones on the page.

TIP

Because a Web Part page can contain only Web Parts, the Insert tab buttons for text and images actually insert a Content Editor Web Part or an Image View Web Part, respectively, for those selections.

3. **Select the Web Part you wish to add and then click the Add button.**

    The Web Part is placed on the page.

4. **Alternatively, in a Wiki page, click inside a Rich Content area, click Web Part from the Insert tab, and then Add a Web Part to add a Web Part the page.**

    Either select the area from the drop-down list and then click the Add button or drag the Web Part name into the zone or Rich Content area you want to place it in.

TIP

You can also use the Add button under the About the Part section to insert the Web Part into the zone or Rich Content area your cursor is in.

5. **In either page, modify the Web Part properties by clicking the Edit drop-down list (in the far right of the Web Part title) and choosing Edit Web Part.**

   By clicking on the Web Part, additional configuration options may appear in the ribbon. (Skip ahead to "Changing Web Part Properties" later in this chapter, for more about configuring Web Parts.)

TIP

Web Parts can be moved in a Web Part page or a Wiki page simply by dragging them from one zone or area to another.

Choosing the Right Web Part

The SharePoint gallery contains more than 80 Web Parts, as well as List View Web Parts created for any Library or List-based apps you've made. In addition, your company may create custom Web Parts or purchase them from third-party vendors.

REMEMBER

Your company may purchase or create additional Web Parts. Conversely, your company may choose not to make available every Web Part we describe in the upcoming list. Companies may also modify some Web Parts, such as the Content Editor Web Part, to disallow certain styles or JavaScript content.

With so many choices, how do you decide which Web Part to use? If you're like us, we're sure you'll find your favorites. We think about Web Parts as being either specialized or generalized in what they do. We tend to use the more general Web Parts, but in a lot of websites, we want to control how those Web Parts appear. When we're using an internal Team site, we tend to use the specialized Web Parts that contain fewer configuration items.

TIP

A constant source of confusion in SharePoint is that things aren't always as you would expect. For example, you might read about a cool Web Part, but when you go to try it out, it's nowhere to be found. There are a couple of reasons for this. The first is that not all Web Parts are available for every edition of SharePoint. The second reason is that functionality is turned on and off with specific SharePoint features. For example, you might be looking for a Web Part that only becomes available when the related feature is activated for your site. If you read about something and can't seem to find it, your next step should be in figuring out which feature to activate to get what you're looking for.

When you insert a Web Part onto your page, you're presented with the Web Part Gallery or the new Web Part Selector for the new Site page. The Web Part Gallery organizes Web Parts into categories. The top category in the list is always Apps.

These are all of the apps you have added to your site. It also includes custom apps you have developed, such as a custom List or Library app.

The new Site page Web Part Selector in SharePoint Online includes some exciting new connector Web Parts such as Salesforce and Trello, and more are being added all the time. The traditional Web Part Gallery includes the usual Web Parts and groups them into categories as outlined as follows.

WARNING

You might not see all of the Web Parts listed since they appear and disappear depending on whether the right SharePoint feature is activated or not. You learn how to activate SharePoint features in Chapter 18.

» **Apps:** These Web Parts display items from the List and Library apps on your site. You can use Views to filter, sort, and group the information presented in the Web Part.

» **Blog:** This category includes Web Parts for working with blogs. For example, you can add Web Parts that provide links to older blogs, show blog notifications, or even provide tools for blog owners and administrators.

» **Business Data:** The Business Data Web Parts allow you to display data from external data sources. This category includes Web Parts for displaying Excel and Visio documents in your web page.

» **Community:** These Web Parts are designed for Community sites and include functionality for providing information about the community, joining the community, community membership details, and what's happening information. In addition, there is a Tools Web Part for community owners and administrators.

» **Content Rollup:** This category includes Web Parts for rolling up content from multiple sources. For example, there are Web Parts to aggregate sites, query content, and search for content. In addition, this category contains Web Parts to view RSS and XML feeds. Because more and more content is available in RSS and XML formats, these Web Parts are especially useful. You use an XSL template to tell the Web Part how to display the RSS or XML content on your web page.

» **Document Sets:** These Web Parts display the content and properties of a Document Set. A *Document Set* is a grouping of documents in a Library app.

» **Filters:** The filter Web Parts provide numerous ways to filter the information displayed on the page. For example, you can add the Choice Filter to a page and then connect it to a List View Web Part so that the list is filtered by the value selected by the user. Your filter options include filtering by the current user who's visiting the page, date, good old-fashioned text values, or a query string. A *query string* is a value that you pass into the page by using a question mark, such as mypage.aspx?filter=somevalue. Another example would be adding a SharePoint List Filter Web Part to your page to only show certain items from a list. The actual list might include every product in your company, but you could add the Web Part to a department page and only show the products for that particular department.

>> **Forms:** There are two Web Parts for displaying forms: the HTML Form Web Part and the InfoPath Form Web Part. An HTML form uses basic HTML code to show a form. InfoPath is a retired Office product that was used to build forms. InfoPath is no longer included with Office. Microsoft is doubling down on forms though and has a feature called Forms that we discuss further in Chapter 16.

>> **Media and Content:** These Web Parts work well when your content needs are simple. Use the Media Web Part to display Windows Media Player on your web page. The Image Viewer Web Part lets you link to an image and display it on your page. If your company has Silverlight applications, they can be played using the Silverlight Web Part. The Content Editor Web Part is a perennial favorite because it allows you to enter almost any HTML, CSS, or JavaScript you want on your page.

WARNING

Some of these Web Parts, especially the Content Editor Web Part, can really make it difficult to manage a site's content long-term. Imagine you have a Team site with ten web pages. On each web page, you've placed three Content Editor Web Parts. That's 30 individual components you have to touch every time you need to change content. Rather than add all this custom HTML and CSS code into a Content Editor Web Part, it would be better to have a developer create a custom Web Part to solve your specific need and to add the custom Web Part to the SharePoint gallery.

>> **Search:** Although these Web Parts may seem specialized, they are actually quite powerful. You can use the Search Web Parts to create a custom search results page that is scoped to the content you want to filter.

>> **Search-Driven Content:** These Web Parts take search to a whole new level. Using these Web Parts, you can build a web page based on search results. This creates a very dynamic page that is constantly updated as content is added and removed from the site. You can use Web Parts for searching and displaying pages, pictures, popular items, tagged items, recently changed items, recommended items, videos, web pages, and Wiki pages.

>> **Social Collaboration:** These Web Parts are designed for displaying social functionality on your web pages. You can add a number of social features to your pages such as contact details, Note Boards, site users, tag clouds, and user tasks. The Note Board Web Part is a particularly cool collaboration function. Dropping this Web Part on your page adds a Social Commenting box so that folks can add comments right inside your web page. Social commenting is part of SharePoint's new social networking features, which we discuss in Chapter 10.

TIP

In addition to the standard categories, you might also see custom or third-party categories. For example, when we develop Web Parts for clients, the Web Parts appear in a category with the client's name and the Web Part name.

WARNING

Any configuration or content that you put inside a Web Part isn't version-controlled. In other words, each time you change the Web Part, you write over any previous configuration or content. That's another reason we caution against using the Content Editor Web Parts. Store your content in lists and libraries where the content is subject to version control and retention policies, rather than placing it directly in the web page. You can export your Web Part's configuration using the Export on the Web Part's menu.

TIP

Content you place inside a Rich Content control on a Wiki page is version-controlled if versioning is enabled in your library.

Changing Web Part Properties

After you select and insert a Web Part into your page, you may want to modify its properties to fit your needs. The number and type of properties you can modify are based on the type of Web Part you use.

Reviewing Web Part properties

When you select the Edit Web Part command by clicking the Web Part menu (in the far right of the Web Part title), SharePoint opens the Web Part tool pane. In some Web Parts, SharePoint creates a link to this tool pane as part of the place-holder text. Following is a list of properties in the tool pane common to List View Web Parts:

>> **Selected View:** The options in the Selected View drop-down list are dependent on the type of library or list and/or other views you may have created.

The Current View is simply what's showing currently. You change view properties on-the-fly using the Edit the Current View link in the tool pane. Your changes are now part of the current view. If you use the Edit in Current View link, you can't revert to a past view.

REMEMBER

The Edit the Current View options are, for the most part, identical to what you see when you create a view in the Library or List app. Make sure you look at Styles and Item limits when creating a view for a Web Part because these options are frequently overlooked.

If the changes you need to make to the view are simple and few, the Edit the Current View link is handy. If you need to consistently apply the same view selections for this Web Part, create a view in the Library or List app so that you can apply the view and don't lose the options you chose.

» **Toolbar Type:** Depending on the Library or List app, this drop-down list allows you the options of Full Toolbar, Summary Toolbar, No Toolbar, or Show Toolbar. For example, in a Document Library app, choosing Full Toolbar enables users to upload the document, check it out, and so forth.

» **Appearance:** The Appearance section allows you to title the Web Part, fix the height and width as necessary, and determine the chrome type. *Chrome* is another word for the Web Part surround; for example, title and border options. Chrome is also the name of the Google web browser that has nothing to do with the Chrome type setting. Don't you love how software seems to re-use the same words over and over for different things?

» **Layout:** In the Layout section, you can change the zone location of the Web Part, as well as hide it without closing it.

» **Advanced:** This section contains many of the options you use to allow users with permissions to modify Web Parts, such as Allow Minimize or Allow Close.

» **AJAX (Asynchronous JavaScript and XML) Options:** This section gives the owner/admin the choice of enabling *asynchronous behaviors.* This means that the data in the Web Part is sent to the page without causing the web page to refresh.

» **Miscellaneous:** Miscellaneous options including sample data, XSL link, and some caching properties.

TIP

In addition to these common categories, a third-party Web Part might have additional categories that are specific to the Web Part. For example, the Portal Integrators Web Parts include configuration categories specific to the purpose of the Web Part.

Editing Web Part properties

Editing Web Part properties is pretty straightforward. Again, experimenting is the key. The most commonly used sections are located at the top of the tool pane: Selected View, Toolbar, and Appearance. Many users don't realize how much they can enhance the user experience with the Web Part by using the options available.

Site page Web Parts are edited by opening the page in Edit mode and then clicking the pencil icon next to the Web Part you wish to edit. We like to think of these types of Web Parts as connectors to online services such as Facebook, GitHub, the

Weather Service, and many others. (Remember that these Web Parts are different than the traditional SharePoint Web Parts. Both use the name *Web Part* so it can often be confusing.)

If you are working with the traditional Web Parts in SharePoint, you can edit them by opening your page in Edit mode and then opening the Web Part tool pane and editing the properties for the one you want to configure.

To open the Web Part tool pane and modify Web Part properties, follow these steps:

1. **Click the Web Part menu on the Web Part and choose Edit Web Part.**

The tool pane opens. You see several of the categories of properties we describe in the preceding list. You may need to click the plus (+) sign to open certain sections.

You need to be in page Edit mode before the drop-down list to select Edit Web Part appears.

TIP

2. **Adjust properties as desired.**

Make your selections based on the categories and options we describe in the preceding list or other options available per the specific Web Part.

3. **Click the Apply button to apply your current changes before modifying others, or click OK to finish modifying.**

Your changes are visible in the Web Part.

Minimizing or deleting Web Parts

You have two options for removing a Web Part from your Web Part page: minimizing a Web Part or deleting it. Minimizing a Web Part leaves the Web Part on the page so you can restore it again for future use. Deleting the Web Part removes the Web Part from your page (but doesn't delete it from SharePoint).

To minimize or delete a Web Part from your page, click the Web Part menu, as we describe in the preceding section, and choose Minimize or Delete.

To restore a Web Part that was previously minimized, open the page in Edit mode, click the drop-down for the Web Part, and choose Restore.

In previous versions of SharePoint, you could also "close" a Web Part. (SharePoint Online may still display this option if you are using a classic view.) Closing a Web Part saves it to a special category in the SharePoint Web Part Gallery. When you want to add a closed Web Part back to the page, you find a category in the Web Part

TIP

Gallery called Closed Web Parts. Clicking the Closed Web Parts category reveals all the Web Parts on the page that have been closed. On the other hand, if you delete a Web Part, it will be gone forever.

TIP

If you spend time configuring a Web Part and want to remove it, it's better to minimize it so that you don't lose all your configuration changes. Keep in mind that having a minimized Web Part on a page causes the same performance impact as if the Web Part was open. So you don't want a ton of minimized Web Parts if you don't need them.

Connecting Web Parts

One cool thing you can do with Web Parts is connect them to each other. This allows you to use one Web Part to filter the values of another Web Part. This is a very powerful feature that allows you to create useful, data-driven web pages in your Team site.

Follow this process to connect two Web Parts:

1. **Add both the Web Parts you want to connect to your web page.**

For example, you can create a custom app called Customers based on the Custom List app. Assume the Customers app contains a column for customer name and a column for customer city. You can then add the associated Customers Web Part to the page along with a SharePoint List Filter Web Part. You must first select the SharePoint List Filter Web Part to which you want to associate the list by selecting the list on the Web Part property window along with the identifying column that needs to be filtered. You must set and save this selection before the Send Filter Values To choice in the Connections menu will be enabled.

TIP

Creating a custom List app is covered in Chapter 11.

2. **Click the drop-down arrow on the SharePoint List Filter Web Part, choose Connections ⇨ Send Filter Values To, and then choose the name of the Customers Web Part you want to filter, as shown in Figure 6-10.**

The Choose Connection dialog box appears. The Choose Connection tab displays the connection type you selected in this step.

If you don't see this dialog box, make sure your web browser is allowing pop-ups from the site.

TIP

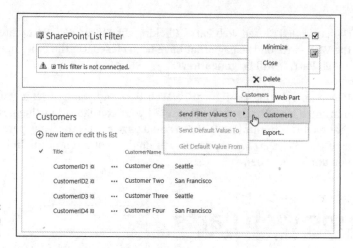

FIGURE 6-10:
Choosing which
Web Part to filter.

3. **Click the Connection Type drop-down list, choose Get Filter Values From, and click the Configure button.**

This is the field that has the set of values you want to match from your filtering Web Part. To filter a Customers list Web Part with a City column, we chose the City field as the Consumer Field Name, as shown in Figure 6-11.

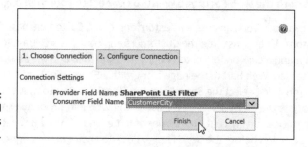

FIGURE 6-11:
Select the field
that contains
your filter values.

4. **Click the Finish button.**

The connection is established.

5. **On the Page tab of the ribbon, click Stop Editing.**

The page exits Edit mode. As you select values in the filter Web Part, the connected Web Part is filtered accordingly, as shown in Figure 6-12.

FIGURE 6-12:
A filtered
Web Part.

Managing Pages

SharePoint pages have commands on the Page tab of the ribbon that are useful for managing pages. The different types of pages have different items in the ribbon on the Page tab. This can get confusing, so you just have to play around and get familiar with each page type. As an example, some of the commands you will find on the Wiki page include the following (see Figure 6-13):

>> **Page History** allows you to easily see all the edits made to the current page.

>> **Page Permissions** lets you set unique permissions on the page.

>> **Make Homepage** sets the current page as the home page for the Team site.

>> **Incoming Links** shows all the pages that link to the current page.

>> **View All Pages** takes you to the wiki library where the page is saved.

After you are in the wiki library, you can use all the standard document library functions to manage the library's settings.

FIGURE 6-13:
Manage Wiki
pages with the
Page tab of the
ribbon.

Categorizing Your Wiki Pages

Wikis often include a way to categorize pages, and SharePoint wikis are no different. By default, the wiki library includes an Enterprise Keywords field that allows you to enter freeform keywords or tags on your Wiki page. These tags can be displayed in a *tag cloud*, a visual representation of tags that indicates how often they occur in relation to each other and can help users find content they are interested in.

To add a tag to your Wiki page:

1. **Activate the Enterprise Keywords column in the settings for the Site Pages library.**

If you are using SharePoint On-Premises (or the classic SharePoint experience in SharePoint Online), you access the Site Pages library settings by clicking Library Settings on the Library tab.

If you are using the newest SharePoint Online experience, you access the Site Pages library settings page by clicking the gear icon and choosing Site Contents and then selecting Settings from the ellipsis drop-down menu next to the Site Pages library. Both approaches take you to the settings for the Site Pages library. Once in the settings window, click Enterprise Metadata and Keywords Settings.

TIP

The Enterprise Metadata and Keywords functionality is not available in all editions of SharePoint.

2. **Select the Add an Enterprise Keywords Column to This List and Enable Keyword Synchronization check box.**

TIP

If you are using SharePoint On-Premises, then you will see an option for social tags; however, if you are using SharePoint Online, you won't see this additional option. This is an example of the slight variations that appear depending on the way your SharePoint environment is set up.

3. **Click OK to save the change.**

4. **Browse to your Wiki page, click the Page tab on the ribbon, and click the Edit Properties button.**

The Edit form appears.

5. **Type tags in the Enterprise Keywords field.**

6. **Click the Save button.**

The web page has your keywords associated with it.

If you aren't sure of the difference between Enterprise Keywords and social tags, be sure to check out Chapter 10 for insights on how to use these important tagging mechanisms.

TECHNICAL STUFF

If you can't save the properties of a page, and you are using SharePoint On-Premises, then it's likely that some services are not running for your SharePoint farm. Ask your farm administrator to check to make sure the Search Host Controller Service and the Search Query and Site Settings services are running. This is done in Central Administration on the Services on Server page.

TIP

If you need your Wiki page to have a consistent layout that displays the Enterprise Keywords field on every page, you should probably use an Enterprise Wiki site template.

Taking a Peek into Custom Page Designs

A recent feature in SharePoint is the ability to create a page using a custom page design. One place you will find it is in the Communication site template.

The Communication site template is also a recent edition to SharePoint, and you can only access it in the SharePoint Admin interface shown in Figure 6-14.

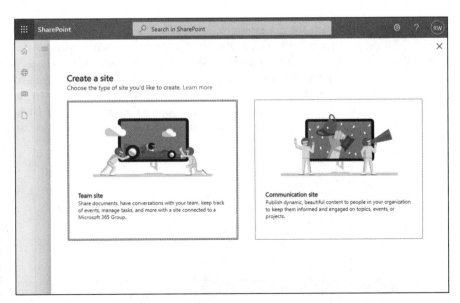

FIGURE 6-14:
Creating a
Communication
site in SharePoint
Online.

Once you create a Communication site, you can click the New button and select Page. As you see in Chapter 5, a new Site page is created. The new custom page designs (think page templates) allow you to pick a predefined look for your new page, as shown in Figure 6-15.

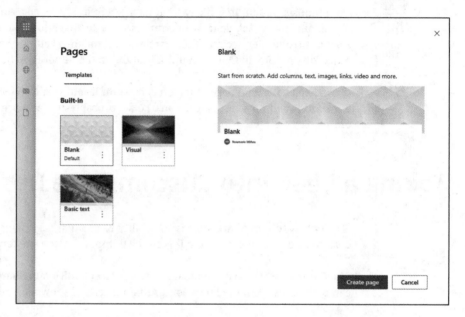

FIGURE 6-15:
Creating a new page using a custom page design.

REMEMBER

You create a Communication site the same way you create a Team site in Chapter 1. When you click the Create Site button on your SharePoint Online landing page, the Communication site is now a standard option. We cover getting to your SharePoint Online landing page in Chapter 1; however, as with most things Microsoft, you can access it in multiple ways. One way is to navigate to `https://admin.microsoft.com` and then open the app launcher (it is in the upper-left corner of the page) and selecting SharePoint from the apps listed.

Chapter **7**

Adding Content to SharePoint

SharePoint became popular for its ability to manage content. Over the years it has become capable of doing many more things, but at its heart, SharePoint is still a place to create, store, and manage all your digital content.

In this chapter, we take a look at SharePoint as a content management system (CMS) and explore how you can use SharePoint to get a handle on all your digital data. We also explore how to create, upload, and view content in SharePoint using both your web browser and the SharePoint Mobile App.

SharePoint as a Content Management System

SharePoint does a really good job at providing a place to store and manage your content. If you have seen file names with extensions such as `financials-reviewed8-12_final_reallyfinal_FINAL_ABSOLUTEFINAL.xlsx`, then you know what we mean. SharePoint provides a number of features and mechanisms to handle content, but at its root, it provides a single source of truth for all content.

SharePoint includes features such as version control and check-in and check-out capabilities, but in its simplest form, SharePoint is a single place to store and organize your content.

As your content grows, the features of SharePoint become more evident. You can organize views into your content (covered in Chapter 14); you can create detailed search optimizations (searching in SharePoint is covered in Chapter 23); and you can report on and share your data. There are many other things SharePoint does to make the digital content in your life easier to deal with.

TIP

As you read about and explore SharePoint, keep in mind how the features can be used with your content. Because SharePoint is a content management system at heart, you can rest assured that most features are there in order to help you deal with digital content in one way or another.

Wrangling the Overwhelming Mountain of Digital Content

To be productive in this day and age, you need a system in place that makes wrangling your digital content as easy and intuitive as possible. Over the last few years, Microsoft has recognized this fact and has poured effort into creating new features in SharePoint (and other products) that help with this goal. Changes we have noticed in SharePoint are features such as the SharePoint Mobile App and increased efficiencies in search capabilities.

One of the most valuable new features in SharePoint that we use every day to help manage content is syncing documents between all devices. This is something a tool such as Dropbox has done for a long time — we even used it when writing some of our previous books on SharePoint (don't tell anyone). Why did we use Dropbox? We used it because we could always find a file on any device and continue working wherever we happened to be at the time and whatever device we happened to be using. In the last few years, SharePoint has achieved the same functionality we loved in Dropbox and we now use SharePoint full time for our writing. Now we get the benefits of having all our files accessible on any device (through SharePoint Online), as well as versioning control and check-in and check-out capabilities, in the same SharePoint format we have come to know and love.

Another innovation we have found incredibly useful is SharePoint's incorporation of activity feeds in places you might need them. An activity feed can be a lifesaver when you are dealing with mountains of digital data. When you are looking at a never-ending list of documents, you can just jump over to the recent activity to open the file you need instead of scrolling or searching for it the traditional way.

One place where activity feeds are especially important is on your mobile device. Your mobile device has a much smaller screen than a computer monitor, and as such, it can be much harder to find things. You don't want to have to type in a search query just to show off something you have been working on. You will find activity feeds super useful in finding content you have recently worked on. An activity feed in the SharePoint Mobile App is shown in Figure 7-1.

FIGURE 7-1:
An activity feed in the SharePoint Mobile App on an iPhone.

Getting Your Documents into SharePoint

There are many ways to upload your documents into SharePoint. You can upload them one at a time, or add a whole bunch in one swoop. You can even upload template files so that you can use them to create new documents within SharePoint based on the template.

Uploading files has become quite easy and intuitive with modern web technologies. If you are using your web browser, you can drag and drop them right into the web browser window. If you are using Microsoft Office, you can save them right into SharePoint without even leaving your Office application (we cover working with Office and SharePoint in Chapter 9). With all these options, you have no excuse to keep your files only on your hard drive and then suffer from a crash!

Uploading a single document

When you have a single document to upload into SharePoint, you can do so easily through a web browser. The easiest way is to simply drag the file onto the SharePoint app and drop it, as shown in Figure 7-2. Dragging and dropping the file into the web browser uploads it automatically to the SharePoint library.

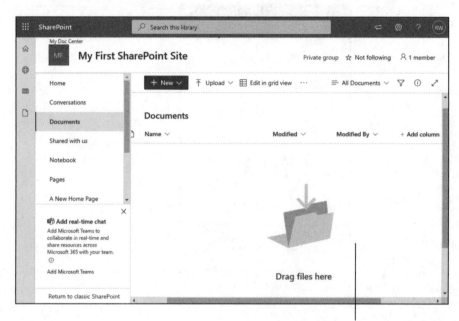

FIGURE 7-2:
Dragging and dropping a document into SharePoint.

Drag and drop to upload a file automatically

In addition to dragging and dropping files directly into SharePoint, you can also click the Upload tab, as shown in Figure 7-3, and select Files to navigate to the file you wish to upload. To see the Upload option, make sure you are at a place within SharePoint that can store documents. In this example, we clicked the Documents link in the left navigation pane. (This link is created by default when you create a SharePoint website.)

TIP

You can also upload documents from directly within the SharePoint Mobile App. We have found this to be useful when we need to upload a document from another file-sharing service such as Dropbox into SharePoint so that we can work on it.

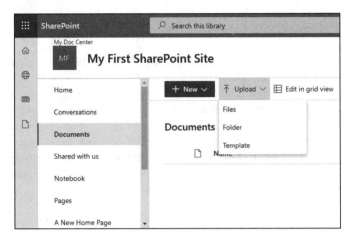

FIGURE 7-3:
Uploading files
into SharePoint
using the
Upload tab.

To upload a file using the SharePoint Mobile App, you first need to navigate to the site you want to store the document. On the Team site, a Web Part shows this on the main page. Swipe down the page to see the Documents section and then tap the small ellipsis that shows up next to the name of that location. (The Document Library called "Documents" in this case.)

Figure 7-4 illustrates uploading a document into the default Documents Library app that comes with the Team site.

FIGURE 7-4:
Uploading files
using the
SharePoint
Mobile App.

Uploading multiple documents

There may be times when you have multiple documents to upload. You can drag and drop multiple documents into SharePoint in the same way you do a single document. To select multiple documents, click the first document then, hold down the Ctrl key as you click additional documents to select as many as you want.

If you want to upload an entire folder of documents, choose the Folder option from the Upload tab and simply select the folder you wish to upload. All the files in that folder are uploaded to SharePoint. This makes it pretty nice when you want to get your content into SharePoint quickly.

WARNING

Uploading multiple documents saves you time getting the documents into your app, but you still need to go into the properties for each document and set the properties for that particular document. Unfortunately, you can't batch-upload properties. To learn about how to update properties for documents you upload, see the coverage of the Edit in Grid View option in the next section. Another option: If you have a developer on hand and need to work with documents in batches, you can ask the developer to work with the SharePoint Application Programming Interface (API) and create a script to make the changes through code.

REMEMBER

Your SharePoint administrator can block the upload of certain file types, such as executable (.exe) files. The reason is to prevent a malicious person from uploading a virus to SharePoint, because any user who clicked the virus file would run the virus. If you try to upload a blocked file type, you see a message letting you know that the file has been blocked from uploading by the administrator.

Updating document properties using Edit in Grid view

You may have noticed that when you upload a document or multiple documents, SharePoint doesn't prompt you to enter the properties of the files you uploaded. The reason is that SharePoint doesn't know anything about these files (metadata) yet, so it requires you to enter this information as you see fit. The result is that you now have documents in your SharePoint app, but you still need to set the properties for each document.

TIP

You can add new metadata to your documents by clicking the Add Column button when looking at a library of documents. When you add a new column, you choose what type of data you want it to be and any default values. Those values are called *metadata* because they contain information about the document itself instead of the data inside the document.

You can update metadata properties quickly using the Edit in Grid view option. To edit properties for multiple documents using Edit in Grid view, follow these steps:

1. **Navigate to the location of the documents and then click Edit in Grid View that appears along the top of the page.**

If you are using SharePoint On-Premises or the classic interface of SharePoint, you will find the Quick Edit button (which is the same thing) on the List or Library tab of the ribbon.

The SharePoint app reloads and shows the documents in an editable grid format, as shown in Figure 7-5.

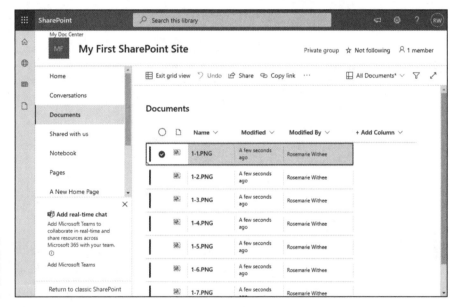

FIGURE 7-5:
Updating document properties using Grid View.

2. **Place your cursor in the field you want to update and make the changes.**

You can also add new columns of information by clicking the + icon in the right-most column.

3. **Move your cursor off the cell you updated, and your changes are saved. When you are done editing, click Exit Grid View to return to the regular view.**

Creating New Content in SharePoint

In addition to uploading content you have already created, you can also create new content from right within SharePoint. The process couldn't be simpler. You just navigate to the location where you want to create the document and then click the New tab and choose the type of document you want to create. For example, you can choose between Word, Excel, PowerPoint, OneNote and others in the default Team site, as shown in Figure 7-6.

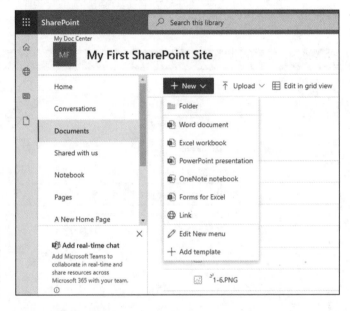

FIGURE 7-6:
Creating a new
document within
a SharePoint
Team site.

In Chapter 9 you discover how to use Microsoft Office with SharePoint. (Sneak peek: You can work with SharePoint without ever having to leave the Office clients such as Word, Excel, and PowerPoint.)

TIP

In Chapter 8 you explore how to use Microsoft Teams and how it uses SharePoint to handle content even though most users might not ever realize it. SharePoint has become a content engine for Microsoft products and knowing how SharePoint works is key to unlocking all of the value Microsoft is pumping into their products.

Using the SharePoint Mobile App to Peek at Content on the Go

When you are on the move and using a mobile device, it can be a real challenge to find the SharePoint content you need to look at. The key to finding content is using the recent activity feed in the SharePoint Mobile App.

The recent activity feed shows all the latest pieces of content you have been working on. Of course, you can also search for content, but we have found the recent activity feed even more valuable than search because generally what we want to look at is something we have recently been working on. For example, let's say you are at work and using a laptop or desktop computer to work on a document. You might then leave your desk to go to lunch and you remember something you wanted to check about the work you were doing. Using your SharePoint Mobile App, you can pop open the recent activity feed and view your work on your mobile device. Granted, actually working on a small smartphone or tablet screen is not something we have had success with. But opening a document and zooming into some details is something we find ourselves using all the time.

Here is how to open a document on your mobile device using the SharePoint Mobile App and finding it in the recent activity feed:

1. **Open the SharePoint Mobile App on your smartphone or tablet.**

2. **Tap the Find tab located at the bottom of the screen.**

3. **In the Frequent Sites list, tap the vertical ellipsis that appears at the right of the screen next to the SharePoint site you wish to access. You will also see a recent files list to go directly to an individual file in any site.**

   In Figure 7-7, you can see the vertical ellipsis to the right of the My First SharePoint site.

4. **Tap the Activity list to see the documents you have recently worked on, as shown in Figure 7-8.**

5. **Tap one of the documents to view it on your mobile device.**

TIP

If you don't see a recent document, drag down on the screen to refresh. It can take a few moments to appear once you upload or work on a document in SharePoint.

FIGURE 7-7:
The SharePoint sites you frequently use shown in the SharePoint Mobile App.

FIGURE 7-8:
Selecting the Activity feed for a SharePoint site in the SharePoint Mobile App.

The SharePoint Mobile App is a window into the work you do with Office from your desktop or laptop computer. We use this feature almost daily, and we especially used it during the writing of this book. When we happened to be away from our computers and discussing something about this book, we could easily pop open a chapter document (we wrote the book in Word) and discuss what we were doing. Granted, we didn't spend too much time inputting content using our mobile devices, but we would take notes and show what each of us was doing.

Chapter **8**

Discovering SharePoint in Microsoft Teams

I f you have not yet heard of Microsoft Teams, you are likely going to hear a lot about this product that is taking the instant communications space by storm. Microsoft Teams is a competitor to such team collaboration products as Slack, Zoom, and others. In addition, Microsoft Teams is replacing Skype for Business in the Office world, and Microsoft has announced that Teams will be integrated into the new Windows 11 by default.

In this chapter, you learn how to use Teams in Microsoft 365 and discover how SharePoint is closely integrated with Teams. You learn that every Teams channel has its own special SharePoint site and how you can work with that site from within Teams. Most users will probably never know they are using SharePoint when they are using features like the Teams wiki, but you will after you read this chapter!

TIP

In this chapter we just touch the surface of Teams. To take a deep dive, check out *Microsoft Teams for Dummies* (Wiley, 2021).

Using Teams in Microsoft 365

When you start your Microsoft 365 trial subscription in Chapter 1, you automatically get the Teams app with it. You can find the Teams app on the App menu, as shown in Figure 8-1.

App launcher   Teams app

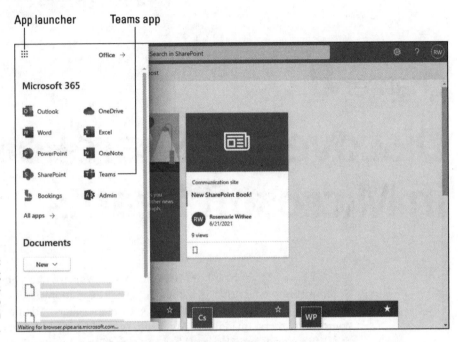

FIGURE 8-1:
Opening
Microsoft Teams
from the app
menu in
Microsoft 365.

You can use Microsoft Teams in your web browser on any supported operating system, and you can also download the actual Teams app to your local computer. When you first log in to Teams, you are presented with a quick tutorial in setting up a team or joining an existing one. Once you finish the tutorial, you can find the button to download the Teams app to your computer in the lower-left corner of the screen, as shown in Figure 8-2. You can also choose to use the web-based app instead. In this chapter, we will use the web app.

TIP

We recommended trying both the web app and the locally installable desktop app for all Office products and then deciding which you prefer. For mobile phones and tablets, we recommend using the installable Teams app from your device's app store.

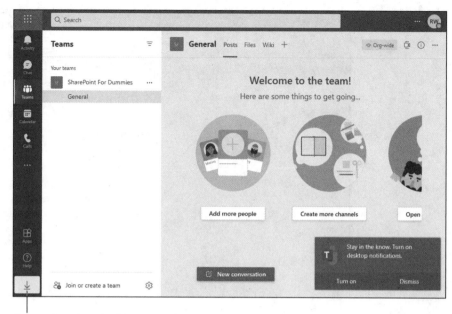

FIGURE 8-2:
The initial Teams
view in the web
browser and the
button to
download the
Teams client to
your local
computer.

Teams client download button

Once you open Teams, you will see the menu items on the left side, which include Activity, Chat, Teams, Calendar, Files and an ellipses for additional options. By default, when you open Teams the Teams menu item is selected, where you will see your teams and channels displayed. Each channel allows you to type to other members of the channel.

You can click on Chat along the left navigation to see a listing of all your chat messages to others, as shown in Figure 8-3.

Both SharePoint and Microsoft Teams are organized around groups of people. This is one of the main reasons Teams is so closely integrated with SharePoint. SharePoint came along first and then Teams was built as a one-stop communications center for people using Microsoft 365. It was a natural fit for Teams to leverage what SharePoint already has to offer, and many new users will be introduced to SharePoint through Teams without ever knowing they are using SharePoint.

WARNING

When creating a new SharePoint site, you may have noticed a new site template called "Team site (no Microsoft 365 group)" and one called "Team site (classic experience)." A Microsoft 365 group is used by other Office apps such as Outlook email or Teams. When you create a new SharePoint site, you can choose whether you want the Microsoft 365 group created automatically or not. Don't be confused with the wording. The word "Team" in the SharePoint site template is completely different from the "Teams" that is the app we are discussing here.

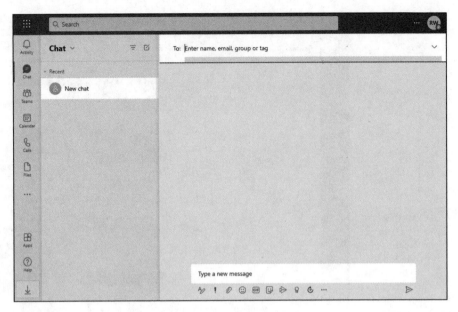

FIGURE 8-3:
The Chat screen
in Teams.

Understanding the Marriage of SharePoint and Teams

Every Microsoft Teams team automatically has a modern SharePoint Team site associated with it. Yes, we realize we've used the word "team" a lot here. That is no accident. Microsoft views Teams as the central product for groups of people working together. Microsoft has even integrated Teams directly into the new Windows 11 release. Because Teams and SharePoint are so tightly integrated, you could even say more people than ever will be using SharePoint without even knowing it.

The SharePoint site that is created for every new team in Microsoft Teams is used for storing content. Two of the most common scenarios are sharing files to Teams and adding content to the Teams wiki.

Accessing SharePoint files in Teams

Microsoft Teams is made up of different channels. A *channel* is just a name for a particular chat that lets everyone know the topic being discussed. For example, you might have a General channel for general topics, a Carpool channel for people wanting to discuss carpooling, a Finance channel for that fun topic, and many others.

Each channel has a tab at the top called Files, as shown in Figure 8-4. You can upload files to the channel and everyone in the channel can see them by clicking on the tab.

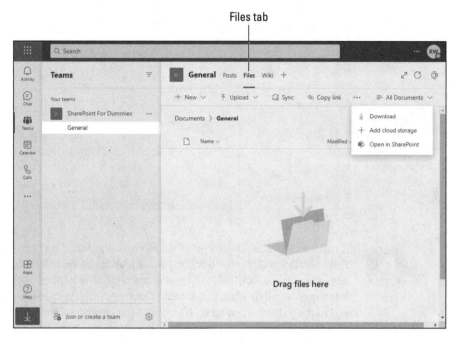

Files tab

FIGURE 8-4:
The Files tab in a
Microsoft Teams
channel.

The Files tab of each channel is associated with a documents folder in the backend SharePoint site. To view the SharePoint site, select the Open in SharePoint link from the ellipsis drop-down menu (shown in Figure 8-4) and the backend SharePoint site opens, as shown in Figure 8-5. Notice that this is a brand new SharePoint site created when the team was created in Teams. This is because we are in the default team, which was created when we created our Microsoft 365 subscription. If we create a new team (in Teams) and then select the Open in SharePoint link, we will see a brand new site is created for the channel with the same name as the Teams channel we created.

We created a new team called "Site From Teams." (You can see the button to create a team in Figure 8-2 at the bottom of the list of channels.) We then clicked the Open in SharePoint link from the ellipsis drop-down menu and now we can see a brand new SharePoint site for our brand new team in Figure 8-5.

Because you opened the SharePoint site from the Files tab, you automatically land in the Documents app of the SharePoint site. Any files in your Files tab on Teams will be stored in this Documents app in the associated SharePoint site.

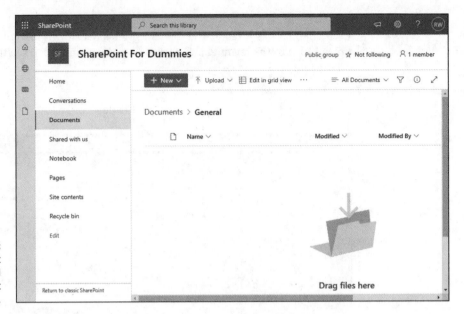

FIGURE 8-5:
The SharePoint site associated with a Microsoft Teams team.

TIP

It can lead to initial confusion when Microsoft automatically creates a Teams team and SharePoint site for you when you sign up for Microsoft 365. We like to take the next step, as we outline earlier, and learn what is happening behind the scenes. Many people stick with the default Teams team and the default SharePoint site and happily use the products. If you read the previous section, then you are already ahead of the pack in understanding how these products tie together.

Using the Teams wiki and finding it in SharePoint

In addition to the Files tab, a Wiki tab also appears on every Teams channel (refer back to Figure 8-4). When you click the Wiki tab, you will see a wiki for the channel. A *wiki* is a shared web page that can be edited and updated by multiple people. Wikis are common throughout the Internet, and SharePoint includes wiki functionality as well. In fact, the wiki in Teams is also part of the backend SharePoint site associated with the team.

Each channel has its own wiki file stored in SharePoint. You can view the wiki content by going to the SharePoint site (by selecting the Open in SharePoint link) and then looking at the Site Contents, as shown in Figure 8-6.

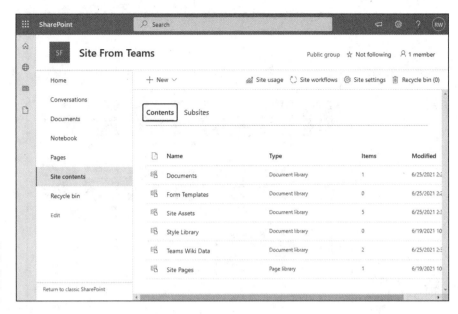

FIGURE 8-6:
The Teams wiki
content in the
associated
SharePoint site.

Adding SharePoint Pages and Lists to Teams

Every channel in a Teams team has a default Files tab and Wiki tab, but you can also add your own tabs to a channel. For example, you might want to add a tab to a SharePoint site or to a specific page within a SharePoint site.

To add a new SharePoint–based tab to a Teams channel, follow these steps:

1. Click Teams in the left navigation menu, expand the channel, and then click the channel to which you want to add a SharePoint-based tab.

2. Click the plus sign to the right of the existing tabs to bring up the Add a Tab dialog box, as shown in Figure 8-7.

3. Click the SharePoint icon to add SharePoint functionality.

4. Select the page or list you want to add.

We are selecting the News page, as shown in Figure 8-8.

5. Click Save.

The News page, which lives in SharePoint, is now added as a tab to the Teams channel, and anyone in the team can now click this tab to view news.

FIGURE 8-7:
Adding a new tab
to a Teams
channel.

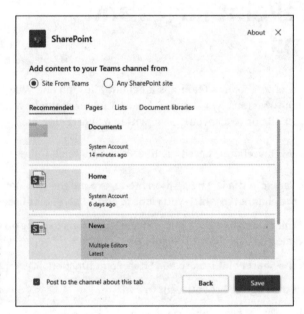

FIGURE 8-8:
Selecting
SharePoint-based
content for a new
tab on a Teams
channel.

TIP

Adding a SharePoint page to a Teams tab provides a shortcut so that people don't need to leave Teams in order to open their web browsers and then navigate to the SharePoint site directly.

You can also add content that is stored in SharePoint and have it displayed directly in the tab. A great example of this is adding a Microsoft Word document, as shown in Figure 8-9. The Word document is stored in SharePoint, but it is displayed, and editable, directly in the Teams channel tab.

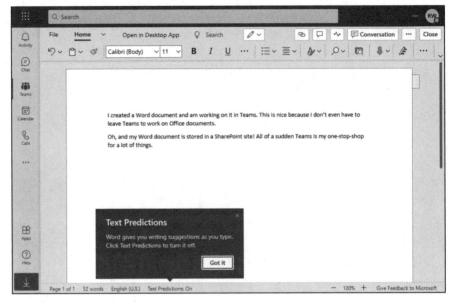

FIGURE 8-9:
Editing a Word document that is stored in SharePoint directly in a Teams channel.

Microsoft has positioned Teams as a central application that everyone will spend most of their workday using. We have noticed that we often switch between Outlook and Teams as we work throughout our day, and we expect at some point we will spend most of our time in Teams even though we are using SharePoint behind the scenes.

Chapter **9**

Working with SharePoint from Microsoft Office

The Microsoft Office suite of productivity apps, which includes Word, Excel, and PowerPoint, is still one of the most used suites of software for working with content. SharePoint is a member of the Office family as well and has embraced Microsoft Office with excellent integration. This is not to say you can't use other suites of software to create and edit your content. You can! But if you are using Microsoft Office, you will be pleasantly surprised at how SharePoint fits in seamlessly with the Office apps you have come to know and love.

In this chapter, we take a look at how SharePoint can be used with the Office productivity apps on desktop computers and laptops as well as on mobile devices. These include Word, Excel, PowerPoint, OneNote, OneDrive for Business, and more.

Getting Familiar with Office Versioning

Just like other Microsoft products, Office is moving to the cloud. This doesn't mean the Office clients are only available in the cloud — you can still download them and install them locally on your computer as a stand-alone client if you wish. What it does mean is that by moving the Office products to the cloud, Microsoft has enabled users to receive continual updates to the Office clients through a subscription-based program called Microsoft 365.

TIP

Microsoft recently rebranded Office 365 to Microsoft 365. You can use these terms interchangeably.

Instead of a one-time purchase of an application (such as Word or Excel) that you download directly onto your computer, with Microsoft 365, whenever a new feature comes out for any of the Office apps, you automatically get that feature as an update. You don't have to wait for the next major release (traditionally every three years) for new features. (And versioning of the Office clients is constantly changing!) The downside to the subscription-based model is that you continue to pay a monthly fee to Microsoft for as long as the subscription is active.

TIP

When you purchase the stand-alone Office clients instead of the Microsoft 365 subscription, the Office suite is simply called Office 2021 (or whatever the latest year is for the Office release).

Working with Office on Your Desktop or Laptop

Let's face it: Most of us still use Word, Excel, and PowerPoint when we create new content. These productivity apps are popular and we love them. The good news is that we don't have to give them up in order to adapt to the new cloud-based future. We can still use them and they now work better than ever in the cloud.

But what does "in the cloud" mean? It simply means that we can open and save content directly to SharePoint (in the cloud) from the Office apps running on our local computer. Let's take a look at how to create new content and edit existing content using Office installed on a desktop or laptop computer.

Installing Microsoft Office

Before we get started working with the Office apps, we need to make sure they are installed. There are two primary ways to obtain the Microsoft Office suite of apps. You can download it as part of your Microsoft 365 subscription or you can buy it outright.

If your Microsoft 365 subscription includes Microsoft Office, you can install the Office apps by doing the following:

1. Open your web browser and navigate to `www.office.com`.

2. Select Sign In in the top-right corner of the screen and sign in to your Microsoft 365 account.

3. Click Install Office in the upper-right corner of the screen and select Premium Office apps, as shown in Figure 9-1.

4. Follow the instructions to download and install the apps.

Once the download and installation are complete, you will find the familiar Word, Excel, PowerPoint, and other apps in your Start menu on your computer (or on Launchpad on a Mac).

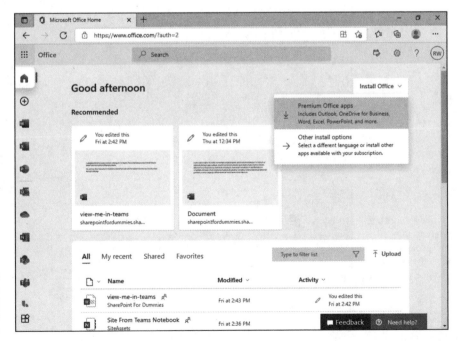

FIGURE 9-1: Using the office. com website to install the Office apps.

WARNING

We cover purchasing a Microsoft 365 subscription in Chapter 1. Be aware: not all subscriptions include access to the Microsoft Office apps. Make sure you choose a subscription that does if you want to use the Office apps on your local computer.

If you want to purchase the Office apps and download them the old-fashioned way, you can do so. Just follow these steps:

1. **Open your web browser and navigate to** `products.office.com`.

2. **Click the Products tab (see Figure 9-2) and select "See all apps and services" in the lower-right corner of the drop-down menu.**

3. **Scroll down the page and under the "Home" section, choose either Office Home & Student or Office Home & Business.**

   Clicking a link will take you to a page where you can purchase Microsoft Office for a one-time charge and then download and install it on your computer. Once installed, the Office clients will show up in your Start menu on your computer (or in your Apps on a Mac).

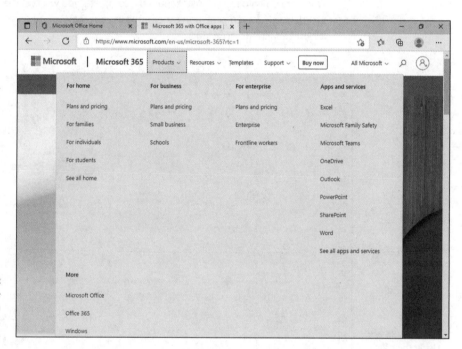

FIGURE 9-2:
Viewing the Office products from the products. office.com page.

Saving a new document to SharePoint

You can create and save a new Office document using the apps on your computer and then save it to your SharePoint site without ever needing to leave the Office app. Let's do that now with a new Excel workbook.

1. **Open the Excel app on your computer.**

If you've just installed Office, Office will ask you to sign in and register your device and agree to some terms and conditions, as shown in Figure 9-3.

::: Microsoft

Hello Rosemarie, welcome to Office

Sign in to activate Office with this account

info@sharepointfordummies.onmicrosoft.com

Change account

Continue

FIGURE 9-3:
Activating Office
for the first
time with
Microsoft 365.

2. **Create a Blank Workbook.**

3. **Enter some data.**

4. **Choose File ⇨ Save.**

Because this is the first time saving this file, the Save As menu opens where you will see the SharePoint sites in your Microsoft 365 tenant. If you recall from Chapter 1, we set up ours with the name "SharePoint For Dummies," as shown in Figure 9-4.

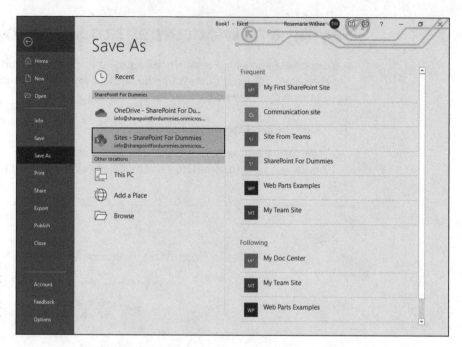

FIGURE 9-4:
Selecting
SharePoint as the
location we want
to save our
spreadsheet.

5. **Choose the site you want to save the document in, give the new spreadsheet a name, and select the Library you want to use, as shown in Figure 9-5.**

Note that in our example we only have the default Documents library.

TIP

In this example, we chose Documents because it is the only Document Library in the SharePoint site we selected. If there were other Libraries in the site, they would show up as options, too. You must choose a document location. If you forget to choose a library, you will get an error message that says you cannot save in that location. The reason for this is that a SharePoint site by itself doesn't have any place to store the content. You need a Library, such as Documents, in order to save the content into. We cover creating these Libraries in Chapter 11.

6. **Click Save to save your spreadsheet.**

Your file will be saved and you can keep working in Excel. As you work on the document your changes will be saved into SharePoint and thus into the cloud. The result is that even if your computer is lost or stolen or crashes, your Excel file will always be available in SharePoint and you can access it from any other device.

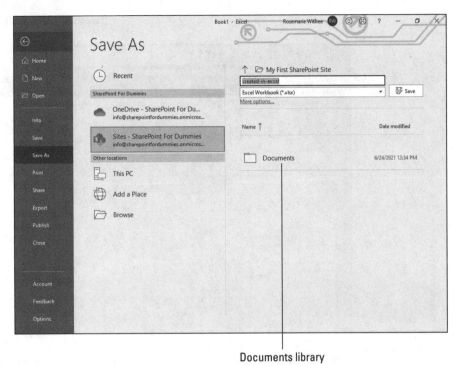

Documents library

Opening a document from SharePoint

You can open an Office document that has been saved to SharePoint in one of two ways. First, if you are browsing the SharePoint site, you can click a document and view and edit it in your web browser using the Office web apps. Second, if you want to open the document in the Office app on your local computer, you can click the Open In [app] button that appears in the top middle of the screen, as shown in Figure 9-6. Here, when you click Open in [app], the app on your computer opens and you can continue to work on the document. When you save the document, it is automatically saved back to the same SharePoint location so you will never lose your work.

In addition to opening an Office file from within SharePoint, you can also open the Office app on your computer first and then browse to a file that is located on SharePoint. For example, with Excel, when you first open the app, click the Open tab on the left. You will see the SharePoint locations and recent files, even those that are stored in SharePoint, as shown in Figure 9-7. Microsoft has done a great job of making working with the cloud-based content stored in SharePoint feel just as easy as working with files that are saved locally.

TIP

In these examples we used Excel, but you can follow the same process with any of the Office apps.

Click to open the file in the desktop app

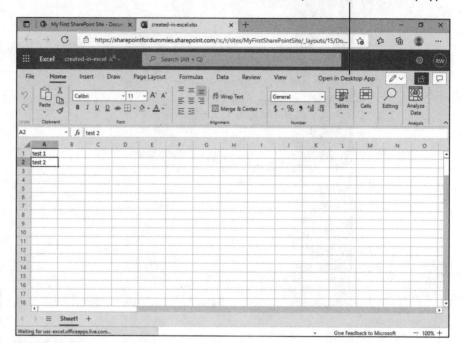

FIGURE 9-6:
Opening an Excel
file directly from
SharePoint.

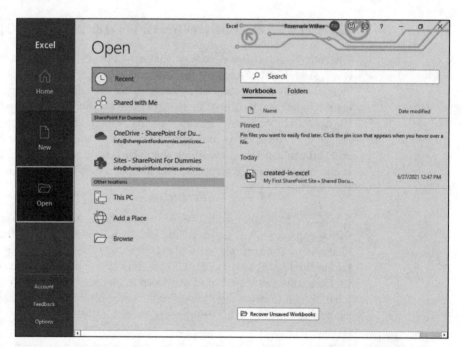

FIGURE 9-7:
Opening an Excel
file stored in
SharePoint.

Working with Office on Your Smartphone or Tablet

In addition to working with the Office suite of apps on your desktop or laptop computer, you can also work with the popular Office apps on your iOS- or Android-based mobile device.

Saving a new document to SharePoint

When you create a new Office document on your mobile device, you can choose to save it to your SharePoint site. This happens by default if you have already signed in to the app when you first opened it.

To create a new Word document on your mobile device and save it to SharePoint, follow these steps:

1. **Open the Word app on your mobile device.**

2. **Choose to create a new blank document.**

3. **Enter some text and then tap the ellipsis in the upper-right corner of the screen and tap the Save button, as shown in Figure 9-8.**

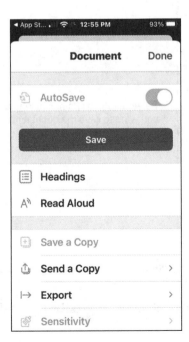

FIGURE 9-8:
The Save button in the Word app on an iPhone.

4. **Give your document a name and then choose your SharePoint site, as shown in Figure 9-9.**

TECHNICAL
STUFF

If you have already logged in to Office on your mobile device, you will automatically see the SharePoint sites in your subscription. If you haven't, then you can log in by tapping your user icon in the top left of the screen and then selecting Add or Switch Accounts. For the example we are using throughout the book, we are using the Microsoft 365 credentials we set up in Chapter 1, which has a username of info@sharepointfordummies.onmicrosoft.com.

Alternatively, you can add SharePoint as an option by choosing to add a place and then scrolling down and selecting SharePoint. For example, we added a place and gave the address of our Microsoft 365 SharePoint site as https://sharepointfordummies.sharepoint.com. If you logged into your Microsoft 365 subscription, you will see an option for OneDrive (which is integrated with SharePoint). If you added a SharePoint place without signing into your Word app with your Microsoft 365 credentials, you will see the SharePoint place you added. You can see we did both in Figure 9-9 to show the difference.

FIGURE 9-9:
Choosing a
SharePoint site to
save a Word
document from
an iPhone.

5. **Select the location within the SharePoint site where you want to save the document.**

In this example we will choose Documents, as shown in Figure 9-10.

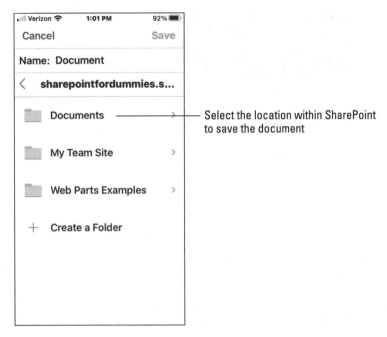

Select the location within SharePoint to save the document

FIGURE 9-10:
Selecting the
Documents
library within a
SharePoint site.

6. **Tap Save in the upper-right corner of the screen.**

   Your file is saved to your SharePoint site. You can now access it from any other mobile device or even open it from Word installed on your desktop or laptop computer.

Opening a document from SharePoint

Opening an Office document on your mobile device is no different than opening a locally saved file. When you open Word or any other Office app, you will see a Recent tab at the bottom of the screen. Tap that tab and you will see all your recent documents, including those saved to your SharePoint site, as shown in Figure 9-11.

To open a document, just tap on it and make edits. When you save the file, it is automatically saved back to SharePoint — you don't have to do anything extra. This is a nice feature that has saved us multiple times when we have dropped or otherwise rendered a phone unusable!

FIGURE 9-11:
All your recent
Word documents
are located on
the Recent tab.

Chapter **10**

Getting Social

The folks at Microsoft got to thinking about how SharePoint is a lot like social networking communities on the web. *Social networking* services build online communities of people who share interests and/or activities and consist of services and sites such as instant messaging (IM), discussion boards, wikis, posts, bookmarking sites, Facebook, LinkedIn, Flickr, Twitter, and so on (and on).

Some people use them all. We just can't. And neither should you feel like you have to use all the social networking options in SharePoint. Focus on picking the right tool(s) for you and your team. You can still be cool (and productive) using just a few. There are good and specific reasons for using discussion boards, posts, news, and wikis, and even more reasons for using alerts, notifications, and feeds. And SharePoint even has a What's Happening feature similar to the on-the-fly updates of Twitter.

SharePoint offers other social networking features that all site visitors can use and some features (such as wikis, news, posts, and discussion boards) that a site owner must set up for a team to use.

In this chapter, we discuss social networking tools that let individuals and groups communicate, collaborate, share, and connect. Depending on the culture of your organization and the projects you work on, these tools may find greater or lesser use; we encourage you to experiment with them all. Organizations generally experience some anxiety and growing pains around the less structured communications that social networking facilitates, but after a period of adjustment, we often find that those who were initially most reluctant become social networking advocates as they discover the value these tools can bring to productivity, collaboration, and morale.

Sharing and Following SharePoint Sites

It is easy to follow a SharePoint site and receive updates about what happens on that site. With the latest release of SharePoint, the option is as simple as clicking a star icon on the main page of a SharePoint website, as shown in Figure 10-1. And if you are using the SharePoint Mobile App, tap the ellipses in the upper-right corner and select to follow the site, as shown in Figure 10-2.

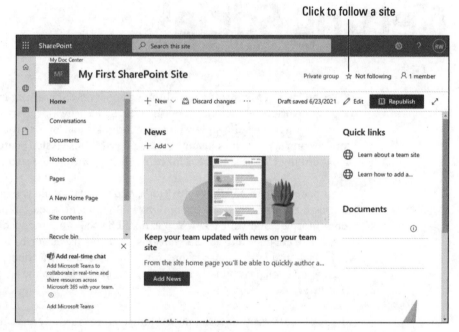

FIGURE 10-1:
Click the star on a SharePoint site to follow the site.

Once you follow a SharePoint site it will show up on your main SharePoint dashboard — the main dashboard you see when you sign into Microsoft 365 and click the SharePoint app. (See Chapter 1 for more about the dashboard.) You can always get back to the dashboard by clicking the app menu (the waffle icon in top-left corner of your screen) and clicking SharePoint.

When you follow a site, you will receive all the news and updates and activity on your main SharePoint dashboard. To see your sites, select My Sites from the left side of your SharePoint dashboard. In Figure 10-3, you can see the list of sites that we frequent along with the sites we are following. We like this because we don't always frequent sites but we still want to follow what is going on with them when they do have activity.

If you are using the SharePoint Mobile App, you will see a News tab on the main screen. This tab shows all of the news and activity from the sites you are following. The News tab is shown in Figure 10-4.

REMEMBER

The same news article that was shown in the web browser in Figure 10-3 is also shown in Figure 10-4 in the SharePoint Mobile App. As we discuss in Chapter 4, this is a recurring theme. The SharePoint Mobile App displays the same content you will find when using SharePoint in your web browser. It is just a mobile version designed to be easier to use on small devices.

TIP

The SharePoint dashboard will only be available if you are using SharePoint as part of Microsoft 365. If you are using SharePoint On-Premises, check with your IT department to find out if there is a consolidated site they have for notifications and activity.

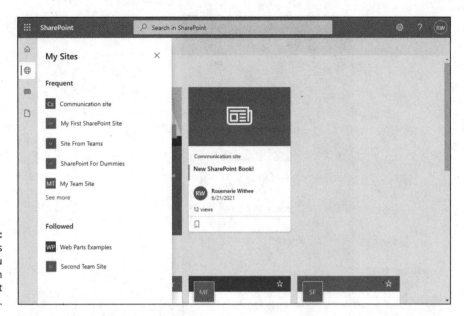

FIGURE 10-3:
Frequent sites
and sites you
follow appear on
your SharePoint
dashboard.

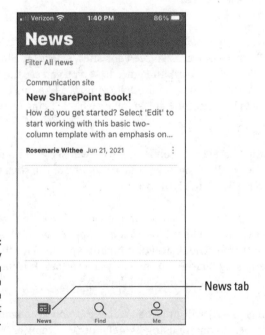

FIGURE 10-4:
News and activity
from sites you
follow appear on
the News tab in
the SharePoint
Mobile App.

News tab

Setting up alerts

In addition to following a site, you can also set up alerts for other areas of Share-Point. For example, documents are stored in a special SharePoint container app called a Library. The Documents app that shows up on the left navigation of your default Team site is an example. *Alerts* are a great way to keep track of the changes your teammates make to documents and items.

TIP

You must have an email address configured in your SharePoint profile in order to receive alerts. If your SharePoint server is located in your network, that's usually not an issue. However, Microsoft 365 may not be integrated with your network and email information. In those situations, your administrator can either manually configure your email address or grant you permission to do so.

To set up an alert for content in the Documents app, follow these steps:

1. **Open your web browser and navigate to `www.office.com`.**

2. **Sign in if you are requested.**

    Remember, this is the site we set up in Chapter 1.

3. **Select your SharePoint site to open the site.**

4. **Select the Documents app that appears in the left navigation pane.**

5. **At the top of the Documents app click the ellipsis and then click Alert Me, as shown in Figure 10-5.**

    The Alert Me When Items Change dialog box opens.

TIP

    If you are using SharePoint On-Premises and you don't see the Alert Me button, chances are your administrator has not configured outgoing email settings. If outgoing email settings are not configured in Central Administration, the Alert Me button simply will not appear to users. If you are using SharePoint Online, however, then outgoing email has already been configured by Microsoft and you are good to go.

6. **In the Alert Title text box, enter a name for the alert.**

    We suggest making the name something meaningful to you in your inbox, such as Documents Modified Today – Budget Team Site. Otherwise, you have no meaningful way to tell one alert from another.

7. **In the Send Alerts To text box, enter the names of people in addition to you who should receive the alert.**

    That's right, you can subscribe other people to an alert! You must have the Manage Alerts permission, which is granted by default to site owners.

TIP

Organizations and site owners may want to subscribe multiple users to an alert to make sure they get important updates, as well as encourage them to contribute to a discussion board, blog, or wiki. Users can still opt out by modifying settings in their Alert settings.

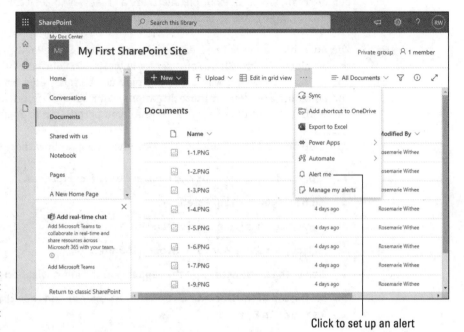

FIGURE 10-5:
Selecting the Alert
Me option in a
SharePoint
Documents app.

Click to set up an alert

8. **In the Delivery Method section, select whether to receive alerts via email or text message to your cellular phone.**

   Text messaging requires your SharePoint administrator to configure this service through a third party, so you may not be able to send alerts to your phone.

9. **In the Change Type section, select the option that matches the type of notifications you want to receive — All Changes, New Items Are Added, Existing Items Are Modified, or Items Are Deleted.**

   If you're responsible for managing an app, we recommend receiving an alert any time items are deleted.

10. **In the Send Alerts for These Changes section, choose when to receive alerts.**

    The options you see here vary based on the kind of app you're working with. For example, a Tasks app allows you to receive an alert when a task is marked Complete or any time the status of a high-priority task changes.

11. In the When to Send Alerts section, choose the frequency of your alert delivery.

You can receive them immediately, once a day, or once a week. We like to receive a daily summary; otherwise, we get too many emails.

12. Click OK to create your alert, as shown in Figure 10-6.

FIGURE 10-6: Creating a new alert for a SharePoint Documents app.

TIP

You need the Create Alerts permission to create alerts. This permission is granted usually with the out-of-the-box configuration of the *Site* Members SharePoint group. (See Chapter 21 for details on working with permissions.)

TIP

Any time users say they need a workflow to receive notification of changes made to project files, try an alert first. You'd be surprised at how often alerts provide the options that are needed.

TIP

If your app has a personal or public view that includes a filter, you can subscribe to changes to just that view. For example, say you want to be notified via text message when an item in an Issue Tracking app has its priority set to High. You would create a view that filters the app for high-priority issues. Select the filtered view in the Send Alerts for These Changes section when you create your alert, and you will receive alerts when items meet the filter criteria.

Managing alerts

You can always go back and adjust alerts. When you click on the ellipsis (shown earlier in Figure 10-5) you can choose Manage Alerts and edit any alerts you have already created. This button takes you to a single page instead of navigating to each app where you have set an alert. Figure 10-7 shows the My Alerts page.

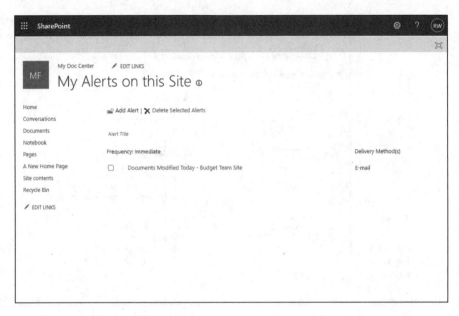

FIGURE 10-7:
Managing your
alerts for an
entire SharePoint
site.

To manage all the alerts you have on a given site and modify or delete them, follow these steps:

1. **Browse to an app where you currently subscribe to an alert.**

2. **From the ellipsis drop-down menu, choose Manage My Alerts.**

    The My Alerts on this Site page appears.

3. **Select the appropriate alert name link.**

    The Edit Alert page appears with all the options you viewed when you first created the alert. Change the settings as desired.

    Didn't set the alert to begin with? You can still read through the settings and change the choices (see the preceding steps). Your changes don't affect the alert settings for others if the alert was created for multiple users at the same time.

4. **Click OK to modify the alert with your new settings or Delete to delete the alert.**

   Deleting an alert that was created for you doesn't delete the alert from other users who are in the group the alert was created for.

TIP

If you're the site administrator, you can manage the alerts of everyone on the site by clicking the User Alerts link on the Site Administration section of the Site Settings page.

When the event occurs that matches your alert — for example, the time or location of a calendar event change — you receive an email in your inbox. The email notification you receive is based on a template. These templates can be modified by your administrator, so they can provide for more detail.

Staying Up to Date with News

A popular feature in SharePoint is the ability to create and show news content throughout SharePoint in areas such as your SharePoint home dashboard, Team sites, Communication sites, hub sites, and even in other Microsoft 365 apps such as Microsoft Teams.

To explore the news feature, we'll use the SharePoint site we created in Chapter 1. News is shown front and center on the main page. You can click the Add button to add new news to the feed and anyone who is following the site will see the news on their SharePoint dashboard. Also, anyone who visits the site will also see the news.

To create a news post:

1. **Open your web browser and navigate to www.office.com.**

   If you are not already signed in, sign in with your Microsoft 365 account.

2. **Navigate to the SharePoint site you created in Chapter 1.**

3. **Click the Add drop-down and choose News Post, as shown in Figure 10-8.**

   You can also choose the Add News button as well.

4. **Create the news post just like you would a regular SharePoint site page.**

   You can provide a name for the post, and then click the plus icons to add content. We cover adding content to Site pages in Chapter 6.

5. **When you are ready, click the Create Post button in the upper-right corner of the screen.**

   Your news is now published and everyone who is following the site will be able to see the information.

Click to create a news post

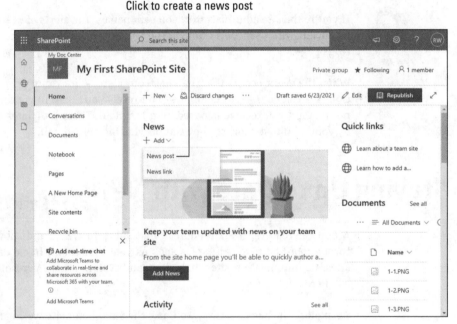

FIGURE 10-8:
Creating a news posting in a SharePoint site.

Information Sharing with Blog Style Sites and Wikis

Published web pages are intended to be mainly one-way communication: An individual or group with an opinion or expertise creates posts (think of a blog post) that others read and subscribe to. Readers can comment, like, and email a link to the post, but the posts themselves aren't collaborative. You often see executives in an organization maintaining blog style sites to communicate to employees, or IT departments to provide helpful posts that address FAQs.

Microsoft has decommissioned the Blog template for SharePoint Online sites. We suspect it is because a blog is really just a place to publish content. And you can publish a new page of content in any SharePoint site.

Wikis, on the other hand, are specifically collaborative efforts: Information is added to, and maintained by, a network of users. Perhaps the most well-known wiki is *Wikipedia* (www.wikipedia.org), a web encyclopedia of information about any topic imaginable, editable by anyone in the Wikipedia community. A wiki is a very flexible and democratic way for individuals to work together to share, refine, and collect information.

Good candidates for wikis include corporate encyclopedias, dictionaries, and training manuals so that many individuals can add their knowledge and examples.

Creating a blog-style site

To create a blog-style site in SharePoint using the Communication site, you create a top-level site on your main SharePoint landing page. (We discuss creating new sites in Chapter 5.) As a reminder, to access your SharePoint landing page, log into www.office.com and then select SharePoint from the app launcher that appears in the top-left corner of the page. From there you click the Create site button and select the Communication site template.

Publishing a new post

Creating a new post is fairly straightforward as long as you have the right permissions. One way we have seen people create blog style posts is using News. The default Communication and Team sites have a section for news where you can create a News post or News link. The post or link shows up on the default main page and others can click them to read the full article just like a blog post. Once on the post readers can interact with the author by liking and commenting.

If you prefer to create new pages for each posting, you can do that by navigating to the library where the pages for the site are kept and selecting Page from the New button. We covered how to do this in Chapter 6. However, to keep things simple for authors and information flow, we recommend sticking with using the news functionality for creating new posts.

Comments and likes (if any) are displayed below the post to which they apply. The Comments link and the Add Comment field allow users to comment on a post by titling their comment (optional) and adding body text. The Comments link also shows the current number of comments. The Like button creates a smiley face and shows the number of likes, along with an Unlike button if you change your mind.

You will see options on the toolbar across the top of the post and you can email a link using email or Yammer. If you are the author of the post you will see options catered to you such as viewing the analytics for the page and editing the page.

Using wikis to collaborate and coauthor

A *wiki* app is a library of pages that can be edited by any member (Contributor) of your site. As we describe earlier, encyclopedias, dictionaries, and training manuals are all good examples of wikis for an organization. These examples are entities that provide structure to what is being accomplished but benefit by input of a group.

Creating a wiki app

A wiki app in SharePoint is a library of Wiki pages. Create the wiki the way you would any other app, which we describe in Chapter 12, by selecting Wiki Page Library app.

Adding pages to a wiki

Two pages are created by default in your new wiki app, Home and How to Use This Library. Both provide predefined instructions that may be helpful when you first create the wiki. Most users change the home page content before launching the wiki, but you can keep the How to Use This Library page or delete it, depending on its usefulness.

To add other pages to your wiki, follow these steps:

1. **Navigate to the home page of the wiki app by using the link on the Quick Launch menu, if available.**

    You can also navigate to the Site Contents page (from the gear icon in the upper-right corner of any SharePoint site) and open the app.

2. **Click the Page tab of the Ribbon and click the View All Pages button located in the Page Library section.**

    You see the list of pages.

3. **Click the New drop-down at the top of the page and select Wiki Page to create a new Wiki page.**

4. **Type your new page name in the New Page Name text box and then click the Create button.**

   The new page appears, ready for editing, as shown in Figure 10-9. Just click in the page and then the Format Text tab appears.

   You can now edit the page, or repeat the steps to create multiple pages before editing.

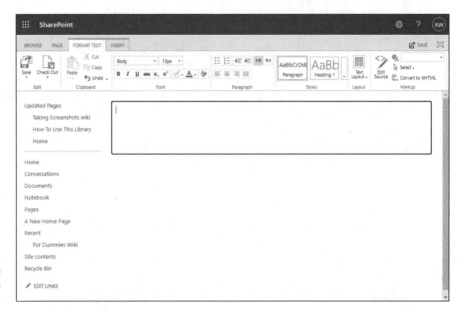

FIGURE 10-9:
A Wiki page in
Edit mode.

TIP

Another easy way to create additional pages is to create a link to them first in a Wiki page, save the page, and then click that link. A dialog box appears for adding a new page and you can click Create. The new page is created automatically with the name found in the link. For example, type **[[My New Page]]** to create a link to the My New Page page. The link to an uncreated page appears underlined with dashes. If users click the link, and then clicks the Create button on the Page dialog box, the page is created for editing and the link turns into a normal hyperlink. To create a link to a page and have the name be different than the wording of the link, type a pipe character (|) after the page name and type the display text. For example, type **[[Resources|Resources for You]]** to create the Resources link that points to the Resources for You page.

Editing a Wiki page

When you first create a Wiki page, the page appears in Edit mode, as shown earlier in Figure 10-9. When you want to come back to a Wiki page and edit later, follow these steps:

1. **Access the page from the Quick Launch menu or Wiki Library Page list.**

2. **Click the Page tab of the Ribbon and click the Edit button located in the Edit section.**

TIP Like other documents, check out the page if you don't want others to be able to edit at the same time and perhaps overwrite your work. See Chapter 22 for details.

Editing a Wiki page is similar to working in a word processor. You can type or copy text, indent, make bullets, apply bold and italics, and insert various other types of content such as tables and images. To stop editing, click the Save button on the Edit tab of the Ribbon. You need to check in your wiki as a separate step if you checked it out.

TIP You can also find an Edit link in the upper-right corner of the Wiki page. Clicking it moves you the page into Edit mode for you.

After switching a page to Edit mode, you can also change the text layout. By default, text layout is one column (full page width), but you can change the layout by choosing one you like from the Text Layout drop-down list on the Format Text tab. (*Note:* You must be in Edit mode to see the Format Text tab.) Now you may have multiple text containers to work with.

WARNING You can switch layouts at any point. But be careful — if you switch to a layout with fewer containers than your current layout, SharePoint combines content in one container with content in another. You won't lose the content, but you'll probably have to make some edits to fix the combined content.

TECHNICAL STUFF Changing the text layout of a Wiki page isn't the same as changing the layout on a Web Part page or the page layout on a Publishing page. Wiki pages, Web Part pages, and Publishing pages all behave slightly different and have different purposes. See Chapter 6 for a more thorough discussion on SharePoint's web pages. By the way, if you can articulate the differences among these different kinds of SharePoint pages, consider a career as a SharePoint consultant!

Communicating with Discussion Boards

Discussion boards, along with alerts, are the granddaddies of social networking services. Discussion boards have been around since before the World Wide Web and consist of text postings by individuals with others posting replies to the original subject or to other replies. A discussion board post and the responses to it are one *thread.*

One of the benefits of a discussion board (versus a long email chain, and you know what we're talking about) is the ability to find and search posts easily for information. Threads provide a useful history of the comments on a topic. Users generally have various levels of expertise in organizing and searching their email, but SharePoint discussion views and search make it easy for users to both find and read posts.

TIP

One of the benefits of a team discussion board is (should be) the less formal approach in posting questions and answers — a discussion board exchange resembles a true discussion. Blog-style sites and wikis are more formal, so discussion boards are generally where team members can ask questions and share thoughts.

Creating a Discussion Board app

Adding a Discussion Board app is a fairly straightforward process. You simply choose the Discussion Board app template when creating a new app. Adding apps is covered in more detail in Chapter 11.

You can add as many discussion boards to your site as you like. You might find it beneficial to create a discussion board for each functional area to keep the discussions on topic. On the other hand, you might find that it is better to just have a single discussion board for the team and to get people using it and interacting with their ideas. As with most things in SharePoint, the way you work with the functionality is up to you. SharePoint just provides the platform, and it's up to you and your SharePoint consultant to determine the best way to use it.

Posting and replying to a subject

To create a new subject in a discussion board, follow these steps:

1. **Browse to your discussion board and click the New Discussion button.**

The New Discussion page appears.

2. **Type a subject for the new discussion in the Subject text box.**

   This needs to be a short phrase that teammates can relate to as a topic.

3. **Type the detail of your post in the Body text area.**

   You have all the editing options of Rich HTML in this area. Use the Editing tools to format your text with the toolbar and styles, as well as insert tables, images, and links. You can upload files using the Insert tab.

   You also have a spell checker in this dialog box!

4. **Select the Question check box if you're asking a question.**

5. **When you're finished with your post, click the Save button.**

   Your new post appears and shows the subject title, who created it, the amount of replies, and when it was updated last. Note that the amount of replies shows on the details of the discussion page.

The Discussion Board app shows a number of different views into the discussions: Recent, My Discussions, Unanswered Questions, Answered Questions, and Featured.

To reply to a subject or another reply, follow these steps:

1. **Click the Subject Title link for the discussion.**

   The subject appears in Flat view with a Reply button. If you're the owner of the discussion posting, you also see an Edit button. You can also click the ellipsis to be alerted to additional replies, mark the discussion as Featured, or delete the discussion.

2. **Click the Reply link or click in the Add a Reply text box.**

   The Reply text box activates, and you can type your reply. By default, the Reply text box shows only a Body field.

3. **Type your reply; if desired, use the Rich HTML features (as we describe in the preceding step list).**

   Remember that you can attach files, upload files, and add all sorts of text formatting.

4. **When you're finished with your reply, click the Reply button.**

Connecting with Others Using RSS Feeds

An *RSS feed* is a feed formatted in a special way to be read by a Really Simple Syndication (RSS) reader. Every SharePoint list or library app has the ability to display its data using an RSS feed.

Viewing RSS feeds

Nowadays, most websites publish a syndication feed, or *RSS feed*, of their site's content. SharePoint sites are no different. In fact, every app in SharePoint can publish an RSS feed. You can even create RSS feeds based on views, which means you can filter what gets published to the RSS feed. If you subscribe to the feed, you're *pulling* the information. However, you can also subscribe to alerts to make SharePoint *push* updates to you.

RSS feeds are a popular way for people to keep track of updates to a website without visiting that site.

To use RSS feeds, they must be enabled for the site. To enable RSS, go into the Site Settings of the site and click the RSS link under the Site Administration link. This is a SharePoint administrator task and we cover how to work with Site Settings in Chapter 18.

In addition to enabling RSS feeds for the SharePoint site you must also enable them for the List or Library app, too. To enable RSS feeds for your app, follow these steps:

1. **In the site that contains your app, click the gear icon in the top-right corner of the screen and then click Site Contents. Then click the ellipsis next to the list or library and select Settings.**

    The settings page appears.

2. **In the Communications section, click the RSS Settings link.**

    If you don't see the RSS Settings link, RSS isn't enabled for your site. You can enable RSS settings for your site by clicking the RSS link in the Site Administration section of the Site Settings page. RSS must also be enabled for your web application by the SharePoint farm administrator.

3. **On the Modify RSS Settings page, select the Yes radio button under the Allow RSS for This List option.**

    You can also use this page to configure the settings for the apps default RSS feed, such as the feed's title, columns, and item limit.

4. **After you finish configuring the default settings for your app's RSS feed, click OK to save your changes.**

REMEMBER

Each app has its own RSS feed. Therefore, you must configure RSS for each app where you want to use RSS.

After you enable RSS feeds for your app, you can view the RSS feed as follows:

1. **Browse to the app where you want to view the RSS feed, click the All Items drop-down menu, and select Edit Current View (see Figure 10-10).**

2. **Click the RSS feed logo, as shown in Figure 10-11.**

   The RSS feed is displayed in your web browser. The URL in your web browser is the actual link to the RSS feed.

   Most browsers display the RSS feed using a built-in style sheet for formatting.

3. **Subscribe to the feed using your browser as a reader or paste the web address for the feed in the feed reader of your choice.**

   See the section, "Reading RSS feeds with Outlook," later in this chapter, for instructions.

FIGURE 10-10:
Editing a view
to get to the
RSS feed.

TIP

RSS must be enabled for the farm, site, and app. In other words, you can't use RSS feeds if they aren't turned on. You can also turn off RSS feeds for a given app or site if you don't want people to use them. The default option is to allow RSS feeds. At the site level, RSS feeds are enabled in the Site Settings page. The RSS settings for an individual app are managed in the List Settings or Library Settings page for that app, respectively.

RSS feed logo

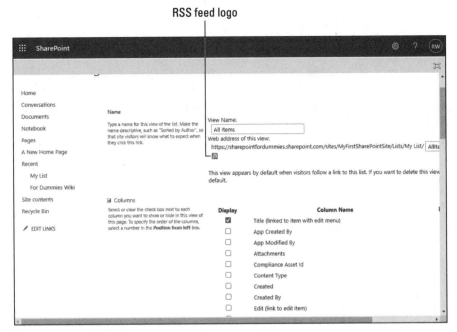

FIGURE 10-11:
Clicking the RSS
feed icon to
display the
feed URL.

Reading RSS feeds with Outlook

Your email application, and specifically in terms of SharePoint integration, Micro-soft Outlook, is still the bedrock of online communication for most business users. As in the past, you can still integrate Outlook with SharePoint calendars, contacts, and tasks using the Connect to Outlook button in the Ribbon of a calendar app. You might prefer following a SharePoint app using RSS.

To add a SharePoint RSS feed to Outlook, follow these steps:

1. **Open Outlook and on the Ribbon, click File, then Info, and then select Account Settings from the Account Settings drop-down menu.**

2. **On the RSS Feeds tab, click New.**

The New RSS Feed dialog box appears.

3. **Type (or copy and paste after getting it in the previous steps) the URL of the RSS feed.**

4. **Click the Add button.**

The feed is added to the list of subscribed feeds on the RSS Feeds tab.

3

Customizing SharePoint

IN THIS PART . . .

Understand the concept of an app, how to add them to your SharePoint site, and how to develop your own.

Take control of your SharePoint experience by customizing your SharePoint profile, keeping track of your favorite sites, and organizing your documents with OneDrive for Business.

Get a handle on your SharePoint documents by creating views into the content so that it is easily accessible, filterable, and readily available for you and others to consume.

Find out how to build a workflow using Microsoft Flow and connect that workflow to other services.

Understand how to use Microsoft Forms and how to integrate them with SharePoint.

Chapter **11**

Customizing SharePoint with Apps

The concept of an app is relatively new in SharePoint. An *app* in SharePoint is Microsoft's attempt to help stem confusion because getting your head around lists and libraries is difficult, especially when you start customizing them. For example, say you start with a custom list and then add columns to make it specific to customers. Is it still just a custom list or is it a Customers list or what? Microsoft posed this question to a number of focus groups and found that people were more comfortable with the concept of an app than a list or library. The result is that every list and library is now called an *app*.

Apps don't end at lists and libraries, though. Web developers can create apps that do all sorts of cool things. Because SharePoint is built using HTML standards, a web developer can take any web functionality and roll it into a SharePoint app. Third parties can put up their apps for sale on the online SharePoint App Store, which you access from within SharePoint.

In this chapter, you delve into apps. You find out how to add apps to your SharePoint site and how to configure apps. You find out that most apps are based on lists. And finally, you see how to configure these List-based apps.

Introducing SharePoint Apps

The concept of an app in general is nothing new. If you use a smartphone, you're surely familiar with apps. Each type of smartphone has millions and millions of apps available. SharePoint has jumped on the app bandwagon and embraced the concept of an app. A SharePoint app can be simple or complex. For example, you might create an app by customizing the Custom List app. On the other hand, you might hire a web developer to build a complete accounting system as a SharePoint app.

An app displays differently in your browser depending on whether you are using a classic experience or the new user interface updates. In the classic experience, an app displays commands on the ribbon that provide additional configuration options. These commands are *contextual* because the commands that appear depend on the context of where you are in the site. For example, the Document Library app contains a Files tab and a Library tab in addition to the Browse tab. In the newer user interface the ribbon is removed in favor of a more simplified view of things at the top of the app. For example, for a library containing content, you probably add new things to it frequently. So the first button at the top is called New and you can add new documents with it. Oh by the way, the New button is also a bright color so it is easy to find. The next button over is what you also probably do frequently, which is upload new documents.

You can select between the new and classic experience for an app on the Advanced settings page. To find it, navigate to the app. Then select List or Library settings from the gear icon drop-down menu located in the top-right corner of the page. On the app settings page, select Advanced settings. You will find the selector between new and classic experience at the bottom of the list of advanced settings available. The section is called List Experience and you can choose the New Experience option, the Classic Experience, or the Default Experience. The Default Experience will use whatever is set for the site collection as a whole by the administrator.

TIP

As we mention frequently throughout the book, Microsoft likes to change the user interface of things fairly frequently. The ribbon at the top of an app is a great example. If you are using the classic experience in SharePoint, you will see the ribbon. If you are using the latest version, you won't see the ribbon. The same functionality is there behind the scenes, but the way things look and the way you work with them has changed. It is a common theme with Microsoft in general and it takes some time to get used to these changes when they happen. In our experience, the good news is that the changes are usually for the better and we come to enjoy them after the initial shock of the change wears off.

Adding Apps to Your Site

When you create a new SharePoint site, you choose a template. Depending on the template you choose, your site already has a number of apps by default. You can add more apps to your site, however. For example, you might want to add a Survey app to your site.

TIP

The SharePoint site you created in Chapter 1 uses the Team Site template.

You can add an app (for example, the Survey app) to your site by following these steps:

1. Click the Settings gear icon and choose Add an App.

The Your Apps page appears, showing all the apps you can add to your site. (See Figure 11-1.) There is a Noteworthy section at the top for the most common apps.

2. Scroll down and click the Survey app.

The Adding Survey dialog box appears.

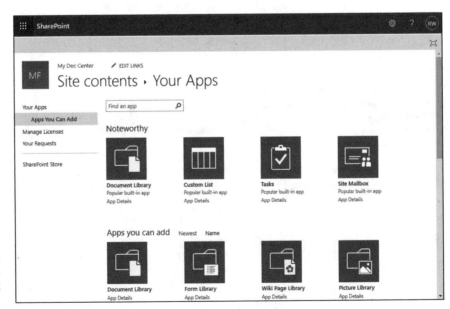

FIGURE 11-1:
Add a new app to your SharePoint Team site.

3. Provide a name for your Survey app.

You can also click Advanced Options to set app specific options. In this case, you can choose to show usernames in the survey and also choose whether you want the Survey app to allow multiple responses per user.

4. Click Create to create the app and add it to your site.

The Site Contents page is displayed, which shows all the apps on your site. Notice you now have a new Survey app with the title you provided in Step 3. Figure 11-2 shows the app on the Site Contents page.

FIGURE 11-2:
A Survey app on the Site Contents page.

You can access an app by clicking on it in the Site Contents page. If you click an app you just created, it will display on the screen.

Accessing App Settings

Most apps are based on a list or library. A list or library has a settings page where you can configure your app. To view or change the configuration settings of your Library app or List app, use the Library Settings page or the List Settings page. This page is the hub where you can find all the options for configuring and customizing your List or Library app to meet your business requirements.

Follow these steps to access the Library Settings or List Settings page:

1. **Navigate to your library app or list app by clicking the name of the library or list on the Site Contents page.**

You can access the Site Contents page from the Settings gear icon.

2. **Click the Gear icon (in the upper-right corner of the page) and select Library (or List) Settings (whichever appears), as shown in Figure 11-3.**

The Library Settings page or the List Settings page appears. (You may have already accessed this page when completing the steps in other chapters in this book.)

The Library (or List) Settings page is divided into several sections. Each section contains many configuration choices, as shown in Figure 11-4. We suggest you spend some time browsing this page. Some of the sections you see include

- *List Information:* Displays the library (or list) name, web address, and description.

  You can change the list's name and description by clicking the List Name, Description, and Navigation link in the General Settings column.

  The web address is set to the list's default view. Change the default view by scrolling down to the Views section of the Library (or List) Settings page.

  When you link to a list or library, use the root of the web address. That way, you can change the default view any time you want without needing to change any links that target the list. For example, to create a link to the Shared Documents library, you would use the following:

  ```
  http://intranet.portalintegrators.com/Shared Documents
  ```

- *General Settings:* Includes list name and description as well as settings for Versioning, Advanced, Validation, Column Default Value, Rating, Audience Targeting, and Form. See Table 11-1 for a complete list of General Settings.

- *Permissions and Management:* Includes saving the library or list as a template as well as settings for Permissions, File Management, Workflow, Information Management Policy, and Enterprise Metadata and Keywords. You can also generate a file plan report from this section. (See Chapter 21 for more about security settings.)

- *Communications:* Configure RSS and incoming email settings for the library or list.

- *Content Types:* If you have configured your library or list to allow for content types, a Content Types section appears. Use this section to associate content types with your list or library. With content types, you can reuse columns across sites, as well as across lists and libraries. (See Chapter 14 for a more thorough discussion of content types.)

- *Columns:* Create, view, add, and modify columns for the library or list.

  You can create your own column for this list only, add a site column from the preconfigured SharePoint site columns, or create a new site column of your choosing that can be added to multiple lists.

- *Views:* Display and modify the library or list views. You can also create new views.

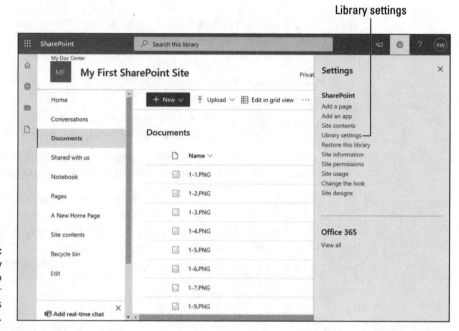

Library settings

FIGURE 11-3:
Select Library
Settings to
change your
library's
configuration.

Many site owners never change the default settings options; some simply change the List name or delete the list. For others, this level of optional setting detail is what they want to know first! Microsoft supplies descriptions on the how and/or why to use the settings on each of the individual settings pages; however, this chapter may become one of the most dog-eared chapters in the book because there are so many options to remember!

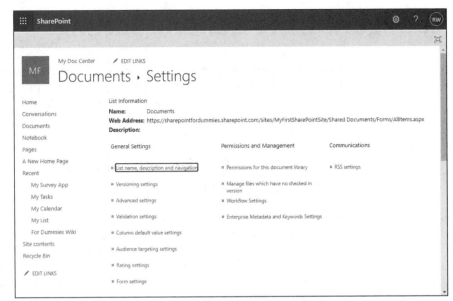

FIGURE 11-4:
The Library
Settings or List
Settings page.

TABLE 11-1 **General Settings Configuration Options**

Setting Name	What You Can Accomplish
List Name, Description, and Navigation	Just like it sounds! (See the section, "Changing the title, description, and navigation," later in this chapter.)
Versioning	Configure item approval, versioning (major and minor), and require check-out.
Advanced	A plethora of options, including allowing for the management of content types, search visibility, allowing for folders, or datasheet view.
Validation	Allows you to create formulas that compare two or more columns in your library or list.
Column Default Value	Add or edit default values for columns indicated in the library or list Validation settings.
Audience Targeting	A check box to enable audience targeting and a check box to enable classic audience targeting. These allow the library or list to use audience targeting. Enabling audience targeting creates a Targeting column for this list. Some Web Parts can use this data to filter list contents based on whether the user is in the audience.
Rating	A Yes or No option that allows items in the library or list to be rated.
Form	The Form options let you select between using the default SharePoint form for working with a List or Library app or creating a custom form in PowerApps. We cover PowerApps in more detail in Chapter 17. Using PowerApps you can customize the form that is used to create or edit items in a List or Library app. In the past, you would use a tool called InfoPath; however, that tool is no longer available and PowerApps is used instead.

Configuring the General Settings

The General Settings area of the Library or List app has recently been expanded to include multiple new settings, including Validation, Column Default Value (for libraries), Audience Targeting, Rating, and Form. See Table 11-1 for an overview to see what you can do with each of these options.

Changing the title, description, and navigation

The General Settings page is a simple, self-descriptive settings page. Most of these options are what you configure when you first create the Library or List app, including whether the app appears on the Quick Launch navigation.

WARNING

Changing the title does *not* change the web address (URL) of the app. If having the title match the URL is important, or less confusing to your team, consider re-creating a new app with the desired title and deleting the old one. Of course, this works better early in the process, before you upload documents or create apps!

TIP

If you already have many items in your app, you can copy documents from one Library app to another, or export an existing List app to Excel and re-import into a new one. However, this shouldn't be taken lightly. Some column configuration settings, such as a Choice column, need to be re-created along with all the app settings we discuss in this chapter. If you're unsure what you want to name an app when you create it, take some time to consider your terminology before creating the app.

Versioning settings

The Versioning Settings area contains some of the most sought-after settings in any app. Versioning settings cover most of the document management or content management choices. So your new document/content management mantra is *approval, versioning,* and *check out.* You can say it in your sleep. By default, Approval, Versioning, or Check Out Requirement settings are *not* turned on in a Team site.

The reason versioning is turned off by default is that it takes up a large amount of space in the database. Each time a new version is created, the database grows. However, versioning is important for any real work, so we recommend you turn it on.

TIP

If you want to have these options enabled when your sites are configured, consider using a publishing site instead.

Before selecting these options, make sure you know the business processes of your team. If documents are thoroughly vetted and approved outside the SharePoint process, you may not want or need Approval settings or Check Out enforced. If your documents are images, you may or may not want to apply versioning if the versions don't matter to you and you would not need to revert to an older version.

TIP

Consider using multiple Document Library apps and apply different settings based on need. For example, if you have 100 documents in a Library app and really only need versioning and approval on 5 of those documents, perhaps they can be placed in a Library app with extra configuration.

Versioning can be one of the most misunderstood features of SharePoint document management. Versioning is a helpful protection mechanism because you can revert to a previous version of the document if necessary. *Versions* in SharePoint are copies of the same document at different intervals during editing.

TIP

We suggest adding the Versions column to your views so that users can quickly see the version of the document. Otherwise, you end up with users appending versioning information to the document's name or title, such as Employee Handbook v1.0, Employee Handbook v2.0, or my favorite, Client_Proposal_Final_v3.0_FINAL_KW-edited_RW-reviewed_FINAL-DO-NOT-REVISE_02-06-2019_ROSEMARIE-SIGNED-OFF-FINAL_FINAL.

Follow these steps to apply or modify Versioning settings:

1. **Click the Versioning Settings link in the Library Settings or List Settings page.**

   The sections of the Versioning Settings page include Content Approval, Document Version History, Draft Item Security, and Require Check Out (Library apps only).

2. **Next you need to choose whether you want to require content approval for submitted items. You make this selection by choosing the Yes or No radio button on the Versioning Settings page (accessed in Step 1).**

   If you selected Yes in answer to Require Content Approval for Submitted Items?, individuals with the Approve Items permissions can always see draft items.

   Items that aren't approved yet (meaning they are draft versions) aren't visible to site members or visitors. You can designate who you want to view drafts in the Draft Item Security section. See Chapter 22 for details on content approval.

3. **In the Document Version History section, select a radio button to indicate whether to use No Versioning, Create Major Versions, Create Major and Minor (Draft) Versions, or (optional) specify the Number of Versions to keep by entering a number.**

   The default for a List or Library app is No Versioning. You can select Major Versions (1.0, 2.0, 3.0, and so on) or Major and Minor Versions (1.0, 1.2., 1.3, 2.0, and so on). Selecting either of the last two options enables you to designate a limit for the number of versions of each type by entering a number up to 10,000.

4. **Choose who can see draft items by selecting a Draft Item Security radio button in the Draft Item Security section.**

   This section is disabled unless you allow for minor (draft) versions or require content approval of your documents or list items. Here are the three options for who can see draft items — Any User Who Can Read Items, Only Users Who Can Edit Items, or Only Users Who Can Approve (and the Author of the Item).

5. **Determine whether to require check out for users editing documents by selecting the Yes or No radio button.**

   Although it can sometimes be a hassle (we often forget we have checked out a document, sometimes months ago!), requiring check out is another good safety mechanism that makes sure the other users don't see a document in mid-modification or have multiple users editing at the same time (last save wins).

TIP

   Consider adding the Checked Out To column to your views so that users can quickly see who has an item checked out.

6. **Click OK.**

   After you click OK, your Versioning settings are applied. Go try them out!

When viewing documents in a Library app, you can click the ellipsis to see a contextual menu, as shown in Figure 11-5. This menu allows a document's editor to check out/check in the document, approve, set off a workflow, and so forth. Because the menu is contextual, if approval isn't set on the library or list, for example, Approve doesn't appear on the menu. If a document is checked out, the option to Discard Check Out appears.

TIP

In most cases, team members navigate to the site using a browser to work with list apps. However, think about how your team interacts with documents. They may be navigating to an app using the browser, but they may also be linking from a bookmark or opening the document directly from the editing application (such as Word, Excel, or PowerPoint). Although current versions of Office support and interact with SharePoint Library app settings, users may not know where to find these app settings.

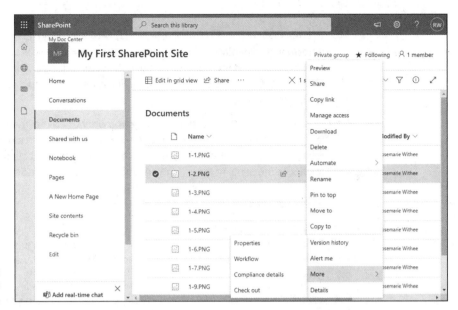

FIGURE 11-5:
A document's
context menu.

REMEMBER

Avoid frustration by taking a little time to review the settings and options with your team. Training on these document management options is one of my number one recommendations for SharePoint collaboration success, especially for teams with many members or contributors.

Advanced settings

Advanced settings include many powerful configuration options for Library and List apps:

» **Content Types:** Allows you to add and remove content types associated with the app. See Chapter 14 for details on creating your own content types.

» **Document Template (Library app only):** Allows you to specify the default template, such as a Word, Excel, or PowerPoint template, that is used when someone clicks the New button to create a new document.

TIP

You can also associate document templates with content types, so you can use multiple content types with a library to associate multiple document templates. Sounds confusing, but in a nutshell, having multiple document types and templates enables you to have multiple options for creating a document when you click the New button. For example, you might have a Word template for expenses and a Word template for vacation requests. These can both show up in the New drop-down list (located in the ribbon on the Files tab) using content types.

>> **Opening Documents in the Browser (Library app only):** Enables you to determine the behavior of the browser when someone clicks on a document to open it. If you don't want to use the Office Web apps, disable the opening of documents in the browser. This also allows users to send direct links to the documents if necessary.

>> **Custom Send to Destination (Library app only):** This is a great option that lets you add your own web address to the Send To menu on a document's Edit menu. Your SharePoint administrator can also add global addresses that appear in the Send To menu in every document library. The Send To command sends a copy of your file to another location, such as another Team site where you want to share the document.

>> **Folders:** Indicates whether users can create new folders in the Library app. We like to turn off this option so people don't go folder crazy. You can always turn on the option so you can create folders when necessary and then turn it back off.

>> **Search:** Specifies whether items in the app should appear in search results.

>> **Index Non-Default Views/Reindex Document Library:** Options for indexing non-default views and re-indexing the document library. Indexing provides extra data for searches so that searching the library is faster. There is some overhead with indexing, though, so SharePoint makes available some options to control it.

>> **Offline Client Availability:** Allows you to specify whether users of desktop client software, such as Outlook, can download content for offline viewing.

>> **Site Assets Library (Library app only):** Allows you to designate the Library app as a Site Assets library, which makes it easier for users to browse to the Library app to find multimedia files.

>> **Quick Property Editing:** Lets you specify whether Quick Edit can be used on this library. Quick Edit lets users open the view in a grid and make edits to metadata on the fly. This is much like editing the metadata (data about the documents in the library) on the fly in an Excel type interface.

>> **Dialogs:** By default, list and library forms launch in a dialog box. This option lets you specify that forms should open in the browser window as a page instead of a dialog box.

In addition, List app advanced settings include item-level permissions and attachments.

Follow these steps to apply or modify Advanced settings:

1. **Click the Advanced Settings link in the Library Settings or List Settings page.**

The Advanced Settings page appears, as shown in Figure 11-6.

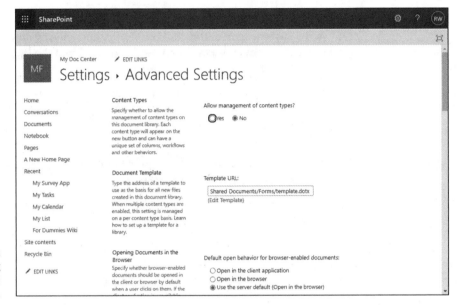

2. **Choose whether to enable management of content types by selecting the Yes or No radio button.**

If you select Yes, after applying, your Library Settings or List App Settings page will contain a new section for Content Types. The default is No.

3. **Change the document template (Library app only) by specifying a template URL in the Template URL text box.**

Library apps have a default template for new documents. Remember, you can create a new document in a Library app, as well as upload documents that have been created previously. For example, the document template for a Document Library app is the default Word template. You could change this to an Excel or PowerPoint template. You could also change it to a custom template you created in one of these applications.

If you're working with content types, you can enable a different template for each document type. For example, your library may house contracts and have three content types for different contracts, all with a different template available on the New button.

If you opt for a different document template, upload the template to the Forms folder in Document Library app and change the Template URL in the Document Template section of the Advanced Settings page.

4. **Choose when to open documents in the browser (Library app only), the client application, or as the server default by selecting a radio button in the Opening Documents in the Browser section.**

If the client application is unavailable, the document opens in the browser.

5. **Add a Custom Send to Destination (Library app only) by entering the name that should display on the Send To menu and the URL destination.**

Similar to Windows commands (for example, Send to Desktop), you can create an option to appear on the Edit menu for documents in this Library app to be sent to another SharePoint destination. Supply a short name to appear on the contextual menu and a URL for the destination in the Destination Name and URL text boxes.

6. **Select whether folders can be created in this app by selecting the Yes or No radio button in the Folders section.**

Selecting Yes or No determines whether the New Folder command is available on the New menu. The default is Yes.

We usually disable folders unless we have a good reason to use them. In our opinion, the only good reason to use folders is when you have a set of documents that require unique permissions but must remain in the same app. If you leave folders enabled, people will use them.

7. **Determine the search visibility for this app by selecting the Yes or No radio button in the Search section.**

Selecting No for the Search option can keep the items in the app from being presented in search results, even if the site or app is included in Search settings. The default is Yes.

8. **Enable offline client availability by selecting the Yes or No radio button in the Offline Client Availability section.**

The Offline Client Availability option determines whether items in the app can be downloaded to offline client applications, such as Outlook. The default is Yes.

9. **Add app location to the Site Assets Library (Library app only) by selecting the Yes or No radio button in the Site Assets Library section.**

This new Site Assets Library option specifies whether this Library app appears as a default location when uploading images or other files to a Wiki page. This can be especially beneficial for Document Library apps that contain images or a Picture Library app. This keeps wiki editors from searching all over for the images they should be using. The default is No.

10. **Determine whether the app can be edited using Quick Edit by selecting the Yes or No radio button in the Quick Property Editing section.**

This option determines whether Quick Edit can be used to bulk-edit data on this app. The default is Yes.

11. **Indicate whether forms should launch in a modal dialog box by selecting the Yes or No radio button in the Dialogs section.**

Modal dialog boxes get old pretty quickly, so we suggest you select the No option on this section quite often.

12. **Click OK to apply your selections.**

Other advanced configuration settings available in a List app (not in the Library app) include a Yes/No option for allowing attachments for a list item (default is Yes) and item-level permissions. The default for item-level permissions in a List app is for all members (contributors) to be able to read and modify all items. You can adjust these settings for users to either read only their own items and/or edit only their own items.

Validation settings

Validation is a formula or statement that must evaluate to TRUE before data can be saved. SharePoint has two different types of validation: column-level and app-level validation. The difference between column and app validation is that column validation compares only the data in that single column to some test, such as whether a discount is less than or equal to 50 percent.

```
= [Discount] &lt; = .50
```

On the other hand, validation settings in the app level compare two or more columns that must to evaluate to TRUE before the data can be saved. You can set a rule that [Discount] < [Cost] so customers don't get an item for free (or get money back!) because they buy an item with a discount.

To use validation settings, follow these steps:

1. **Click the Validation Settings link in the Library Settings or List Settings page.**

The Validation Settings page has two sections, Formula and User Message. The Formula section is the test your comparison of the columns must pass for the item to be valid. The User Message section is what the user receives if the test fails. Users can then adjust the values until the test passes.

2. **Create a formula for the validation by entering it in the Formula field.**

The formula needs to compare (or validate) one or more columns in your app. The App Settings page provides an example and a link to learning more about the proper syntax.

A selection list of columns in your app is available for use in your formula.

3. **In the User Message text box, enter a message to be shown to users who enter an invalid item.**

4. **Click Save to apply your validation to your list.**

Validations aren't retroactive. They apply only to new and modified entries on the specified columns.

Audience Targeting settings

The Audience Targeting setting includes options to select either Enable Audience Targeting or Enable Classic Audience Targeting for the app. Enable Audience Targeting is used for new Web Parts, such as News, and Enable Classic Audience Targeting is used for all the existing Web Parts we have come to know and love. In other words, the classics. Certain Web Parts, such as the Content Query Web Part, can use this column to filter list contents based on the user's inclusion in a specific audience.

Audience Targeting isn't the same thing as permissions. Users can still access content even if they aren't included in an audience. Audience targeting is simply a way to filter the presentation of content to certain groups of people.

Rating settings

Rating settings is a simple Yes/No option to allow the items in the app to be rated by users. The Rating feature is a much-requested feature. When enabled on your app, a Rating field appears, as shown in Figure 11-7. The Rating field allows users to select a star rating.

Instead of rating items with a star rating, you can instead choose to approve of items by using a simple Like button. If you are familiar with social-networking sites like Facebook, then you'll know how the Like button works. Changing from a star rating to a Like button is accomplished on the Rating Settings page when you enable ratings.

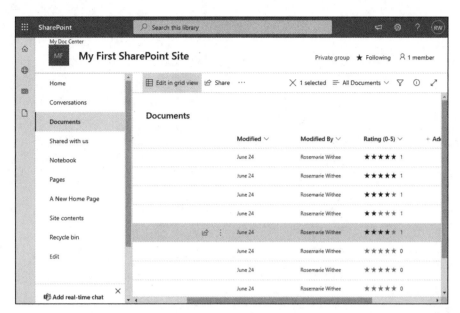

FIGURE 11-7:
Rating a
document.

Form settings

The Form Settings option lets you configure whether to use the default SharePoint form or create a custom form using PowerApps. We cover PowerApps in detail in Chapter 17. You can opt to allow customization of the form using PowerApps by selecting the Use a custom form creating using PowerApps radio button.

WARNING

Forms used to be customized using a product called InfoPath. However, Microsoft has replaced the functionality with a relatively new and expanded platform called PowerApps. If you are using an older On-Premises version of SharePoint, you might still see the InfoPath option.

Chapter **12**

Developing a Custom App

SharePoint ships with a number of useful apps, including apps for calendars, tasks, pictures, links, announcements, contacts, discussions, issues, surveys, assets, and even reports, just to name a few. These apps are useful, but there comes a time when you need to create your own app for very specific data. To create a custom app based on a list, use the Custom List app.

Creating your very own SharePoint app may sound a little daunting. The good news is that creating and customizing an app couldn't be easier. The easiest way to create your own app is to start with a Custom List app and then customize it for your particular need.

In this chapter, you find out how to create your own app. You see how to add columns to store data, create views into the data, validate data, and import data into your app. Finally, you explore the SharePoint Store, where you can search for and purchase third-party apps, and discover that your own organization can even have its own private SharePoint Store.

Planning Your App

Capturing information is nothing new. Ancient civilizations (millennia ago) used stone or clay tablets, pre-computer organizations (decades ago) used typewriters, and many organizations still use Excel. Often, the problem with data is not in collecting it but in sharing and aggregating it.

Excel does a great job with data aggregation but not such a great job with sharing. SharePoint is all about sharing (hence the name). A SharePoint app is a centralized container of data that is easy to manage and maintain. In addition, by the very nature of a centralized web portal, the data is easily shared and viewed by anyone in the organization with access.

Creating an app specifically for your data needs is important. You need to determine the columns of data you will capture and how the data will relate to each other. In addition, you need to determine which data will be valid and which should be rejected.

Planning a custom list is similar to starting a new spreadsheet in Excel or a table in Access. In all cases, a little up-front planning saves time in the long run. Plan ahead so you know what order you want the columns to be in and what options you want in drop-down lists.

TIP

Already have a spreadsheet that you think would make a good list in SharePoint? Make sure you check out the section "Importing a Spreadsheet as an App," later in this chapter. That section can help you create a custom app in no time.

REMEMBER

Columns can also be called *fields* (for those used to database terminology). When these columns are used to describe files (usually documents in a Document Library app), they're also referred to as *metadata* or *properties (of the file)*.

TIP

One of the neat features about SharePoint is the ability to add columns to the predefined apps. The process for adding columns is the same in Library and List apps. However, in a Library app, your columns capture information about a *file*, such as its category or author. List apps generally are all data columns and are used for tracking and communication.

Creating Your App

You create a custom app using the Custom List app. The Custom List app creates a basic list app that you can then customize for your particular scenario.

Follow these steps to create a custom app:

1. **Click the Settings gear icon, select Add an App, and then choose the Classic Experience link**

   The Your Apps page is displayed. Microsoft is moving towards simplifying SharePoint and one of the recent changes is creating a catalog of apps for you instead of letting you create any type of app by default. A catalog of apps is a subset of apps that anyone can create. The benefit to this simplification is that an administrator might want people to only be able to add a few apps that they have preapproved as opposed to any of the apps in the classic experience. Personally, we still prefer the classic experience.

2. **Click the Custom List app on the Your Apps page.**

   The Adding Custom List dialog box appears.

3. **Provide a name for the app in the Name text box.**

   To make things simple, you only need to give your new app a name. However, if you want to provide a description, you can click the Advanced Options link and then type the description in the Description box on the page that appears.

REMEMBER

   The name you type here is used in the app's web address. Avoid using spaces in the name when you create the app. You can change the app's name to a friendlier name after you create it, as described earlier in the chapter.

4. **Click the Create button.**

   SharePoint creates your new app and takes you automatically to the Site Contents page, as shown in Figure 12-1.

Adding columns to your app

A new custom app displays a single text Title column. The list also contains several behind-the-scenes columns that you can't see, such as ID and Version. To make the custom app your own, you have to add columns to the app.

Columns are like fields in a database table. When you add a column to your app, a data entry field appears in the app's New Form to give you a place to enter data into that column.

REMEMBER

A little planning goes a long way. You created a plan for your custom app, right? Because now is when you start adding the columns to your app that you listed in your plan.

You can also add columns to the predefined SharePoint apps.

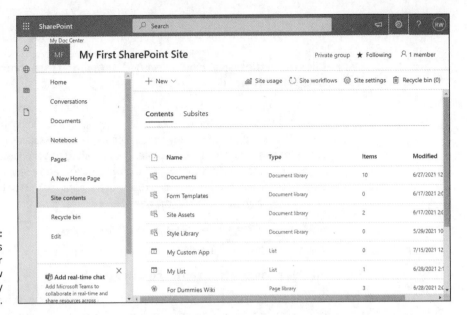

FIGURE 12-1:
The Site Contents page after creating a new app called My Custom App.

You can add a new column by clicking Add column in the heading of where you would expect a new column to show up. When you click Add column, a drop-down menu appears where you then choose the type of data the column will contain.

You can also add a new column using the classic experience. We prefer this method because it provides more control and it also lets us see more detail about the hidden columns that are already part of the list app. Follow these steps to add columns to your custom app:

1. **With your app open in the browser, click the gear icon and select List Settings.**

2. **Select Create Column in the Manage Views group (see Figure 12-2).**

The Create Column window appears.

You can also add new columns with the List Settings page.

3. **Type a name for your new column in the Column Name field.**

The name you type is what users will see, so pick a name that's concise but meaningful. We don't recommend using spaces in your column names when you first create them. You can always add spaces later.

TECHNICAL STUFF

Spaces entered in a column name become a permanent part of that column's *internal name* in SharePoint. Some of these internal names can get quite lengthy and downright nonsensical, which makes referencing them a real pain.

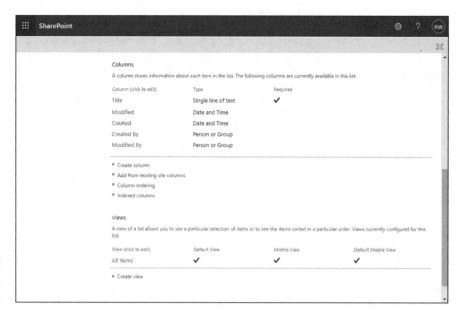

Columns

A column stores information about each item in the list. The following columns are currently available in this list:

Column (click to edit)	Type	Required
Title	Single line of text	✓
Modified	Date and Time	
Created	Date and Time	
Created By	Person or Group	
Modified By	Person or Group	

- Create column
- Add from existing site columns
- Column ordering
- Indexed columns

Views

A view of a list allows you to see a particular selection of items or to see the items sorted in a particular order. Views currently configured for this list:

View (click to edit)	Default View	Mobile View	Default Mobile View
All Items	✓	✓	✓

- Create view

FIGURE 12-2:
Add a new column to your list.

4. Select the type of information you want to store in the column.

The options given here are fairly intuitive — Single Line of Text, Number, Date and Time, and so on. See the later section, "Getting to know column types," for details on selecting the column type.

WARNING

Make sure you determine what kind of data you have when you first create the column. Changing the data type later may result in loss of data, or you may not have as many options when you change the type.

5. In the Additional Column Settings section, select the options that further define your column's type.

The column type you select in Step 4 determines what options you have available for configuring the column.

6. (Optional) If you want SharePoint to test the values entered into your column, use the Column Validation section to enter your formula.

7. Click OK.

SharePoint adds the column to your custom app.

You can change the column properties later and rearrange the order of the columns by using the List Settings page.

TIP

After you first create a custom app, use the List or Library Settings page to modify your app, where you have all the commands at your fingertips to power through the column creation — you can pick site columns, create your own columns, and rearrange them, as shown earlier in Figure 12-2. After your app has been created and you need to add more columns, the Create Column button on the main view of the app is a handy way to add one or two columns without leaving the main page.

Getting to know column types

Columns are used to store data, and unlike a spreadsheet, you need to define the type of column as you create it, as shown in Figure 12-3. For those who work with databases, this is a familiar concept. By defining the type of column, you gain extra functionality based on that type, and you help to control the type of information that can be entered into the column and how that information is presented onscreen. For example, users can enter only a number in a Number column; they can't add miscellaneous text.

SharePoint provides a number of built-in column types that you can select for your apps, such as columns that know how to handle dates and URLs. Third-party companies and developers in your organization can also create custom column types that can be added to SharePoint. For example, if your company needs a column that handles a full zip code (the zip code plus four numbers), a developer could create it for you.

Table 12-1 lists common SharePoint column types and what they're used for.

In addition to the column data types in Table 12-1, other data types, such as Publishing HTML (an even richer form of text), can be selected when creating site columns in publishing sites. Publishing sites are beyond the scope of this book, but we would encourage you to dig further if you are in a large organization and need to have granular control on who can publish to which portions of a page.

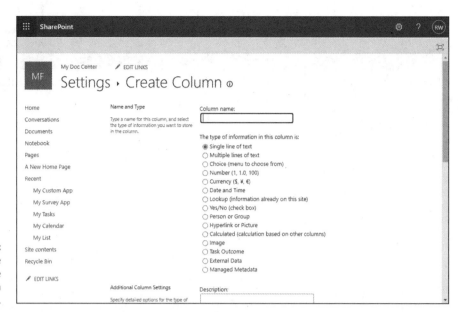

FIGURE 12-3:
The Create
Column page
showing data
type choices.

TABLE 12-1 **SharePoint Column Data Types**

Column Data Type*	What It's Used For	Display on Form
Single Line of Text	Display text and numbers (such as phone or course numbers, or zip code) up to 255 characters.	Single-line text box (the text box may not show all 255 characters).
Multiple Lines of Text	Display multiple lines of text.	Select from Plain Text, Rich Text, or Enhanced Rich Text. Depending on the number of lines you select, this option shows as a text area of that size with additional toolbars to format text.**
Choice***	A defined list of choices; for example, categories or departments.	Drop-down list is the default and most common.
Number	Numerical values that can be used for calculations.	You can identify a min/max value number with a choice of decimal options.
Currency	Numerical values that represent money.	You can identify a min/max value currency. Includes options for decimal places and currency format.
Date and Time	Dates and times.	Date and/or Time-Calendar Picker.

(continued)

TABLE 12-1 *(continued)*

Column Data Type*	What It's Used For	Display on Form
Lookup	Values from another list — for example, categories could be stored in a lookup list for document metadata.	Drop-down list populated with values from another list.
Yes/No	Boolean value of Yes or No.	Check box.
Person or Group	Directory listing information from SharePoint.	The person or group is shown as a hyperlink and can include presence information.
Hyperlink or Picture	Hyperlink (internal or external) or an image.	Hyperlink or picture.
Calculated	Data that can be calculated by formula.	Result of calculation; can be text or numerical.
Image	Image data.	An image for the row of data. For example, a profile picture if the list app contains contacts.
Task Outcome	The outcome of a task such as Approved, Rejected, or Pending.	The Task Outcome presents a list of choices that you can define when creating the item.
External Data	Data stored in a data source; for example, a table or view in an enterprise database.	Usually filled in by the external source and not users.
Managed Metadata	Provides a common set of keywords and terms that can be used across the organization.	Users can simply start typing, and the options will fill in based on their input. The options are pulled from the metadata managed by SharePoint.

Most columns also include property options for Required, Allow Duplicates, Default Values, and Add to Default View.

**Although you may set a number of lines for editing, this isn't a defined limit. Users can type or cut/paste a large amount of text into this control. You may want to use column validation to restrict the length.*

***Choice can also be shown on the form as radio buttons for a single choice or check boxes for multiple choices.*

REMEMBER

When you're creating columns for your custom app, you can change the order of the columns as they're shown in the Columns section of the List Settings page. Changing the column ordering in this section helps with organizing the app flow for owners and how they display on the app's form. However, changing the order on the List Settings page doesn't change the order of columns in the default view — you must modify the view separately.

TIP

Don't underestimate descriptions! Creators of lists often carry a lot of information in their heads about the content in the app. Users aren't mind readers. Make sure to type descriptions to help them understand the intent of the column and the data expected.

Validating data entry

Column validation options allow you to define additional limits and constraints for your data. For example, you may want to ensure that a value in one Date column occurs after another Date column. (So, for example, column validation can ensure that the date in the Date Finished column can't be earlier than the date in the Date Started column — you can't finish a project before it's begun!)

To use column validation on your app:

1. **In your app where you want to validate data entry, click List Settings from the gear icon drop-down menu.**

2. **Under General Settings, click the Validation Settings link.**

3. **Type a formula in the Formula text box, as shown in Figure 12-4.**

The result of the formula must evaluate to TRUE to pass validation. The formula syntax is the same as calculated columns, which is similar to Excel syntax.

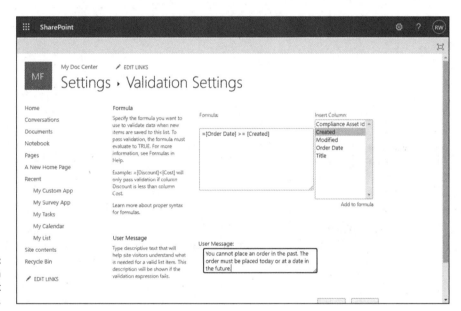

FIGURE 12-4:
Entering a
formula for list
validation.

4. **Enter a user message that you want to appear if the validation formula fails.**

The message should give the user an idea of how the formula works and how to fix the problem. (See the example message in Figure 12-4.)

5. **Click the Save button.**

When users enter data into your form, the validation formula is evaluated. If the formula evaluates to FALSE, your user message appears on the form, as shown in Figure 12-5.

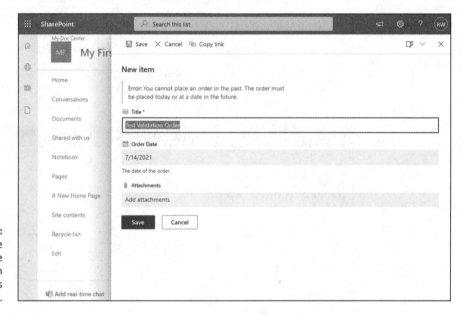

FIGURE 12-5:
A user message appears when the validation formula equals FALSE.

You can add column validation to columns created at the app or site level. Validation created for site-level columns applies everywhere that column is used, although the formula can be overridden at the app where the site-level column is used.

Working with the Title column

Unlike SharePoint's predefined apps, your custom app has only one column when you first create it — the Title column. Unfortunately, you can't delete the Title column or change its data type, but you can rename it, hide it, or make it not required.

To rename the Title column:

1. Click List Settings from the gear icon drop-down menu.

2. Under the Columns heading, click the Title hyperlink.

3. In the Column Name text box, replace *Title* with your own title and make modifications to the other properties as desired.

The Title column is used by the list as a means to access the data entry forms to view and edit the list item. You can opt to hide the Title column so that it doesn't appear on any of the app forms.

TIP

The hidden column will still appear in views unless you remove it from the view.

To hide the Title column:

1. In your list, click List Settings from the gear icon drop-down menu.

2. If the Content Types section isn't visible, enable management of content types by following these steps:

    a. *Click the Advanced Settings link on the List Settings page.*

    b. *Select the Yes radio button under Allow Management of Content Types, and then click OK. The Content Types section becomes visible on the List Settings page.*

3. In the Content Types section of the List Settings page, click the Item content type.

The List Content Type information appears.

If you want to change the Title column in a document library, you click the Document content type. The Item content type applies to custom apps only. In a predefined app, such as a Tasks app, you click the Task content type.

4. Click the Title column.

The Title column's properties appear, as shown in Figure 12-6.

5. Under Column Settings, select the Hidden (Will Not Appear in Forms) radio button and click OK.

The Title column doesn't appear on forms.

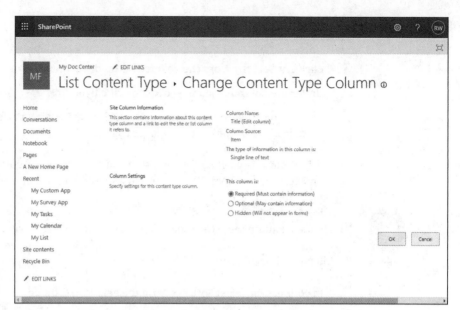

FIGURE 12-6:
Hiding the Title
column.

Importing a Spreadsheet as an App

Already have data in a spreadsheet that you want to be a SharePoint app? You're halfway there! Before you start, make sure you do the following:

>> **Clean the spreadsheet.** Make sure your spreadsheet looks like a table, with no blank columns or rows.

>> **Make sure your spreadsheet has headers.** All columns in the SharePoint app need to have a column title.

>> **Make sure your data is consistent.** For example, if a cell has a comment in it, but it should contain a date, remove the comment text.

>> **Make sure your column heading in the first row is representative of the data.** SharePoint reads the headings in the first row and makes assumptions about the information in those columns.

Figure 12-7 shows an example of a clean spreadsheet ready for importing.

WARNING

SharePoint looks for what it believes is the first text column and uses it as the pseudo-title field (the primary field in the list that has the Edit menu attached to it). Therefore, try to place a text field with unique data in the first column position. Unfortunately, if your unique field is a number, such as a serial number, this can cause issues. To work around the problem, create the app and copy and paste the data from the spreadsheet. (A good example of a first column is a unique name of a person or an item, such as Event Name. A bad example of a first column is the category of an item or a department of an employee.)

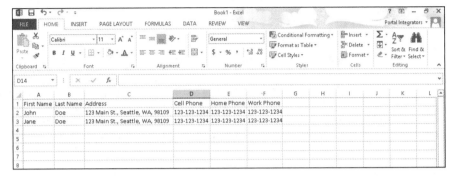

To import your spreadsheet into a custom app:

1. **Click the Settings gear icon, choose Add an App, and then choose the Classic Experience.**

You can also click the Site Contents link on the Quick Launch toolbar and then click the Add an App icon.

TIP

This feature requires the use of a browser that supports ActiveX. If you run into issues with this feature, such as seeing an unexpected error, then ActiveX Controls are not working properly with your browser.

2. **Select the Import Spreadsheet app from the list of apps you can add.**

3. **In the Name text box, enter a name for your app.**

Follow the naming conventions outlined in this book for app names: Keep them short and eliminate spaces.

4. **(Optional) In the Description text box, enter a description of the app.**

5. **Click the Browse button, browse to your spreadsheet, select it, and click the Import button.**

A dialog box appears that asks how your range is designated. The default is Table Range, but other options are Named Range or Range of Cells. If you haven't named the data as a range in Excel or set it as a table, select the Range of Cells option.

6. **If you chose the Range of Cells option, click the Select Range field in the dialog box, and then click your spreadsheet and highlight the desired cells.**

7. **Click the Import button in the dialog box.**

After you import your spreadsheet, verify the column types SharePoint chose for you. Generally, SharePoint assumes text, number, and dates. You may want to change some text fields to Choice, Yes/No, and so forth.

TIP

Don't have the patience to create all your custom columns one by one — but you don't have a current app in another format either? Create a spreadsheet with your column headers and at least one row of data, and then import this spreadsheet and modify the column properties as necessary.

Taking Your App to the Next Level: Calculated and Lookup Columns

Calculated columns are especially powerful for automatically generating data. Don't be intimidated — the web is full of great formula examples for SharePoint calculated columns. Some common uses include

>> Adding days to a Date column to calculate an Expired or Due Date column

>> Adding Number or Currency columns to get a total

>> Using the Me function to automatically add the username to a field

Creating a calculated column

To create a calculated column, follow these steps:

1. **Select the Calculated column type in the Name and Type options in the Create Column dialog box.**

   The Additional Column Settings area changes to support entering a calculation (see Figure 12-8) and specifying column options.

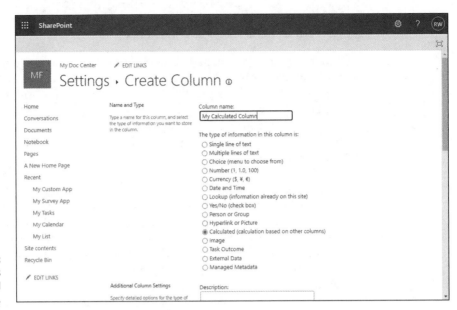

FIGURE 12-8:
Column settings
for a calculated
column.

2. **Type your formula using the proper syntax in the Formula text box.**

If you're basing your calculation on another column in the app, you can reference that column using the square brackets reference syntax.

For example, to calculate a Shipping Deadline value, add five days to the Order Date value in another column by entering [Order Date]+5 in the Formula text box.

3. **Select the proper data type for the returned value and other data type property options, if available, from the Additional Column Settings section of the page.**

REMEMBER

Not all return values are of the same data type as the input columns. For example, if you subtract one date from another, your returned value is a number (the number of days' difference between the two dates).

Other examples include

- Adding the current username to a field. Simply type the constant **[Me]** in the Formula text box.

- Using today as a date in a calculation to create a new date by entering **[Today]+7** in the Formula text box.

Using a lookup column

Maintaining all your options in a Choice field can be cumbersome and prone to error. SharePoint uses a similar model to relational databases by separating the *lookup* information from the *transaction* app. Think of all the lookup data that could be maintained in separate apps. For example, computer hardware inventory lookup apps could include hardware type, maintenance contract, and department location. These apps can be maintained independently of the transaction app — the inventory itself.

For example, you could create a Customer custom app with a single field — Title — and populate it with the names of customers. Then build an Order app (to track orders that customers place). Customer is a column in the Order app. Rather than build a Choice field, you could use the Lookup data type to connect to the Customer app and use the Title field as data for the Customer column in the Order app. The end result is that all your customers are separated from the orders. If customers need to change their name (maybe a customer got married, or their name was misspelled) you can just change the name in the Customer app instead of in every entry in the Order app.

You can also add other columns from the lookup app to the drop-down list to help users select the proper choice. When a user selects the value from the drop-down list, values for the additional columns also display. Figure 12-9 shows a scenario that uses a lookup column to display a customer's sales territory. The customer's name and sales territory are stored in one app and displayed in another app using a lookup column. Figure 12-9 also shows the use of inline editing in a Web Part.

FIGURE 12-9:
Selecting a value
from a lookup
column.

TECHNICAL STUFF

For users familiar with databases and referential integrity, SharePoint includes additional options to support this implementation. Lookup columns can also be used to create a chain of joined apps that can be used to query and display values from additional columns.

Keeping Track of Locations

SharePoint includes a column type specifically designed for keeping track of a geographic location. Have you ever browsed a mapping service such as Bing Maps or Google Maps and seen the pushpins marking specific locations? This is exactly the type of data the new column type is designed to store. Unfortunately the only way we found to enable this column type was through code such as PowerShell or C#, so you will need a developer here. However, if you have an app that needs geo location data then at least it is an option.

A scenario where this would be valuable would be when a field worker needs to track location information along with other data. For Ken's graduate thesis (more than a decade ago), he developed a field biology application that collected data using a handheld GPS. At the time, SharePoint was not yet available, so he uploaded the data to an Excel spreadsheet. That same application today could store the data directly, and instantly, to a SharePoint list using a mobile device. (On one field trip with a biologist in the San Francisco wetlands, he nearly lost his leg to a muddy sinkhole and can remember dipping the device underwater. Having saved his leg, he didn't really care much about the data until he made it back to campus.)

Ken spent months developing his application to collect data and store it. SharePoint, along with modern cellular technology and powerful smartphones, makes a similar scenario available right out of the box.

Downloading Apps from the SharePoint Store

In addition to the apps that come with SharePoint, you can also add apps from third parties. These third-party apps appear in the SharePoint Store. If you're using SharePoint Online, then you have access to the full store. If you're using SharePoint On-Premises, then your local IT administrators may have locked down the apps that you can add for security reasons. If you read about an app but don't see it in your store, you can contact your administrator to get it added.

The SharePoint Store can be found on the page where you add an app, as shown in Figure 12-10. You access the Your Apps page by clicking the Settings gear icon and then selecting Add an App. Take a look and see what SharePoint apps you have available in the store.

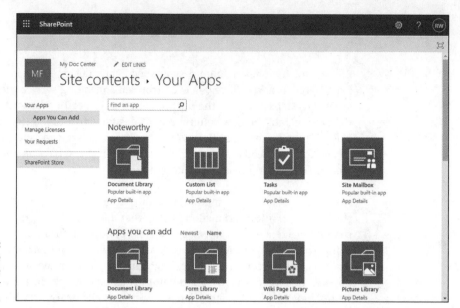

FIGURE 12-10:
Accessing the SharePoint Store from the Your Apps page.

You can choose to view all apps or only those that are free by selecting the Price refiner on the left side of the page. You can also sort apps by clicking a category link. If you want to purchase an app, click it and then click the Buy It button. After you click the Buy It button, you have to log in with your Microsoft account. If you already have a credit card on file with your Microsoft 365 subscription, then you can purchase and download the app. Otherwise, you are prompted to enter your credit card information.

Chapter **13**

Taking Control of Your Profile and Content

Throughout this book, you can read about SharePoint sites and how they can be used with teams and organizations. SharePoint also provides individualized benefits designed specifically for you. In particular, you can customize your own individual space and take control of your SharePoint experience.

In this chapter, you explore how your personal SharePoint space works. You find out about some pretty cool apps and explore how to work with these apps using only your web browser. You discover how to aggregate news and create a personal site, sync and organize documents with OneDrive for Business, and add and follow specific sites. You also explore and set up your personal profile.

Organizing Your Personal Content with OneDrive

Your personal cloud storage location, also known as *OneDrive*, is where you store and organize your documents. You access OneDrive by clicking on the waffle icon (officially called the app launcher) in the upper-left corner of your screen and then choosing OneDrive, as shown in Figure 13-1.

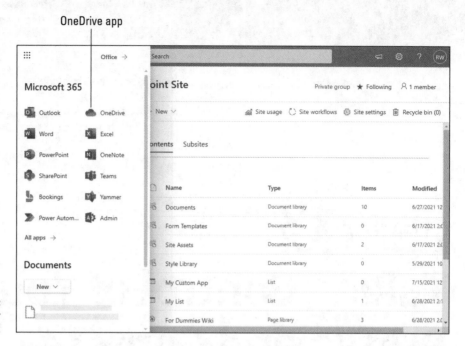

OneDrive app

FIGURE 13-1:
Accessing your
OneDrive site.

When you land on your OneDrive site, the heading, OneDrive, appears at the top of your browser, and your personal site loads, as shown in Figure 13-2. Congratulations, you are now working in your own personal SharePoint storage location! This is your own personal domain, and everything here is private unless you choose to share it with others.

FIGURE 13-2:
The personal
SharePoint
storage location
called OneDrive.

TIP

There are some slight differences between OneDrive in SharePoint Online and OneDrive in SharePoint On-Premises. One example is the action bar (New, Upload, Sync, Automate, More). It is found below the search bar at the top in the Online version, but in the On-Premises version, it is found below the Documents heading.

OneDrive includes a number of features right out of the gate that you access in the left-hand navigation tools. You have an app called My Files in which you can store documents. You can also use the left navigation to view recent files and see the files you have shared with others. You also have a Recycle Bin for anything you deleted that you want to recover.

Saving stuff with OneDrive

Your personal storage location, known as OneDrive, is designed as a place to store, organize, and share your documents, such as a carpool list you're working on or a potluck spreadsheet. You might also be working on business documents that don't really fit into any specific app in SharePoint. Your OneDrive is the catch-all place you can store it.

Think of your OneDrive as your personal Documents folder on your computer. The difference is that the personal Documents folder on your computer is only on that single computer. If you're using a different computer, you can't access those documents. In addition, if your computer crashes and you have not backed up your Documents folder, then those files are lost. OneDrive is designed to be a secure and safe place to store all your documents. What if your device crashes or is stolen? With your documents stored in OneDrive, you just log in again from a different device and continue working on your documents.

WARNING

Your OneDrive files are only secure and backed up if your IT team sets up the infrastructure that way. If you're using SharePoint Online, then you can be assured that Microsoft is doing this for you. If your local IT team is running SharePoint for you, then check with them to make sure they backup and secure your OneDrive documents.

Your OneDrive is designed to live in the cloud and to be accessible by any device you happen to be working on. For example, if you start a document at work and then have to stop working on it when you leave to pick up your kids, you can log in and continue working on the document when you get home. And if you later have to take your mother-in-law to the doctor, and you take your tablet with you, you can log in from your tablet while you're waiting in the doctor's office. Finally, if you drop off your mother-in-law and make a quick stop at the grocery store, and you get an email on your smartphone asking about a detail in the document you have been working on, you can connect to your OneDrive on your smartphone and view the document so you can respond to the inquiry. Being this connected isn't always the best way to spend your off-time, but OneDrive enables you to decide when and where you want to work. The idea behind OneDrive is that when you need your documents, you can access them as long as you can connect to the Internet.

TIP

OneDrive has been a source of confusion in the past because there was a separate OneDrive for Business and a OneDrive for personal use. Microsoft has been making changes to try to reduce this confusion. Now, when you sign up for a Microsoft 365 subscription, you can choose either a home-based subscription or a business-based subscription. And OneDrive is included with all available subscriptions. There is even a free Microsoft 365 subscription called Basic, which includes 5GB of OneDrive storage. OneDrive is similar to other cloud storage services such as Dropbox and Google Drive.

Creating or uploading documents in your OneDrive

When you first land on your OneDrive page, you are presented with a notice letting you know some tips about OneDrive such as accessing recent documents. You can add documents to OneDrive by following these steps:

1. **Navigate to your OneDrive page by clicking the waffle icon in the top-left corner of your screen and choosing OneDrive rom the menu (refer to Figure 13-1).**

TIP

   If you are using SharePoint Online, you won't have any trouble finding OneDrive because Microsoft has already set it up for you. If you are using SharePoint On-Premises, you will only find the waffle icon and the OneDrive app in the waffle icon if your administrator has set it up for you. If you don't see the waffle icon, or if you don't see the OneDrive app in the waffle icon, then contact your administrator to get things set up.

2. **Click the New link at the top of the page and select the type of document you want to create, as shown in Figure 13-3.**

   If you are using SharePoint Online, you already have the Office document types (Word, Excel, PowerPoint, and OneNote) integrated with your OneDrive site because Microsoft has already set it up for you. If you are using SharePoint On-Premises, you will only see these document types if they have been set up. If the integration has not been set up, you will see a dialog box that lets you choose to upload an existing file already.

3. **The blank document opens, ready for you to add content.**

New link   Sort options

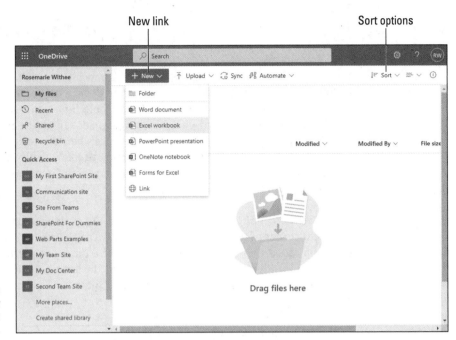

FIGURE 13-3:
Creating a new
document in
OneDrive.

4. **On the other hand, if you want to upload an existing document, click the Upload button and then choose Files or Folder instead of the New button (Step 2), browse to the document you want to add to OneDrive, and click OK to add the file.**

You can choose to overwrite the document if a document with the same name already exists. If versioning is turned on, a new version of the document will be created and the existing document will become the previous version. If versioning is turned off, then overwriting will result in the loss of the existing document with the same name.

TIP

The OneDrive site contains a number of ways to sort your documents. You can sort the documents by type, name, modified date, modified by user, and file size. You can also choose to do the sorting in ascending or descending order. In addition, you can view the documents as a list, a compact list, or as tiles. You find these options in the top-right corner of the screen (refer to Figure 13-3).

Expressing Yourself with Your Profile

People are central to any business, no matter how big or small. Without people, a business wouldn't run. How people interact with each other creates the culture of a business, and part of that culture is how people figure out who does what job, who knows who, who knows what, and how someone might be able to help you do your job better. That culture, to some extent, can be reflected in SharePoint user profiles, and the better the user profile, the more likely you're going to get your job done more effectively. And, the more likely others are going to be able to find you easily when they need to.

You access and configure your personal profile by clicking your name icon in the top-right corner of the screen and selecting My Office Profile. The page that loads is an app called Delve, which is where you *delve* into your personal information. You access your information by selecting Me in the left navigation pane. This page also opens by default when you navigate into Delve using the My Office Profile link.

In the Delve app you can also keep track of your recent documents and email attachments. Delve also shows you what other people in your organization are working on as long as you have access to view those documents. We like this feature because content in most organizations quickly becomes a flood of information; we use Delve to see the most recent things people have worked on.

Creating a holistic profile experience

Depending on the size of your organization, it can be really beneficial to set up your profile so that others can learn about you and get to know you.

Your email, name, phone number, and contact information is automatically pulled in when you set up your Microsoft 365 user account. You are able to make updates by selecting the Update Profile button (see Figure 13-4), which takes you to a page where you can upload your picture and enter information about yourself, such as things people should ask you about, your past projects, skills, schools you attended, your birthday, and your interests.

TIP

The other option that appears from your profile icon drop-down menu is View Account. This option takes you to your Microsoft 365 account page where you can configure things like security, view devices that have logged in with your account, and change your password.

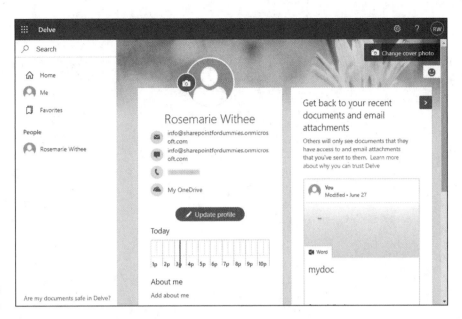

FIGURE 13-4:
Your Profile page.

Filling in your profile information

It seems like practically everyone in the world is familiar with social networking sites such as Facebook, Twitter, and LinkedIn, and Microsoft has taken some cues to extend that social networking functionality into SharePoint. It all starts with sharing some information about yourself so that other people in your organization can find you and read a little about you. That's where the basic profile information comes into play.

Along with the really basic information that comes preset with your profile, you also see "about me" information, your profile picture, and recent content, as shown earlier in Figure 13-4. These items are shared with everyone, unlike some of the extra information we cover next.

To edit your profile, click the Update Profile button and fill in the profile information, as shown in Figure 13-5.

REMEMBER

The information you share in the profile fields should be what you want people to know about you as it relates to what you do at your company. There's really no need to share your love of pet rats (unless your business caters to owners of pet rats). Rather, share a little bit about where you came from, what you like to work on, and when you started at the company — keep it simple and useful for others.

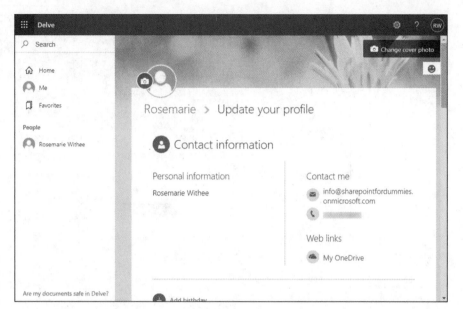

FIGURE 13-5:
Updating your profile information.

Put in what you're really good at, work-wise, and things that people might want to know more about you if they knew you had the same interests or a particular knowledge of something they need to know more about. But again, keep it business-related, because this information is shared with everyone.

For your picture, we recommend one of you in business attire rather than the one of you sunburned and on the beach. Remember, the picture you share here shows up in SharePoint, attached to documents you've created, or when you show up in search results. A picture is really helpful, for example, if you work in a large organization, and even a small- to medium-sized organization where people don't work in the same location. Maybe all the employees of your company are so distributed that they don't all get together but once every year or two, so being able to place a face with a name can help bridge that gap of unfamiliarity. (We've been in many situations where the voice doesn't go at all with the eventual face when we met them in person — a profile picture helps to alleviate some of that awkwardness.)

TIP

For administrators and managers, remember that if one person in the organization updates her profile, it's a start, but it's really not that useful. If everyone does, it becomes a great place to get to know who you work with, what motivates people, and what they're good at. Your challenge is to come up with a contest or some type of incentive program for getting employees to fill out their profiles. Filling in the rest of your profile is up to you.

Tracking Your Favorite Sites

The number of sites being used throughout your organization can be overwhelming. You might be a user on sites for sales, human resources, various departments, carpools, child care, product development, and so on. As SharePoint gains momentum in your organization, the number of sites you might participate in will grow quickly. The Delve app is designed to help you solve this site overload issue. You access the Delve app by clicking Delve in the waffle icon. (If you don't see it right away, then click the All Apps and scroll to find it.) The Delve app loads and a navigation reminder appears at the top of the page that says Delve. You can also access the Delve app by clicking the Favorites link on your Profile page.

TIP

As with many things in SharePoint, there are multiple ways to achieve the same outcome. Delve is what powers the Favorites functionality you will find within your Profile page. You can access the favorites functionality through Delve directly or by going through your Profile page. Whatever is easiest to remember. Just don't get in an argument with someone on how to do something in SharePoint since you both might be right!

The Favorites page is shown in Figure 13-6.

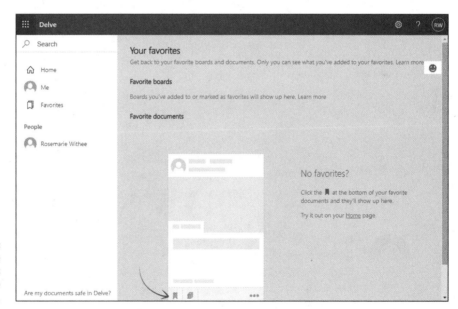

FIGURE 13-6:
The landing page
for the Favorites
page of the
Delve app.

To help you keep track of your sites, the Delve app aggregates all the sites you follow. In addition to keeping track of your sites, the Delve app allows you to create new sites and even suggests sites you might be interested in following based on the sites you currently follow. In other words, the Delve app is a one-stop sites shop and a sites dashboard.

TIP

To follow a site or document, click the bookmark icon at the bottom of the site or page. It looks like a bookmark flag. You can see an example at the bottom of Figure 13-6.

Chapter **14**

Organizing and Viewing Content

You may remember Bill Gates proclaiming that "content is king" back in the mid-1990s. Nearly three decades since, it still couldn't be more true. The rate at which modern organizations are generating digital content is staggering. One of SharePoint's sweet spots is managing content, which is why many organizations adopt the platform in the first place.

In Chapter 7 you learn how to get documents into SharePoint. In this chapter, you delve into organizing and viewing those documents. You discover how to customize SharePoint apps based on libraries (library apps are covered initially in Chapter 7 and are covered in more detail in Chapter 11) and how these apps are used to manage documents. Finally, you learn how to create views into your content so that your content is easily accessible, filterable, and readily available for you and others to consume.

Working with Documents

After you upload your documents to an app (which we do in Chapter 7), you need to be able to work with them. This includes adding descriptive properties and letting other teammates know where the documents are stored.

SharePoint provides different methods for working with documents. If you are using the classic experience, you have actions on the ribbon and actions on the ellipsis menu. If you are using the new experience, you use the ellipsis menu.

REMEMBER

We cover the classic and new experience for apps in Chapter 11. As a reminder, you can change between the two experiences for a list or library app in the Advanced settings of the app. To find it, navigate to the app. Then select List Settings or Library settings (as appropriate) from the gear icon drop-down menu that appears in the top-right corner of the page. On the app settings page, select Advanced settings. You find the selector between new and classic experience at the bottom of the list of advanced settings available. Make sure to refresh the page to view the new experience.

In the classic experience, each document has a set of actions contained in the ribbon that can be targeted to the document. The ribbon actions appear when you select the radio button next to the document, as shown in Figure 14-1. In addition, you can click the ellipsis next to the document (see Figure 14-2) to see a menu of actions for the document. For example, you can check out a document, edit it, and check it back in. In the new experience, Microsoft has moved away from the ribbon in an attempt to simplify the experience. In the new experience, you only use the ellipsis next to a document as shown in Figure 14-2. Note that you can also use the ellipsis in the classic experience, too.

Using the ellipsis

Accessing the menu for a specific document is accomplished by clicking the ellipsis next to the document, as shown in Figure 14-2.

With the ellipsis menu, you have quick access to common things you might want to do with the document. You can open the document with either your Office programs installed on your computer or using an online version using your browser. You can preview, share, or copy a link to the document so that you can share it with others. You can manage who has access to the document. You can also download a copy of the document, delete it, create a workflow using Flow (covered in Chapter 15), and many other things.

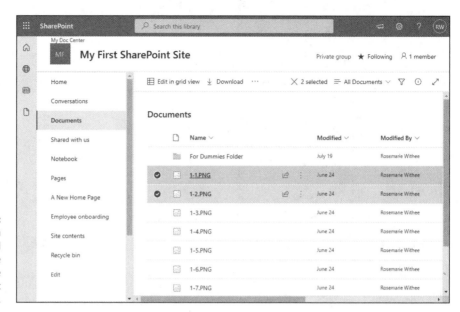

FIGURE 14-1:
Selecting a document and viewing the ribbon in the classic experience.

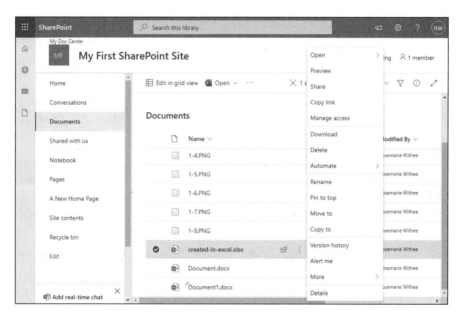

FIGURE 14-2:
Using the ellipsis context menu for a specific document.

To see the details for this particular document, click the Details button at the bottom of the list. The details pane opens on the right side of the screen, as shown in Figure 14-3.

The details pane shows key information about the document such as who has access to it, the document properties, the activity on the document, and even a small preview.

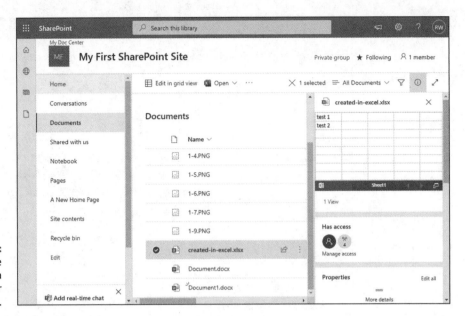

FIGURE 14-3:
Viewing the
details of a
particular
document.

Using the More menu item, you can view and edit properties, interact with work-flows for the document, view compliance details, and check out the document.

Some options in the ellipsis menu depend on how your app has been configured. For example, if versioning is enabled for the app, you see a Version History option in the menu. If versioning is not enabled, then you won't see the Version History option. All items and documents in apps follow this same paradigm. The actual options depend on the type of app you're using and how you configured it.

TIP

Your organization can add custom menu items to the menus, so don't be surprised if your menus look different than the one shown earlier in Figure 14-2. The point is that you can use the ellipsis menu to access a list of actions that you can take on the selected document.

Editing a document's properties

You can edit a document's properties in a number of ways. By default, SharePoint asks only for these two properties:

>> **Name:** This is the filename. For example, if you upload the file, myspread-sheet.xlsx, that's the value you see as the filename.

>> **Title:** A caption that describes the document. If a title already exists in the document, SharePoint uses that. Otherwise, you can enter your own descriptive title.

The app owner can add more properties to describe the document. For example, the owner might add a Category property that allows you to apply a category to the document. Properties are actually just new columns that you add to your app.

The easiest way to view a document's properties is to use the ellipsis menu:

1. **Click the ellipsis next to a document.**

2. **Click the More item from the menu and then click Properties.**

The document's properties are displayed.

Figure 14-4 shows the properties page for a document. In the classic experience, this window includes its own View tab on the ribbon. The View tab includes buttons for managing the document and actions for working with the document. In the new experience, the properties page is simplified and the ribbon is gone (as we discuss earlier). Instead you have a drop-down menu at the top of the page with options for editing columns, configuring the layout, and customizing the app with Power Apps (which we cover in Chapter 17).

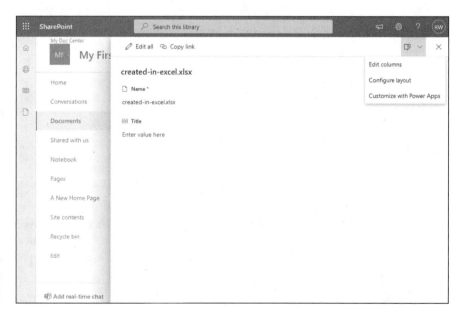

FIGURE 14-4:
The properties page for a document.

TIP

The properties of a document also go by a couple of other names. You will often hear the term "metadata" to refer to properties. Metadata just means data about data. The document itself contains data in the text in a Word document or the values in the cells of an Excel document. The properties are separate from what is inside of the actual document; thus, the properties are metadata. In SharePoint, you see the properties as columns in a list, so you may also hear people refer to properties as columns.

Viewing documents in the browser

Microsoft 365 also includes web-based versions of Office that you can use to view and edit documents in the browser. The experience happens automatically, so you just have to click the filename in the app to open the file. Figure 14-5 shows a Word document displayed using an online version of Word in the web browser.

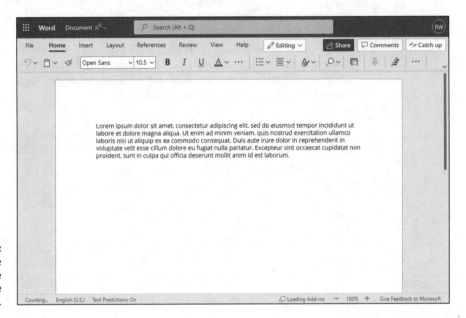

FIGURE 14-5:
Office Online
displays Office
files in the
browser.

Using your web browser to create and edit Office documents is especially useful when you don't want to install the Office clients on your local computer. It also makes quickly browsing document contents a breeze because the file opens right in the browser.

TIP

You can also work with documents right in Microsoft Teams. In fact, we wrote much of this book without ever leaving the Teams client! To learn more about Teams, check out *Microsoft Teams For Dummies* by Rosemarie Withee (Wiley, 2021).

TIP

Office Online is also available in the consumer version of OneDrive as well as Dropbox. Using OneDrive or Dropbox, you can open your Office documents right in the browser. And each has a free version available!

Sharing Your Documents

You're probably familiar with *network file shares:* the file systems that enable people to upload files to a shared network drive so that other people can access and use them. File shares, when they were invented, revolutionized the ability of organizations to keep files in relatively secure locations and manage who had access. But SharePoint has done the file sharing one (okay, a whole bunch) better.

SharePoint apps based on libraries let you store and share files securely, and they also add features that help you manage things such as *document workflow* (the processes that let people edit, comment on, and approve documents) and *version histories* (what happened to a file, and who did what). And although file shares give you one path through folders to your document, SharePoint Library apps give you other paths to expose content. You can access documents directly through the browser, you can display them in Web Parts, and you can sort and filter them by their metadata and content types. And with Library apps, you can expose files by their title, not just their filename.

To share your document with others, they must know where to find the document. One way to do so is to send them the web address of the SharePoint site. You can also send them a link directly to the document itself.

To obtain the URL to a document in SharePoint, follow these steps:

1. **Click the ellipsis next to the document to view the pop-up menu.**

   The document options are displayed.

2. **Click the Share option and provide the person's email address or name. (You can also copy the URL link to the document in this dialog box, too.)**

   Alternatively, click the Copy Link option to copy a direct link to the document into your clipboard. You can then paste it into an email or chat so the person receives it. As long as your team members have network access and permissions to the document, they can click the link and open the file.

Recovering Deleted Documents

It is often said that SharePoint delivers on the promise of making people more productive through software. Although that's not always true, one feature of SharePoint that truly delivers is the Recycle Bin. When you delete a document from an app, it isn't gone forever. Nope. The document just moves to a holding place in your site — the Recycle Bin.

Go ahead and try it. Go to an app and delete a document. You can use the ellipsis menu to access the Delete command. You can also select the document and then use the Delete button in the ribbon. Either way, you're prompted to confirm the deletion, and then your document appears in the Recycle Bin.

TIP

The Recycle Bin works for items in apps that use the Custom List app template as well.

Follow these steps to restore a document from the Recycle Bin to its original location:

1. **Go to the Recycle Bin by clicking the Settings gear icon and choosing Site Contents.**

   The Site Contents page is displayed.

2. **Click the Recycle Bin button in the upper-right corner to display the Recycle Bin.**

3. **Select the deleted document, and then click the Restore link, as shown in Figure 14-6.**

   The file is restored to the app.

Restore link

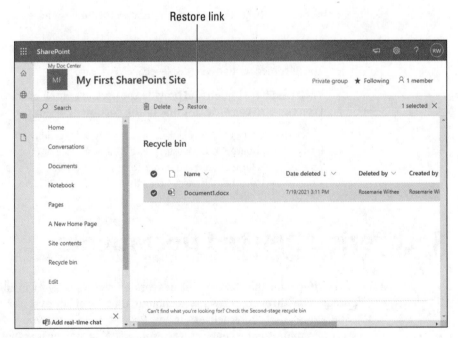

FIGURE 14-6:
Restoring a document from the Recycle Bin.

You can click the Delete link in the Recycle Bin to remove the file from your Recycle Bin. Doing so, however, doesn't permanently delete the file. Instead, the file is moved to *another* Recycle Bin that can be accessed by the site collection administrator.

If you are a site collection administrator, you will see a link at the bottom of the Recycle Bin called Second-Stage Recycle Bin. If you click that you will see the Recycle Bin for all the SharePoint sites in the collection. This is a feature of SharePoint that gives additional power to site collection administrators. So if a regular user accidentally deletes something and then goes into the Recycle Bin and accidentally deletes it from the Recycle Bin, a site collection administrator can still get the content back.

Files remain in the Second-Stage Recycle Bin for a period of 30 days or until they're deleted by the administrator, whichever comes first. When removed from the Recycle Bin, the fate of your documents depends on your company's business continuity management plan. That's a fancy way to say, how does your IT team back up data? SharePoint stores your documents in databases. An administrator can connect to a backed-up copy of the database and select individual documents to restore.

Uploading Documents into a Folder

You can use folders within your apps as a means to organize your documents. We show you how to create a folder and upload files into it, but we urge you to first read the sidebar, "Why folders in SharePoint are evil."

Perhaps you have an app and you have a subset of files that only supervisors should see. You could put those files in a separate app and set the permissions on it. But say you already have one app set up the way you like and it seems silly to create another one. Instead, you can use a folder to separate the restricted files from the rest of the files in the app.

To create a folder within an app:

1. **Browse to the app where you want to create the folder.**

2. **Click the New button in the ribbon and click the Folder option.**

The Create a folder dialog box appears. If you don't see the Folder button, folders are disabled for the library. Use the Advanced Settings option in Library Settings to enable or disable folders in your app. In the classic experience the option is called New Folder and in the new experience (outlined above) it is called Folder. As we mentioned previously, Microsoft often changes the user interface and names of things in SharePoint however the functionality is often the same. This is a great example. You want to create a folder and the exact buttons and label names might be different but the functionality (creating a folder) is the same.

3. **Type the name of the folder in the Name text box and click the Create button.**

   The folder appears in the app.

To upload files into the folder, follow these steps:

1. **Click the folder name to navigate inside it and click the Upload button at the top of the app.**

   TIP

   The File Upload window appears. You can also just drag files from your computer into your browser when your browser has the folder open. Note that in the classic experience, you will see an Add a Document dialog box that has an OK button. In the new experience, outlined above, the naming is slightly different.

2. **Choose Files, Folder, or Template and then browse to the what you want to upload to the folder.**

WHY FOLDERS IN SHAREPOINT ARE EVIL

Resist the urge to use folders in your apps; this file-share paradigm generally causes nothing but problems. One reason to use SharePoint instead of a file share to begin with is so that you can add properties to describe your documents. Properties allow you to view your documents in different ways. If you dump your files into folders just like they were arranged on the file share, ignoring properties, you probably won't be very satisfied with your SharePoint experience.

As well, nested folders in SharePoint are just as hard to navigate as nested folders in file shares (and nested URLs in folders inside apps get unwieldy quickly). Instead of replicating your file structure in SharePoint, we recommend you flatten the folder hierarchies by replacing them with *views*. If you decide to use folders and find yourself going more than two layers deep, stop and ask yourself if you should create another app instead.

The only reason to use a folder in an app is to separate a group of documents to give them separate permissions. For pretty much everything else, we recommend you use properties to organize your documents.

3. **Make sure the Destination Folder text box lists the folder where you want to upload the document.**

   If the folder is incorrect, click the Choose Folder button to select the right folder.

4. **Click OK to upload your document to the folder.**

You can work with folders the same way as you work with documents. That is, the rules about working with properties and the ribbon also apply to folders.

Follow these steps to restrict access to your folder so that only certain groups can access it:

1. **Click the ellipsis next to the folder and choose Share from the pop-up menu, as shown in Figure 14-7.**

   The Send link dialog appears. Note that the ability to share folders must be enabled. If it is not enabled, then you must manually disable the limited access lockdown mode feature for the site.

Choose Share from the pop-up menu

::: SharePoint	🔍 Search this library	⤴ ⚙ ? (RW)

My Doc Center

MF **My First SharePoint Site**   Private group ★ Following 👤 1 member

Home	🔲 Edit in grid view ⤴ Share ⋯	✕ 1 s	Share	⌄ 🔽 ⓘ ⤢
Conversations			Copy link	
Documents	Documents		Manage access	
Shared with us			Download	Modified By ⌄
Notebook	☑ 📁 For Dummies Folder ⤴ 🗐 ⋮		Add shortcut to OneDrive	osemarie Withee
Pages	🖼 1-1.PNG		Delete	osemarie Withee
A New Home Page	🖼 1-2.PNG		Automate ❯	osemarie Withee
Site contents	🖼 1-3.PNG		Rename	osemarie Withee
Recycle bin	🖼 1-4.PNG		Pin to top	osemarie Withee
Edit	🖼 1-5.PNG		Move to	osemarie Withee
	🖼 1-6.PNG		Copy to	osemarie Withee
	🖼 1-7.PNG		Alert me	osemarie Withee
✕ 📱 Add real-time chat			More ❯	
			Details	

FIGURE 14-7:
Sharing a folder in an app.

2. **Enter the names of the people you want to share the folder with in the text box.**

3. **Click the Permission Level drop-down list (it looks like a pencil) to set whether they can only view or can also edit the documents.**

4. **Click the Send button to share the folder.**

We discuss permissions management in detail in Chapter 21.

SharePoint apps are discussed in Chapter 11. When these apps are based on the Library template, you can refer to them as Library apps. In addition to uploading documents direct, as you saw earlier in this chapter, Library apps give you multiple choices about how the documents get into them, too. You can save a document to a Library app using a Microsoft Office client such as Word or Excel, or you can email documents to Library apps or drag and drop from Windows Explorer. And you can create documents directly in the app. You can even use other Microsoft 365 apps such as Teams to get files into SharePoint as is discussed in Chapter 8.

TIP

Every Teams channel has a SharePoint site behind it, which also includes a Library app. If you see someone storing files in Teams (the tab at the top that says Files) then they are actually using SharePoint. They might not even know that is the case, but you will!

No matter how you get your documents into SharePoint's Library apps, just get them there — it's so much easier to share documents with your coworkers in an app than it is to use file shares or email attachments.

REMEMBER

SharePoint apps can be confusing. An app based on a list is designed to store data in columns. An app based on a library is designed to store documents and data about those documents in columns. SharePoint tries to simplify the whole discussion of list and library and just calls everything an *app*. When you create the app, you give it a name and choose an app template. From that point on, you just call your app by its name. For example, you might create the Sales Pitch app. The app is designed to hold sales pitch documents. Because the app holds documents, it uses the Document Library app template. After your app is created, you wouldn't call it the "Sales Pitch app based on the Document Library App template." That would be a mouthful! If you're a seasoned SharePoint user, this new app stuff might take you a while to get your head around. It did us! But when you realize that most users don't think in terms of lists and libraries, and instead think about what a list or library does, it really is much easier to just call everything an app.

TECHNICAL
STUFF

An app can also be built from scratch by a web developer as a standalone app, so such an app isn't based on a list or a library.

Discovering SharePoint Views

A number of apps ship with SharePoint, and you can also create custom apps (as we discuss in Chapter 11). SharePoint also lets you create additional pages, or *views*, that you can use to customize the display of the information in apps. In Excel, you might hide rows and/or columns to create a new view of the data. In a database, you may query only certain fields and use criteria to create a specific snapshot of data. The concept is similar with views.

Common reasons for creating new views include showing only active items, only tasks associated with a certain person, only documents in a certain category, and so on. These views help users find or focus on certain data in the app without having to see everything, all the time.

Next, you discover how to manually create new views and how to modify existing views.

Switching the view

Each SharePoint app comes with at least one view, the All Items (or Documents) view, which is a public view available to app users. Document Library apps start with the All Documents view. Certain apps come with several more predefined views, such as the Discussion Board app, which has special views for showing threaded discussions.

You use the View drop-down menu to access the options for changing an app's views. Figure 14-8 shows the drop-down menu for working with views. You can see the commands available for changing the current views or creating new views.

You can easily switch among views in an app. The current view is displayed as selected in the drop-down menu, and additional views are available to select as well. You can see that for documents you can switch to a compact list or tiles. The tiles view is shown in Figure 14-9.

TIP

We prefer the full List view since it provides the most information and functionality but others may prefer the tiles or compact list view to keep things simple and clean.

Anyone with Design and Full Control permissions (Designers and Owners) can make Public and Personal views for the app. However, site members (contributors) can create only Personal views for their own use.

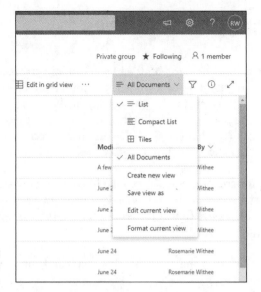

FIGURE 14-8:
Working with
views.

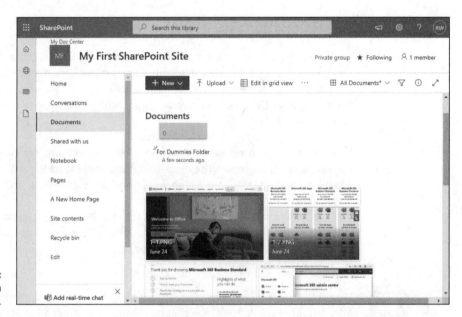

FIGURE 14-9:
Switching to a
tile-based view.

TIP

Use a view instead of folders. When you organize files on your network, folders are the predominant method of subdividing your content. In SharePoint, you gain great power in using columns in combination with views to hide or show what users need to see. Folders take extra effort for the user to drill down and then navigate back up to look for other content. Views coupled with built-in sorting and filtering header options enable the user to easily and quickly find different content by toggling back and forth between views.

Getting to know view formats

If you are working with the new experience, you can quickly create a view starting as a List, a Calendar, or a Gallery. The List is the standard basic list view. The items appear as a list. The Calendar displays a calendar and is similar to the calendar view type in the classic view. The Gallery view shows the items as tiles, as shown earlier in Figure 14-9. You will find this quick create functionality on the same drop-down menu where you change the view. Later in the chapter we show you how to create a new view from the settings page of the app that provides you the same options as the classic experience.

If you are working with the classic experience, SharePoint provides four predefined formats for creating new views. These formats jump-start your view creation experience by determining how information appears on the web page:

» **Standard:** This is the default view when you first access an app. The document or title item is in hyperlink format with an Edit menu for accessing properties and other options. The rest of the list resembles a table without borders.

» **Datasheet:** This is an editable spreadsheet format. Although any app has the option to edit information in a datasheet format using the Quick Edit button on the List or Library tab, certain views may make sense to be created in this format if users will edit multiple items at a time.

» **Calendar:** As you would expect, this view displays as a calendar. You need at least one date field in your app to create a Calendar view.

» **Gantt:** If you are familiar with project management charts, you recognize the Gantt view as showing tasks along a timeline. This view makes it possible to do simple project-management tracking using a SharePoint app.

In the rest of the chapter, we walk you through creating a view using each of these view formats.

Creating a Standard View

The most common kind of view you create in a SharePoint app is a public, Standard view (called List view in the new experience). A public view can be used by anyone to view the contents of an app.

Standard views have the following traits:

>> They're accessible by all browsers, including Firefox, Chrome, and Safari.

>> They have the most configuration options, such as filtering, grouping, and editing options.

>> They're available for all apps.

>> They don't require any special columns for configuring the view. Other view formats, such as a Calendar view, require date columns.

To create a new Standard view:

1. **Browse to the app where you want to create the new view.**

2. **Click the gear icon in the top-right corner of the page and click List Settings or Library Settings to open the settings page.**

   If you are using the classic experience, you find the List Settings or Library Settings on the List or Library tab in the ribbon.

3. **Scroll down to the Views section and click the Create View button.**

   A list of view format options appears.

4. **Click the Standard View link to create a view that looks like a web page.**

   After you select your view format, the Create View page displays your options for creating the new view.

5. **In the View Name field, type the name you want to call this view.**

   The View Name field has two purposes:

   • It provides the friendly name that can be selected to display the view.

   • It provides the filename for the web page, which is part of the web address.

   We suggest giving the page a name that's easy to remember. For example, if your view will group products by department, entering the name, GroupByDepartment creates a web page named GroupByDepartment.aspx. You can change the friendly name after the filename has been created.

6. **To set this view as the default view for the app, select the Make This the Default View check box.**

   If this isn't the default view, users can select the view from a drop-down list on the ribbon.

7. **In the View Audience field, select the Create a Public View radio button.**

Optionally, you can create a personal view that only you can see. You must have at least Designer or Owner permissions to create a public view.

8. **In the Columns section of the page, select the Display check box next to each column you want to display, as shown in Figure 14-10.**

You can also indicate the relative order that columns appear on the screen by selecting the appropriate number in the Position from Left drop-down lists. See more on choosing columns in the "Choosing columns for your view" section, later in this chapter.

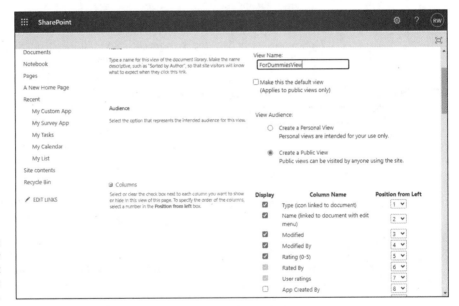

FIGURE 14-10:
Create a new view and select the columns you want to show.

9. **(Optional) In the Sort section, use the drop-down lists to select the first column you want to sort by and then select the second column to sort by.**

The default sort option is ID, which means that items will be sorted by the order they were entered in the list.

10. **Select the remaining options to configure your view, such as the columns you want to filter or group on.**

For example, you can

- Select Tabular View to include check boxes next to items for bulk operations.

- Select the style that the view will take. For example, Boxed, Shaded, Newsletter, Preview Pane, or Basic style.

- Select which columns to aggregate using Count, Average, Minimum, and Maximum functions in the Totals section.

- Specify whether items should appear inside folders or flat as if the folders don't exist in the Folders section.

- Limit the items displayed on a single page with the Item Limit option. This can improve the performance of the view.

We discuss additional options in more detail in the "Filtering apps with views" and "Grouping results" sections, later in this chapter.

11. **Click OK to create the view.**

The new view appears in the browser.

If you created a public view, SharePoint creates a new web page using the name you specified in Step 5. Users can select this view from the drop-down list in the Manage Views section of the ribbon.

Experimenting with all these options is the best way to discover what works for your site. Item Limits, for example, is great for when you want to control the amount of space a Web Part takes up on a page.

Choosing columns for your view

When you choose the columns to display in your view, you see many columns that are usually behind the scenes, including Edit menu options. For a List-based app, these options include

>> **Edit (Linked to Edit Item):** Displays an icon that a user can click to edit the item. This column is useful when you don't want to display the Title column.

>> **Title (Linked to Item):** Displays the Title column with a hyperlink to the list item or document. When a user clicks the hyperlinked title, a web page opens and displays the app item or opens the document.

>> **Title (Linked to Edit with Edit Menu):** When users hover their mouse over this column, the Edit menu appears.

We may want Edit menu columns on our app page for a member to modify items, but we generally don't want them in our app Web Parts on home pages and publishing pages (in that case, we just want users to click a link to open a document or only view the app data as a table).

Other columns you may have available to add to your view include

>> **ID:** Displays the identity number of the item. The ID number is used to display the item's values in a form.

>> **Version:** Displays the version number of the item or document. This allows you to easily see what the latest version of a document is.

>> **Checked Out:** Shows who has the document checked out. Document Library based apps will have this column by default.

>> **Folder Child Count:** Displays the number of folders contained within a folder.

>> **Item Child Count:** Displays the number of items contained within a folder.

>> **Content Type:** Displays the content type associated with the item or document.

When you create a view, you often realize that you want to display a column that's based on a value calculated from another column. For example, if your app displays an anniversary date, you may want to calculate years of service. You can do that by creating a new column and then displaying it in your view.

Filtering apps with views

You can use the filtering options of views to limit the items displayed. You can choose which columns to filter on and how to apply the filter. You can use filters to display app data where a certain column is equal to some value or not equal to some value, or where an item was created between certain date ranges.

You can create filters using columns that are based on String, Number, Currency, or Choice data types. However, you can't filter on lookup columns or multiline text fields.

Building a filter is like writing an equation; for example, $x > y$. In this case, x is the column you want to filter on, and y is the value you want to test the column contents against. The operator in between determines what the test evaluates. This test gives the system a TRUE or FALSE response to your equation.

Available operators are

>> **Equality:** Is Equal To or Is Not Equal To

>> **Comparison:** Is Greater Than or Is Less Than

>> **Substring:** Contains or Begins With

The filtering equation is evaluated for each item in your app. If the equation is TRUE, the item is included in the view; if the equation is FALSE, the item is excluded.

TIP

If you don't see the results you expect to see in your view, your filter is probably evaluating to FALSE.

For numerical values, you usually use the Equality or Comparison operators. When you create filtered views based on string (text) values, you want to be familiar with your data before trying to create the filter. For example, if you want to filter a Contacts app to display only those contacts in the U.K., you have to ask how the value for the U.K. has been entered in the app. Is it U.K., United Kingdom, or both? You can use a Datasheet view to quickly scan the data to determine the range of possible values.

TIP

One way to get around this problem is by validating your data when it's being entered. You can use Choice columns to do that or use SharePoint's validation features.

Say you discover that your data include both values — U.K. and United Kingdom. You could go through and make all the data consistent. Or you could filter for both values using the Or option, as shown in Figure 14-11.

You can also use the constants Today and Me to filter your columns.

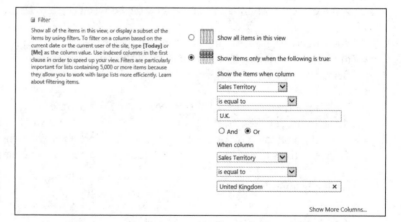

FIGURE 14-11:
Select the column to filter the view.

Grouping results

You can configure your view to group together items based on a common value in a column. For example, you can group a listing of contacts that all share the same department or company.

Figure 14-12 shows the grouping options. You can indicate whether to automatically collapse or expand grouped items and how many items to display per page. When you group based on a column you can then see all items with the same column value and use the toggle arrows to the left of each group header to expand or contract the grouped items.

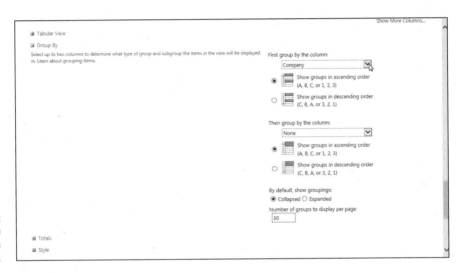

FIGURE 14-12:
You can group
items based on a
shared value.

Don't forget the Totals option! Often when grouping data, you want to create totals. For example, grouping on Inventory by Category and totaling the Quantity creates subtotals for the Category grouping as well as an overall total for the app.

Quickly edit app data with Edit In Grid View (a.k.a. Quick Edit)

In SharePoint, inline editing functionality is baked right in to every app in the form of Edit In Grid View. In the classic experience, this same functionality is called Quick Edit. Edit In Grid View is available on every app based on a list or library and appears at the top of the app, as shown in Figure 14-13, or as a button on the List or Library tab of the ribbon called Quick Edit.

When you select the Edit In Grid View option, you're presented with the data in the app in an easily editable form. You can make changes right on the pages and with multiple items. An app displaying data in grid view is shown in Figure 14-14.

Edit in Grid View option

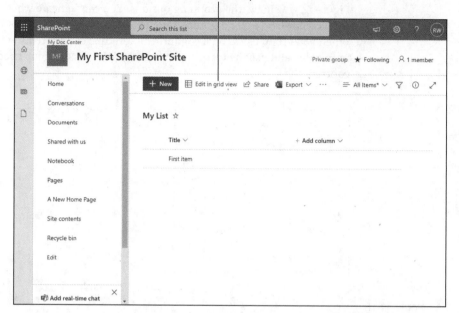

FIGURE 14-13:
The Edit In Grid
View option at
the top of an app.

FIGURE 14-14:
Using Edit In Grid
View in an app.

Choosing a display style

SharePoint provides several preformatted view styles that you can use to control the display of your view. The default view style displays your app data in rows. You can use several additional styles. Many of these are especially helpful in configuring app Web Parts:

>> **Basic Table** displays app data in a simple table.

>> **Boxed** and **Boxed, No Labels** display items as a series of cards, with or without column labels. This display is similar to the Address Card view in Outlook.

>> **Newsletter** and **Newsletter, No Lines** display a table with a streamlined format.

>> **Shaded** displays items in rows, with each alternate row shaded.

>> **Preview Pane** displays items on the left and previews the details on the right. This is a great way to display a lot of information in a compact display.

TIP

Many users overlook these effective display styles. Again, experimenting is the best way to find out how a display style can improve a user's experience with the data.

Figure 14-15 shows the style options you can choose from when configuring your view.

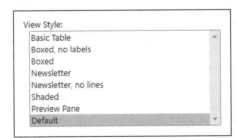

FIGURE 14-15: You can change the format of the view.

Managing App Data in a Datasheet View

Datasheet views are great for performing bulk updates on items and document properties. A Datasheet view displays app data in a web-based spreadsheet.

With Datasheet views, you can

>> Support most column types including Text, Choice, Date, Number, and Lookup columns. Not all column features work as expected in a Datasheet view. In short, when Datasheet views work, they work great. You just have to test your column types before getting overly ambitious.

>> Use the arrow keys to move around in the view like a spreadsheet.

>> Copy and paste values, which is another great way to make bulk updates to an app. We often use this approach instead of importing a spreadsheet as a custom app.

>> Choose View App Data in a Datasheet view on the fly from any Standard view by clicking the Quick Edit button on the List tab of the ribbon.

You create a Datasheet view just like you create a Standard view, although you have fewer configuration options. You can sort, filter, display totals, and set the item limit on Datasheet views.

Think of the Datasheet view as a configurable launcher for the Edit In Grid View functionality (described previously). When you create a Datasheet view you are creating a view that will launch you into the Edit In Grid View functionality but you can adjust all of the properties on the view when you create it.

Using Ad Hoc Views

Users can make Ad Hoc views in any Standard or Datasheet views by using the headers of the columns to sort and filter the data on the fly. These ad hoc changes aren't saved with the app the way defined views are. Helping your users be productive by using these ad hoc options may involve training tips or help support.

Follow these steps to create an Ad Hoc view:

1. **Hover over a column heading and click the down-arrow that appears on the right of the header.**

   This can be done in Standard or Datasheet view.

   A drop-down list appears on the column header cell.

2. **From the drop-down list, select whether you want to sort ascending or descending, or to filter the list based on data in that column.**

   Clicking the column header also toggles the sort order between ascending and descending.

Filtering options appear as distinct data from the values in the column (for example, if Marketing appears ten times in the column, it appears only once as a filter choice).

3. **Select a value from the Filter list.**

Filtering hides rows that don't contain that value.

A Filter icon appears in the column header to indicate a filter is applied.

4. **To remove the filter, click the drop-down list again and select Clear Filter from *[Column Name]*.**

TIP

If you want to access your Ad Hoc view again, simply click the View drop-down and select Save View As and then give it a name. Your personal view is now saved and you can return to it anytime you want by selecting it from the View drop-down.

Creating a Calendar View

To create a Calendar view, you must have at least one Date field in your app. The predefined SharePoint Calendar app, not surprisingly, uses this view as its default. A Calendar view helps users visually organize their date-driven work and events.

To create a Calendar view, start as you'd begin to create a Standard view (refer to the earlier section, "Creating a Standard View"), but in Step 4, click the Calendar view link. Like the Gantt view (which we describe in the following section), you see new options on the Create View page. You have a section for Time Interval, where you select the date column to use as the Begin and End fields for the view.

You also have selections to make for Calendar columns, including Month/Week/Day Titles and Week/Day Sub Heading Titles (optional). Choose the columns of data you want visible on those days in the different calendar layouts.

There is also a scope option for the default display — Month, Day, or Week. As expected, several options aren't available for Calendar views including sorting, totals, item limits, and styles; however, filtering choices are important and are often used with Calendar views.

TIP

Calendar views can also be used with Calendar overlays, which allow you to display more than one calendar view in a calendar.

Displaying Tasks in a Gantt View

To create a Gantt view, your app needs to contain task/project management information relative to that view format. The predefined SharePoint Tasks app contains these default types of columns, including Task Name, Due Date, and Assigned To.

The Create View page includes Gantt view options not seen in other views based on the five columns mentioned previously.

The Gantt view is a *split view* (see Figure 14-16), where you see a spreadsheet of data on the left and the Gantt chart on the right. A split bar between the two views can be moved by users to see more or less of one side. You can create a custom list or modify the Tasks list to add more columns for this spreadsheet side if you want.

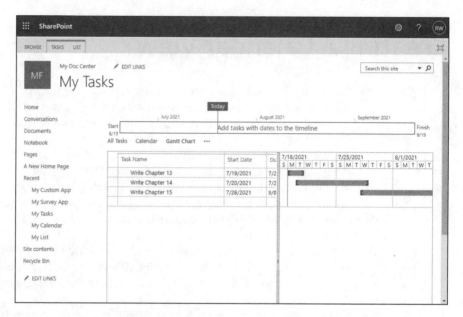

FIGURE 14-16:
The Gantt chart columns available in Gantt view.

TIP

You can synchronize tasks with project plans in Microsoft Project. In Project, choose Save & Send ⇨ Sync with Tasks List and enter the URL for your tasks list.

Managing Existing Views

Chances are you'll want to modify your views over time. In the following sections, we explain how to modify your views and set one as the default view that users see when they browse to an app. SharePoint also provides a couple of built-in views that you may want to customize.

Modifying your views

After creating your new view, you may find you need to change it. Maybe you forgot a column, it doesn't sort the way you want it to, or the grouping is just all wrong.

To modify a view, follow these steps:

1. **Browse to the app where you want to modify the view.**

2. **Display the view you want to modify.**

Select the view from the Views drop-down menu.

3. **Click Edit Current View from the Views drop-down menu.**

A View Properties page similar to the Create View page appears, enabling you to edit the view's properties.

4. **Make your desired changes to the view, such as selecting or removing columns or setting sorting or filtering options as described earlier in this chapter.**

5. **Click OK to save your changes to the view.**

REMEMBER

Public views are visible to everyone, but private views can only be used by the person who creates them.

Setting the default view

To change the default view, select the Make This the Default View check box when you create or modify a view. If you are modifying the current default view, you don't see the Make This the Default View check box.

Most apps have only one default view; the exception is the Discussion Board list, which has both subjects and replies as default views. Keep in mind that if you make a view a default view, it must be a Public view.

Other SharePoint built-in views

In addition to the other view formats we discuss earlier in this chapter, you should also be aware of the Mobile views. Mobile views are simplified, text-only views of your apps for use on a mobile device. Mobile is actually a section on the Create View page. You can enable a view to be a Mobile view or set it as the default Mobile view. (Mobile views must be public.) You can also set the number of items to display for Mobile views. If you don't see the Mobile section in your Create View page, this type of view can't be displayed in Mobile format.

Displaying Views via Web Parts

Throughout this chapter, we make references to app Web Parts to point out what view properties are helpful and applicable to a view displayed in a Web Part. You want to display your app data with other text and Web Parts in multiple locations, such as Team site home pages, Web Part pages, or publishing pages. In these situations, you don't want your users to interact with the app itself with all the editing options. You just want them to see several columns to access a document or view an item.

Chapter 6 goes into detail about using Web Parts, including linked Web Parts, connections, and master/detail settings. However, you need to know that each app generates a Web Part that can be used on SharePoint pages. Each of these Web Parts has a Properties panel that allows you to change the view in that instance of the Web Part.

Predefined SharePoint apps may have specific views that are defaults for Web Parts (for example, the Announcements app has a special default view that can't be re-created in the browser for other apps). Custom apps generally show all columns when first generated.

After selecting the Edit Web Part command on the Web Part, you can use the Selected View drop-down list in the Web Part Properties panel to apply another view (Current View is selected by default), or you can also click the Edit the Current View hyperlink to modify the view on the fly. Depending on the complexity of your choices, creating a view first to apply to the Web Part(s) may be a better long-term maintenance strategy.

Chapter **15**

Creating Workflows with Microsoft Power Automate

Any organization is made up of processes. Some processes might be very simple, such as checking an email, responding, and then filing it in a folder. Other processes are more complex and might involve multiple people and computer systems. In any case, processes — and workflows — are at the core of an organization.

In this chapter, you explore the workflow options available for SharePoint. You discover how Microsoft Power Automate has changed the game for workflow and expanded it beyond SharePoint, beyond Microsoft 365, and beyond Microsoft. You also find out how to build a workflow using Microsoft Power Automate and connect that workflow to other services. Finally, you explore the traditional SharePoint workflow capabilities that continue to provide you options within the confines of your SharePoint environment.

Understanding Workflow

A workflow can be used to manage a human-centric process or a computer-centric process. For example, you might have a process that involves five people working partly in parallel and partly in sequence. If these five people are all in the same room and accomplish the process in one sitting, then using a workflow to coordinate their activities wouldn't make much sense. If the people are dispersed in different offices or cubicles, or the process takes place over a period of time, then a workflow can be used to coordinate and keep the process on track.

In addition, a process might interact with other computer systems. For example, you might have a process that needs to pull customer data from a Customer Relationship Management (CRM) system. Or you might want to pull data into SharePoint from Twitter and the CRM so that a workflow is triggered whenever someone complains publicly on Twitter about your company. Just about anything you can dream up can be built into a workflow.

Introducing Microsoft Power Automate

Microsoft Power Automate is the next generation of workflow. It was born in the cloud and designed from the ground up to interact with Microsoft 365 products as well as third-party products (external to Microsoft) such as Dropbox, Amazon, Twitter, Facebook, and nearly any other online service in the world. It enables employees to create and automate workflows across multiple applications. When you think of Microsoft Power Automate, think of an online workflow engine that is available to the Internet — not just to Microsoft products.

TIP

Microsoft Power Automate is a rebranding of Microsoft Flow. If you are reading about workflow in Microsoft 365 and see articles outlining Microsoft Flow, you can think of Power Automate now instead. Microsoft has a culture of changing the names of things all the time, so don't worry if you see a new name. Chances are good that the technology is not brand new, just the name.

Signing into Microsoft Power Automate

Microsoft Power Automate is accessed in one of two ways:

>> Select the Power Automate icon in the Apps menu from within any Microsoft 365 service (such as SharePoint), as shown in Figure 15-1.

>> Go to the Microsoft Power Automate web page at https://flow.microsoft.com. Notice the domain still uses *flow* because that was the previous name of the workflow engine.

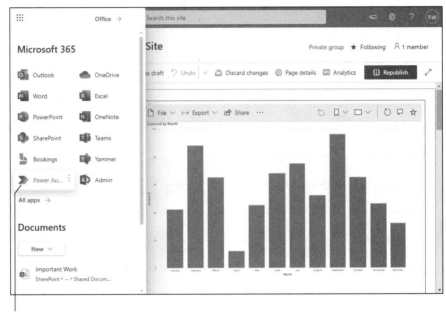

FIGURE 15-1:
Opening Power
Automate from
the Microsoft 365
app launcher in
SharePoint.

Power Automate

Getting familiar with Power Automate

The Microsoft Power Automate service uses your web browser as a design tool for building out automated workflows called *flows*. The design environment is shown in Figure 15-2. Notice the navigation options that appear along the left side of the page: Home, Action Items, My Flows, Create, Templates, Connectors, Data, Monitor, AI Builder, Process Advisor, Solutions, and Learn.

The Home navigational link always takes you back to your start page if you ever get lost. The start page includes overview information and is always a good place to return when working with Power Automate.

The Action Items menu provides a place for approvals and business process flows. Click the Action Items heading in the left navigation menu to display the Approvals link and the Business Process Flows link. Click the Approvals link to display the Approvals page.

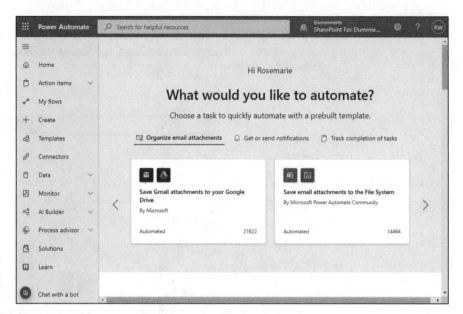

FIGURE 15-2:
The main
Microsoft Power
Automate page.

The Approvals link takes you to the Approvals page, as shown in Figure 15-3, where you can build a new approval workflow or interact with approvals that you have sent or received. You can even see the history of the approvals on this page.

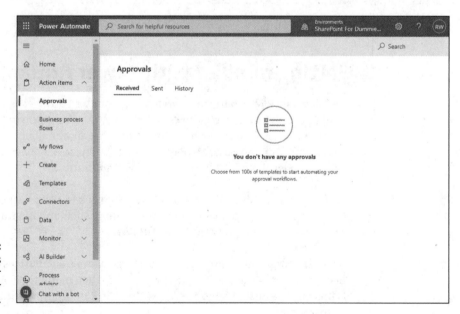

FIGURE 15-3:
The Approvals
page for
Microsoft Power
Automate.

The heart of the Power Automate interface is the My Flows page. When you click this navigational link, you see all your flows and the flows for your team. You will find tabs to group flows by Cloud flows, Desktop flows, Business Process flows, and Shared With Me flows.

>> **Cloud flows** are workflows that are triggered automatically, instantly, or via a schedule based on events that happen in the cloud.

>> **Desktop flows** are workflows for repetitive things that you do on your local computer. For example, organizing your documents and folders or pulling data into an Excel file from the same source each day.

>> **Business Process flows** are designed for human workflows in that users follow the same steps each time. For example, when users open a new account, they should always follow the new account workflow.

>> The **Shared With Me flows** are flows that others have created and shared with you.

The Create navigation item lets you start a new workflow. The next item is the Templates link that takes you to the Templates library. Templates are prepackaged flows that you can use and customize for specific scenarios. For example, there is a flow to send yourself a reminder in ten minutes or start an approval when a new item is added to SharePoint or Outlook. There are an incredible number of templates available, and new ones are added all the time. Chances are, if you already have a workflow in mind, someone has created a template for it.

Next up on the navigational menu is Connectors. Connectors are where Power Automate gets its power. There are connectors that, well, connect Power Automate to all types of services and products. This is where you can build workflows that interact with popular sites and products. Remember when we mentioned Dropbox, Amazon, Twitter, and Facebook? This is where you find connectors for those products, as well as nearly any other online service or product in the world.

TIP

Keep in mind that some services require a premium subscription in order to connect to them.

>> The **Data** navigational link is where you can pull data into your flows so that it can be analyzed and decisions in the workflow process can be made. Once you get up to speed with Power Automate, you will spend a lot of time in this area.

>> The **Monitor** option is where you monitor things regarding your flows. You will see things like notifications, failures, and alerts.

>> The **AI Builder** option lets you enhance your workflows with common AI models. For example, you might train a model to look at incoming invoices and pull out key information. As the model learns it can adapt to new invoice formats without human interaction. There are many different AI models that you can use with Power Automate.

>> Next up is **Process Advisor,** which you can think of as an automated way to visualize your workflows. You can then review the visualizations and figure out how to improve your workflows.

>> The **Solutions** navigational link is where you can bundle flows into a single deployable unit. The deployable unit is called a solution and you can group related flows together for ease of deployment and maintenance. Solutions can be useful in extremely large organizations that have a lot of flows.

>> Finally, the **Learn** navigational link is where you can find step-by-step learning guidance from Microsoft.

Building your first flow

A basic, but useful, workflow is to send an approval email when a new item is added to your SharePoint site. For example, imagine a ticketing app you have built using a SharePoint List (see Chapter 12 for more about creating List-based apps). Whenever someone adds a new item to the app, you want to fire off an approval email to a group of people so that they know a new ticket has been added and someone can approve it. Let's build this workflow using Power Automate.

To build a workflow to send an approval email when a new item is added to your SharePoint List app follow these steps:

1. **In SharePoint, click the Microsoft 365 apps menu in the upper-left corner and select Power Automate.**

   A new tab opens on your web browser and the Microsoft Power Automate page loads.

2. **Click the Templates navigational link on the left side of the page.**

3. **Type** sharepoint **into the search box and press Enter to display the templates that relate to SharePoint, as shown in Figure 15-4.**

   A template is already available to do exactly what we are trying to do.

4. **Click the "Send approval email when a new item is added" template (shown as the last template in the third row in Figure 15-4).**

   The page for this template appears and provides a visual for how the workflow flows. (Pun intended.) You can see in Figure 15-5 that the workflow originates in SharePoint and then moves to Microsoft 365 and Office 365 Outlook (email).

The arrow pointing to the right indicates the direction the data is sent. Farther down the page are the permissions that are required for this email (see Figure 15-6).

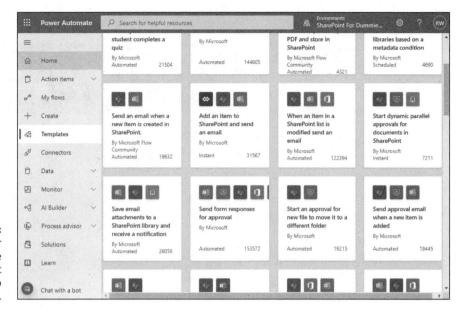

FIGURE 15-4: The Power Automate templates that relate to SharePoint.

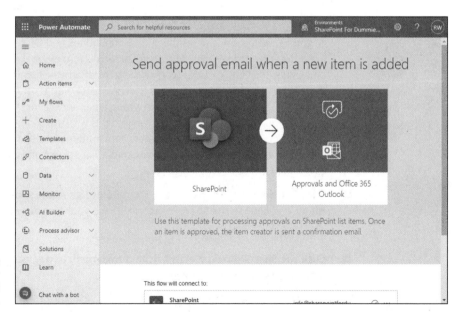

FIGURE 15-5: The data flow for a custom email workflow.

TIP

Something we appreciate about Microsoft services is that authentication is handled for us automatically. If you look at the permissions required for this workflow (Figure 15-6), you will see it actually crosses services. Since our user is part of Microsoft 365, we don't need to set up any extra permissions. It "just works" after we sign into each service from within the flow.

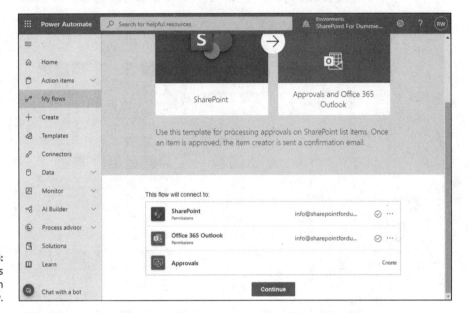

FIGURE 15-6:
The permissions
for a custom
email workflow.

WARNING

A "gotcha" with connectors is that Microsoft Outlook and Office 365 Outlook are different email services. Microsoft Outlook is for personal email addresses and Office 365 Outlook is for work and organization email addresses. If you try to setup an email connector in a flow and receive an error that the account doesn't exist, you might be using the wrong email service for the type of account you are signed in with. We ran into this with the connector that sends an email notification when a new item is added to a SharePoint list. The connector wants the personal Outlook.com email service and we were trying to use the Office 365 Outlook service.

5. **Click Continue and then click the SharePoint Site Address drop-down menu and choose the SharePoint site where your List-based app resides.**

    In our example we chose our For Dummies site.

6. **Click the SharePoint List Name drop-down menu and select the List-based app the workflow will use.**

    In our example we chose My List app, as shown in Figure 15-7.

It can take a little time for a SharePoint site or List-based app to appear in these drop-down menus. If you just created something and it is not showing up, go grab a coffee and check back later.

7. **Fill in the approval details and then click Save to create the workflow and attach it to your SharePoint List-based app.**

Now whenever a new item is added to the list, an approval email will be sent as a notification. You can customize the workflow with the destination email, email message, and timing by editing the flow. You will find it on the My Flows page.

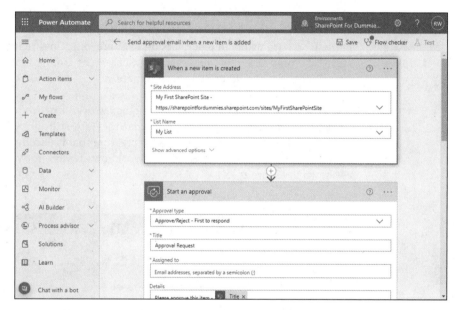

FIGURE 15-7:
Selecting a SharePoint site and List app for a Power Automate workflow.

Using Microsoft Power Automate, you can build workflows that integrate SharePoint with just about any other software you can imagine. Spend some time exploring the templates and when you are feeling comfortable, start customizing the templates to suit your own needs and then move into building your own custom workflows from scratch.

Using the Traditional SharePoint-Only Workflow

Microsoft Power Automate is the future of workflow because it flings open the doors of SharePoint and connects it to the rest of the world. Some organizations might still prefer to use the traditional SharePoint workflow that keeps all workflows within SharePoint itself. In this section, we show you how to activate the traditional SharePoint workflow system so you can decide if you want to stick with it or are ready to jump to the future of workflow with Power Automate.

TIP

SharePoint Designer was a tool used to build the classic workflows in SharePoint. SharePoint Designer has been replaced with Power Automate and is not used anymore. If you are using an older version of SharePoint On-Premises, you still may see SharePoint Designer; however, for SharePoint Online and new versions of SharePoint, you should use Power Automate.

If you're familiar with the out-of-the-box workflows from past versions of SharePoint, you will be glad to know that they are still included in SharePoint. They are now included as a site collection feature that is deactivated by default. To turn them on, you need to activate the Workflows feature for your site collection, as shown in Figure 15-8.

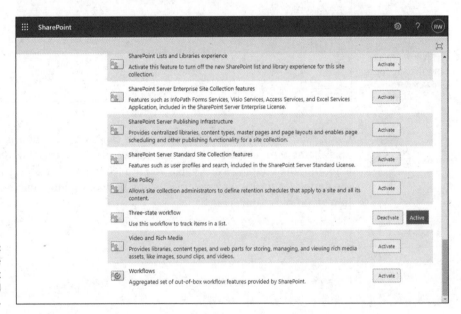

FIGURE 15-8: Activating the out-of-the-box approval workflows.

To find out more about activating features in SharePoint, see Chapter 18.

The out-of-the-box approval workflows use the legacy SharePoint workflow platform. They are turned off by default for performance reasons.

TIP

Unless you have a great reason, like you are being told to use these workflows, we would recommend making the leap to Microsoft Power Automate. You saw earlier in the book how approvals can be setup with Power Automate and you get a lot more functionality.

TIP

The workflow templates that shipped with SharePoint 2010 have been retired. You can achieve the same thing using Power Automate now.

Chapter **16**

Getting Answers with Microsoft Forms

Microsoft Forms is a cloud-based tool for creating digital forms. A digital form is just like a paper form, but you fill it out by opening it in a web browser on your computer. In this chapter, you learn how to integrate Microsoft Forms with SharePoint. You start by learning how to access the Microsoft Forms service. Then, you learn how to create a simple form and display it on a SharePoint page. Next, you see how you can use a form in Microsoft Forms to collect data and send it to SharePoint.

TIP

Forms works with all sorts of Microsoft products and not just with SharePoint. However, Forms and SharePoint are great partners, since the former deals with taking in data from people, and the latter deals with managing digital content.

Signing into Microsoft Forms

Your existing Microsoft 365 credentials (which you create in Chapter 1) are used to sign into Microsoft Forms. If your browser is already opened and you are using a Microsoft 365 app, then you can select the app launcher and choose Forms. Alternatively, you can open your web browser of choice and head over to `https://forms.office.com`. Click the Sign In button. If you are not already logged into Microsoft 365, you will be asked to log in. After you do, a tutorial screen appears with information on how to create a new form, as shown in Figure 16-1.

FIGURE 16-1:
Signing into
Microsoft Forms
and view the
tutorial.

One thing we really like about the direction Microsoft has gone is the linking of all of its online services to your Microsoft 365 credentials. You only need to have a single Microsoft 365 account and you can use all the services with that same login. Microsoft Forms is no exception.

TIP

Now, let's get on with creating our first form!

Creating a Form in Microsoft Forms

From the welcome screen (that you see after you log into Microsoft Forms), click the New Form button to pull up the form creation page, as shown in Figure 16-2.

On the surface, Microsoft Forms might seem trivial and somewhat like a toy. When we first looked at it, we thought we must be missing something. A Microsoft Forms *form* is really just a list of questions! How useful could that be? Well, it turns out, it can be incredibly powerful. Yes, getting started creating a form is trivial, but when you start thinking about collecting data from people by asking questions, you can start to see the opportunity for this simple tool.

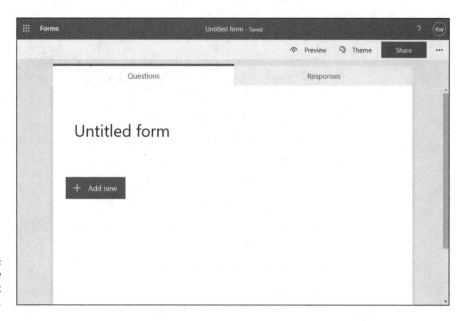

FIGURE 16-2:
Creating a new
form in Microsoft
Forms.

Let's create a simple form to ask folks about SharePoint.

1. **From the form creation page, click the Untitled form text and give the form a name.**

   We called our form "SharePoint For Dummies Survey."

2. **Click the picture icon to the left of the title and select an icon for the form.**

   We chose the famous pencil-headed geek guru of the For Dummies brand.

3. **Provide a description for the form.**

   Now we are onto the primary purpose of the form. Let's add some questions.

4. **Click the Add New button and then choose how you want to collect information.**

   Your choices are: Choice, Text, Rating, Date, Ranking, Likert, File upload, Net Promoter Score, or Section. A Section is a new section to the form as opposed to a question type. We will choose Choice for this question.

5. **Enter a question you want to ask the people taking the survey.**

   We want to know if the person taking the survey has ever heard of SharePoint.

   Once we enter the question, Microsoft Forms is smart enough to give us some default answers. It suggests we add Yes, No, and Maybe.

6. **Click the Add All button to add all of these choices to the answer section.**

    The result is shown in Figure 16-3. You can select some additional options such as allowing multiple answers and requiring this question be answered. Play around with these and the other options.

    Next, let's give the form some attitude.

7. **Click the Theme button that appears in the upper-right corner of the screen and select a theme.**

    We chose an "undersea" theme (see Figure 16-4).

8. **Click the Preview button to preview the form.**

    You can select options to see how the form will be displayed on a computer or on a mobile device.

9. **Go ahead and take the survey and click Submit.**

    Your answers will be recorded, and you will see a success screen that lets you know your response was submitted.

And that is all there is to building a form! Next up, analyzing the data (and don't worry, we are getting to SharePoint integration).

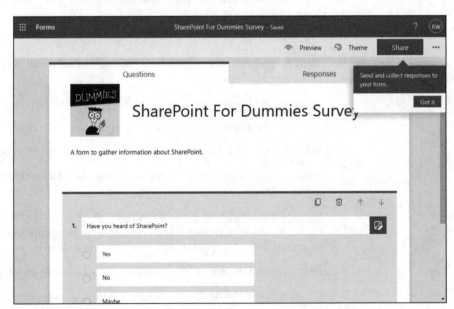

FIGURE 16-3: Adding questions to a form.

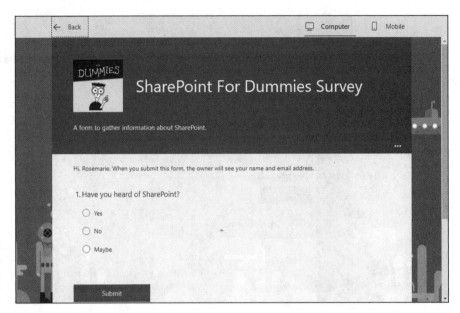

FIGURE 16-4:
A simple
SharePoint
Survey form in
Microsoft Forms.

Analyzing Microsoft Forms Data

In the previous section, you created a new form and then submitted an answer. Over the course of a survey, you may want to check on the form's responses. To view the responses of any form, navigate your web browser to `https://forms.office.com` (or select Forms from the app launcher if you are already using a Microsoft 365 app) and log in to see all of your existing forms. Open the form you wish to view and then click the Responses tab to see all the responses that have come in for this form, as shown in Figure 16-5.

Just like the rest of Microsoft Forms, the Responses tab appears deceptively simple. You can:

>> See the summary of the responses for each question.

>> Click the View Results button to see who responded with which answer, how much time they took to complete the question, delete the response, and print the response.

>> Create a summary link.

>> View the responses in Excel so you can analyze the results.

TIP

By default, people can submit as many of the same form as they want. If you don't want people to stuff the ballot box, you can turn this capability off in the Settings page for the form. You will find this by clicking the ellipsis icon in the top-right corner of the page while editing a form.

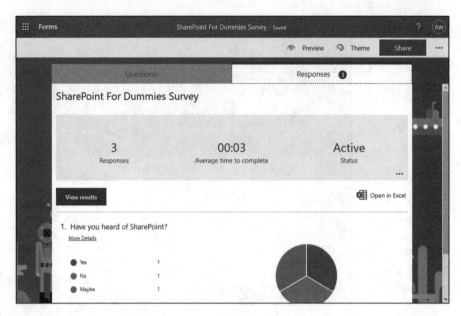

FIGURE 16-5:
Viewing form
responses.

Displaying a Form in SharePoint

To send out a form, click the Share button that appears in the top-right corner of the page. When you click this button, the Share screen is displayed, as shown in Figure 16-6. In the Share screen you can share a link to the form, create a scannable bar QR code, get an embed code for embedding the form in a web page, and email the form to someone. For our purposes, click the Copy button to copy the sharable link.

TIP

You can also share the form as a template so that anyone with a link can create a new form based on your existing form. Or you can get a direct link to the editable version of the form so others can work on building it with you.

All of these methods of sharing a form are nice, but what we have found most useful is displaying a form right on a SharePoint page on an intranet site. That way everyone in the organization can see it when they open the SharePoint site. And if you send them a link to the form, you can actually send them a link to the SharePoint page instead of off to a stand-alone form. This nudges them toward SharePoint and some of the other benefits SharePoint has to offer.

To add a form to a SharePoint page, you add the Forms Web Part and then connect it to the form you want to display. (You learn how to add Web Parts to a SharePoint page in Chapter 6.)

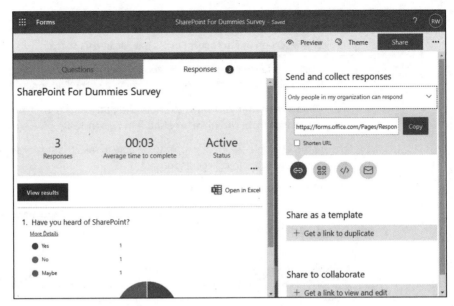

FIGURE 16-6:
The Share screen
for a form.

To add a form to a SharePoint page:

1. **Open the SharePoint page where you want to add the form.**

2. **Click the plus (+) sign to add a Web Part and choose the Microsoft Forms Web Part, as shown in Figure 16-7.**

FIGURE 16-7:
Selecting the
Microsoft Forms
Web Part.

3. **Click Add Existing Form and paste the sharable link you copied from the Share screen in Microsoft Forms earlier in this section.**

   You can also create a brand-new form from the Microsoft Forms Web Part in SharePoint. Clicking that button will take you to the Forms site.

4. **Choose whether you want to show the questions from the form or the responses from the form, as shown in Figure 16-8.**

   In this example, we want people to be able to take the survey so we leave the default, which is to collect responses.

5. **Click OK and then publish your page.**

   Your form is now embedded in your SharePoint page and anyone landing on the page can take the survey.

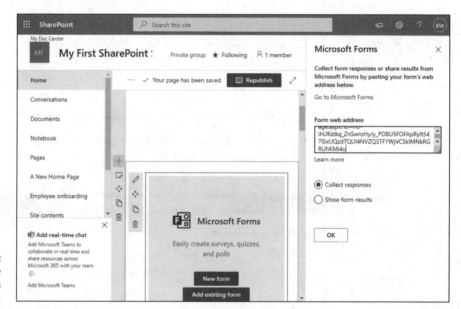

FIGURE 16-8: Configuring the Microsoft Forms Web Part.

Capturing Forms Data in SharePoint

One common question we get asked about Microsoft Forms is regarding data. People love having their data inside SharePoint itself in a List-based app. At first glance you might not think Forms can do this since it appears to be so simple, but that is where Power Automate comes in. Microsoft Power Automate is a workflow tool that you can use to submit your Forms data, or pretty much any other data, into and around your SharePoint site. We cover Microsoft Power Automate in Chapter 15.

4

Becoming a SharePoint Administrator

IN THIS PART . . .

Learn how to build and deploy an app using Microsoft PowerApps.

Add links and customize navigation for your SharePoint sites.

Activate and deactivate features in SharePoint and extend functionality with custom features.

Create and use a client or partner portal based on SharePoint, and see how easy it is to set up a public-facing website.

Manage SharePoint groups, assign permissions, and manage administrative processes to secure your SharePoint sites.

IN THIS CHAPTER

» Gaining an understanding of
Power Apps

» Building your first Power App

» Using a Power App on your mobile
device

» Making SharePoint tolerable on a
mobile phone

Chapter **17**

Building Business Apps with Power Apps

M icrosoft Power Apps is a service that spans many different products. The idea of Power Apps is to provide a platform for non-developers to build apps that people can use on their smartphones and other computing devices. Power Apps is designed for business needs and thus, fits in nicely with SharePoint.

In this chapter, you learn how to build and deploy an app using Power Apps. You also learn how to integrate your app with SharePoint and take a look at Share-Point's mobile environment.

Introducing Power Apps

When we first started using Power Apps, we were excited. It seemed like a plat-form designed specifically for SharePoint. The Power Apps we built we made available to all types of users on their mobile phones. All of a sudden, people started using SharePoint and had no idea they were using SharePoint. They just used an app on their phones and knew that it solved a specific business problem. So we initially thought of Power Apps as a mobile app platform, and we used it almost exclusively with SharePoint. Now that we have some experience under our belts, we realize that Power Apps is more than just making SharePoint apps available on a mobile device (though this is still the biggest value in our opinion).

TIP

Even though we think of Power Apps as primarily a mobile experience, you can also add the Power Apps you build to SharePoint pages as well.

Signing into Power Apps

The easiest way to access Power Apps is by clicking the Microsoft 365 app menu and then selecting Power Apps.

You can also access Power Apps by opening your web browser and navigating to the site directly. The Power Apps site is located at `https://powerapps.microsoft.com`. When you sign into the Power Apps site, you use your Microsoft 365 credentials (see Chapter 1).

Getting familiar with Power Apps

The Microsoft Power Apps service uses your web browser as a development tool for building apps. The development environment is shown in Figure 17-1.

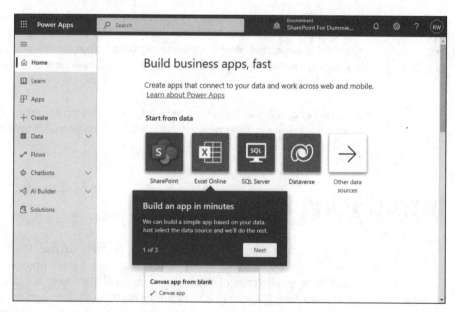

FIGURE 17-1:
The main Power Apps page.

Notice along the left side of the page you have the following navigation options: Home, Learn, Apps, Create, Data, Flows, Chatbots, AI Builder, and Solutions. The Home navigational link is your friend that will always take you back to the beginning if you get lost. The Power Apps home page includes overview information and is always a good place to start when you are developing Power Apps.

Next up is the Learn link. The Learn link includes guided learning, help topics, and a Power Apps community.

TIP

When you first get started with Power Apps, make sure to spend some time to go through the Guided Learning experience found on the Learn page. It is time well spent and will save you lots of frustration and headaches down the road.

The Apps link takes you to a location that shows you all your Power Apps. You will find the recent apps you have developed, apps that have been shared with you, apps you have permissions to edit, and apps that are part of your organization.

After the Apps link is the Create link. The Create link is where you go to create a new Power App. You will use this in the next section when you create your first Power App. After the Create link is the Data link. The Data link expands and includes links for Entities, Connections, Custom Connectors, and Gateways. This is where you can create connections and manage the data you are using in your Power Apps. Data is at the heart of a business app, so you will spend a lot of time here once you get comfortable with building and customizing Power Apps.

After the Data link is the Flows navigational link, which lets you integrate your Microsoft Power Automate workflows directly into your Power Apps. We cover Microsoft Power Automate in Chapter 15.

The Chatbots link is where you can create virtual agents that respond in chats. Think of a chatbot as an automated response system that people can use to interact and have guided conversations. When you expand the menu you have more options such as creating a new chatbot and listing all of your chatbots.

The AI Builder was also mentioned in Chapter 15 on Power Automate. AI Builder is an advanced feature that lets you enhance your apps with common AI models.

Last in the list is the Solutions navigational link. Solutions is a relatively new feature of Power Apps (Microsoft is adding new functionality all of the time). Solutions is beyond the scope of this book, but in a nutshell, a *Solution* allows you to encapsulate a group of Power Apps and move them all at once to another environment instead of one at a time. Imagine a Power Apps solution for a finance team that includes apps used by financial departments. This is the idea behind Solutions.

Building your first Power App

A very simple, but incredibly powerful, use for Power Apps is to let users work with a custom SharePoint List–based app using their mobile phones or tablets. Just about everyone has a smartphone now, and building an app that lets your users interact with a SharePoint list brings your intranet to their mobile devices.

In Chapter 15, we build a support ticketing app based on a SharePoint list. We built a flow to send an approval email whenever a new ticket came into the app. Users could go to the app in their web browsers and submit tickets. Now you will build a Power App so that users can work with the ticketing app from their mobile devices.

To build a Power App for working with a SharePoint list:

1. **Open your web browser and navigate to the SharePoint list.**

   In our case we will use the My Power App List-based app we created in Chapter 15.

2. **Click the ellipsis, choose Integrate, and then on the Power Apps fly-out menu select Create an App, as shown in Figure 17-2.**

   A dialog box displays where you can enter a name for the app.

FIGURE 17-2:
Creating a new
Power App for a
SharePoint list.

256   PART 4 **Becoming a SharePoint Administrator**

3. **Enter a name and click Create, as shown in Figure 17-3.**

Your browser redirects you to the Power Apps development environment called Power Apps Studio.

Power Apps Studio might sound impressive, but it is really just a web page with a lot of functionality for building apps. All you need is your web browser to work with it and build Power Apps. Because we started with an existing SharePoint list, the heavy lifting of creating the Power App was already done for us.

FIGURE 17-3:
Providing a name
for a Power App.

4. **Click the play button, displayed in the top-right corner of the page, to display the app in a preview window, as shown in Figure 17-4.**

The preview shows you what the app will look like when viewed on a mobile phone.

The SharePoint list that contains the data for this app doesn't have any items in it yet so let's create one.

5. **Click the plus (+) sign in the top-right corner of the screen.**

A form that represents the columns in the SharePoint list appears.

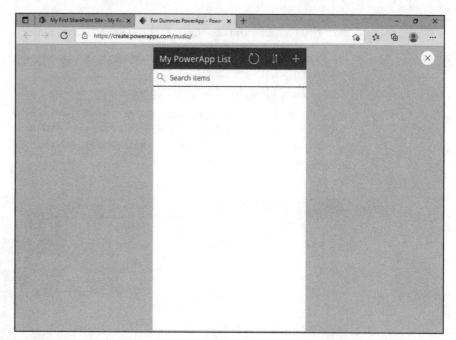

6. Enter information into the form to create a new list item and then click
the check mark in the upper-right corner of the app to create a new item,
as shown in Figure 17-5.

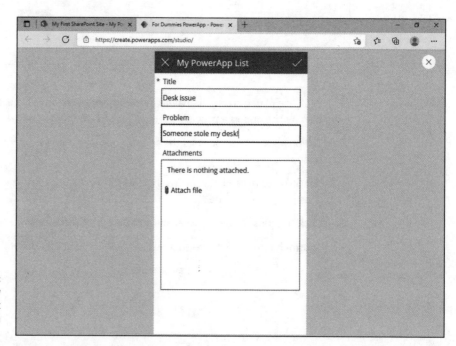

A new list item will be added and the main app page will reload. Let's head back over to our SharePoint list in our web browser to confirm the item was created.

7. **Open the My Power App list in our browser and confirm the new item has been created from the Power App, as shown in Figure 17-6.**

   Note that if you have multiple tabs open to Power Apps on your web browser then you may need to refresh the page to see new items.

   Next, let's create a new item in the SharePoint list in our web browser and then confirm it appears in the Power App.

8. **Click the plus (+) sign (new item in the classic experience or a New button in the new experience) to create a new item in the SharePoint list, then head over to the Power App preview and click the refresh icon (it looks like a circle).**

   Our new item is pulled into the Power App. We can now work with a SharePoint list from a Power App.

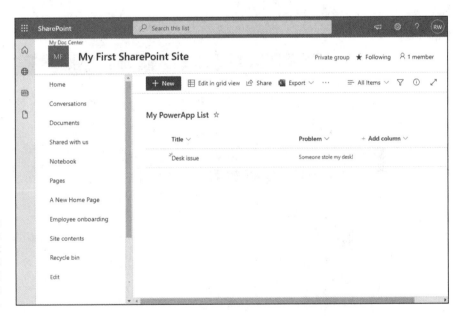

FIGURE 17-6: Viewing a SharePoint list that contains items created from a Power App.

TIP Power Apps can be integrated with Microsoft Power Automate. This combination lets you take SharePoint to the mobile world and also incorporate your workflow at the same time. In our view, this is a game changer in the technology world.

TIP

Power Apps Studio is a complex development environment. It will take some time to get a feel for customizing and creating new Power Apps. Remember to check out the Learn navigational link at `https://powerapps.microsoft.com` to see hands-on training guides and videos.

Sharing your Power App

Now that you have a working Power App, the last step is to share your app so that it is available to use. To share a Power App:

1. **Open the Power App you want to share in Power Apps Studio.**

   If you followed the previous procedure, you will already be viewing the app that was created for the SharePoint list.

2. **Click the File tab and then click the Share button shown in Figure 17-7.**

3. **Enter the name or email addresses of the people you want to be able to use the app and then click Share.**

   An email will be sent with instructions on how to access the app.

FIGURE 17-7:
Clicking the File tab in Power Apps Studio.

Using Power Apps on your Mobile Device

Using apps you have developed in Power Apps Studio is fairly straightforward. You will find the app in both the Apple store and the Google Play store called Power Apps.

Once you have installed the Power Apps app, open it and sign in with your Microsoft 365 credentials. You will see all of the Power Apps that you have created and also any apps that have been shared with you. Tap the For Dummies Power App app we created in the previous section and you will see the exact same app you previewed earlier, except now it is running right on your mobile phone! Notice that all the items we created earlier are displayed and we can create new items or edit existing items. Our SharePoint List-based app is now a full-fledged mobile phone or tablet app thanks to Power Apps.

Embedding a Power App within a SharePoint Page

Most people will use Power Apps from their mobile phones or tablets. However, Microsoft released functionality that lets you embed a Power App directly in a SharePoint page, too. To embed a Power App in a SharePoint page:

1. Open the SharePoint page where you want to embed the Power App.

2. Click the plus (+) sign to add a Web Part to the page and select the Microsoft Power Apps Web Part in the Advanced section.

3. Find the Web link of your Power App by looking on the app details page in Power Apps.

You will find it by selecting the Apps navigational component in Power Apps and then selecting the radio button next to the app you want to embed and clicking Details at the top of page.

4. Copy the URL or App ID of the Power App and paste it into the configuration section of the Web Part.

The Web Part will update with the Power App, as shown in Figure 17-8.

5. Click Republish to publish the page and view the Power App embedded right inside of your SharePoint page.

Note that the Power App was built for a mobile phone. If we wanted to build it for a web browser, we would probably want to increase the width.

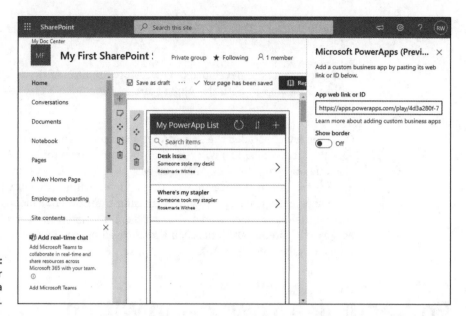

FIGURE 17-8:
Adding a Power
App in a
SharePoint page.

TIP

You can embed a Power App in any HTML web page, not just SharePoint. To do this you can use iframe.

Viewing SharePoint Sites in a Web Browser on a Mobile Device

Power Apps is definitely the way to go when working with SharePoint from a mobile device. However, if there are people who don't want to install the Power Apps app, they can still work with SharePoint using the web browser on their mobile devices.

A SharePoint feature called Mobile Browser View makes it possible to customize how a site will look depending on the dimensions of the web browser being used. When you activate the feature, three different site views become available to mobile devices:

>> **Classic** view shows the site with HTML links to the different navigation components.

>> **Contemporary** view shows the navigation components of the site using tiles that you click on to navigate.

>> **Full Screen UI** is the same view of SharePoint you would see on a regular desktop computer, only rendered in your smaller mobile browser.

Creating views for small screens

When you create a view for your app data, you select whether it should be available on a mobile device. You can even select if the view should be the default view for a mobile device. Chapter 11 walks you through creating a new view and discusses the Mobile section on the Create View page.

The bottom of the app settings page (such as List Settings or Library Settings) shows the views available for the app. A column shows whether the view is available for mobile devices and if it is the default view. Figure 17-9 shows these columns on the List Settings page for an app.

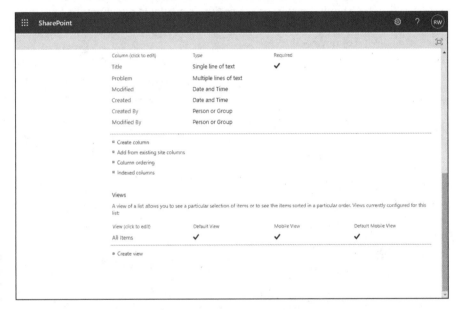

FIGURE 17-9:
The Views section of a List-based app.

Targeting devices using channels

If you have a complex SharePoint site, you might want to render it differently depending on the device being used to view it. You can do this using the Device Channels functionality of SharePoint. Using Device Channels, you can dictate that certain devices should use certain master pages and style sheets. When a particular device, such as an iPad or Android tablet browses the site, it displays in a customized way for that type of device.

WARNING

Creating custom master pages and style sheets is a very technical task and should be done by experienced web developers.

Note: Device Channels are only available for sites with the SharePoint Server Publishing Infrastructure feature activated.

Click the Device Channels link in the Look and Feel section of the Site Settings page to create and configure channels. When you create a new channel, you provide a name, an alias for reference in website design code, a description, and inclusion rules. A web designer can then build the SharePoint master page to display differently based on the channels available. Developing master pages and referencing Device Channels in code is beyond the scope of this book, but you should know that the option is available when you need to customize SharePoint. The result is that SharePoint displays differently, depending on different channels of devices.

Chapter **18**

Realizing You Are a SharePoint Administrator

I t used to be that website administration was done by the same web developer geeks that created the site. This made life simple for the information worker. If something was wrong with the site, call IT! If something needed to be changed, call IT! If a new site needed to be created and developed, call IT!

SharePoint has shifted the paradigm of website administration. No longer do you need to involve IT in your website administration. This relieves the pressure on IT and also empowers you to take control of your own site. Didn't Uncle Ben in *Spider-Man* say, "with great power comes great responsibility"? Well, the same is true with SharePoint. If you are a site administrator, you have great power at your fingertips. Just be prepared; the website users will now come to you instead of IT. No need to fear, though; SharePoint makes website administration straightforward. Everything is done using your web browser from a centralized settings page called Site Settings. Yes, you use SharePoint to administer SharePoint. How convenient!

In this chapter, you go through the settings available for a SharePoint site. You find out how to find the Site Settings page and gain familiarity with the many different settings categories. Next, you discover SharePoint features. You see how a feature works and which features are active by default. You also find out how to activate and deactivate features and explore some of the most common and helpful ones. Finally, you find out how to change the look and feel of a SharePoint site. You see how themes are used for colors and fonts and how composed looks are used.

Changing Your Site's Basic Information

Some of the first things you might want to change on a SharePoint site are the title of the site, the description, and the logo. With these simple changes, your site looks professional and unique to your team or organization. You can then get on with the productivity benefits that SharePoint has to offer.

SharePoint Team sites contain a site icon in the upper-left corner. The default image in a Team site is a square with a couple of letters from the SharePoint site's title. SharePoint has a setting that allows you to change this image.

TIP

In the past, you had to worry about the exact size of your logo. SharePoint dramatically simplifies the process by letting you choose a logo image from your computer or from a Library app somewhere on your SharePoint site. SharePoint then automatically resizes the image to the optimal size for the logo.

To change a site's basic information:

1. **Navigate to the Home page of your site and then click the Settings gear icon and choose Site Information.**

   The Site Information dialog box appears on the right side of the page.

2. **Click the Change button to choose a different logo image.**

3. **Browse your computer for the image you want to use as a logo.**

   When you browse and select an image, SharePoint automatically uploads it to your SharePoint site for you.

4. **Edit the Site Name as desired and type a short description of the site in the Site Description text box.**

   You can also change the site's privacy settings on this screen

5. **Click Save to commit your changes.**

   You see your new logo and title in the header area.

Finding Site Settings

Thankfully, finding the Site Settings page is as easy as a few clicks of the mouse. Click the Settings gear icon and choose Site Contents, then click the Site Settings button, as shown in Figure 18-1.

Site Settings

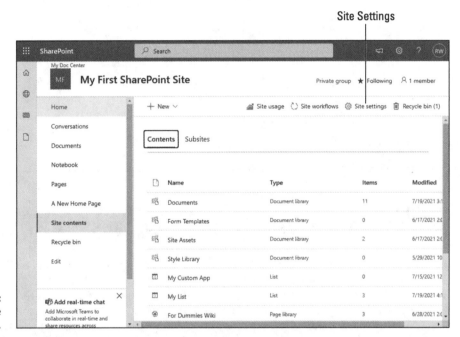

When the Site Settings page loads, you see a number of links all grouped into various categories, as shown in Figure 18-2. The Site Settings page can be daunting and overwhelming. Don't worry, though. As you administer a SharePoint site, you will become familiar with all the various settings pages and become an expert before you know it.

Different settings links appear and disappear, depending on your particular permissions and the type of site you are administering. For example, if you're a site collection administrator, then you see the Site Collection Administration section. If you're not, then you won't see the links or even the entire Site Collection Administration section.

TIP

If you read about a settings page but can't find it, chances are you don't have permissions or you are working with a site that does not have that particular setting. This can occur, for example, if the publishing feature is activated or not. In general, SharePoint shifts around links and names depending on how the site is set up.

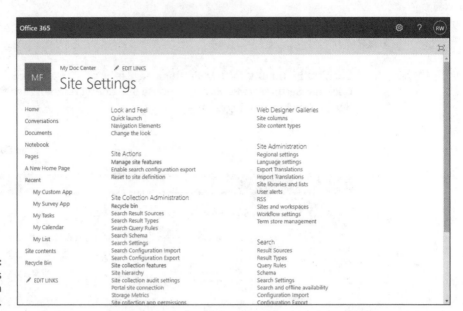

FIGURE 18-2:
The Site Settings
page in
SharePoint.

UNDERSTANDING ADMINISTRATION

SharePoint is a very complex product. This book covers only a small sliver of SharePoint that is the user perspective. In addition to the users of SharePoint, a complete infrastructure also makes up a SharePoint environment. If you use SharePoint Online, Microsoft handles most of the infrastructure (your organization is still responsible for its own Internet access). If you use SharePoint on your own premise, there is a small army of administrator roles that need to be considered.

In this part of the book, you find out how to administer a SharePoint site. In addition to site (and site collection) administration, there are also SharePoint farm administrators. A *farm administrator* takes care of all the settings for the entire SharePoint farm. A *farm* is made up of multiple web applications that can each contain multiple site collections. Depending on the size of your organization, you may have multiple farm administrators.

SharePoint runs on Windows and uses the Microsoft database product SQL Server. These are complicated products in their own right and often have their own administrators. In particular, a database administrator is a very specialized role, and many companies have more than one of them.

SharePoint environments are often made up of multiple servers. And then you have all the users that each have a device that needs to connect to these servers. To make all the communication happen, you need network administrators. Network administrators live in a completely separate world from the rest of the administrators and focus on the wires (and wireless), switches, hubs, and routers that connect all the devices together.

A lot of administrators make up a SharePoint environment. Organizing them all and making everything work properly is one of the reasons SharePoint is considered enterprise-class software. And trust us, mobilizing this army isn't cheap. Using SharePoint on your premises gives you more control over the environment, but using SharePoint Online offers a cost-effective alternative, and SharePoint Online is often the only real choice for small- to medium-sized organizations.

Digging into Site Settings

The Site Settings page for a site based on the Team Site template contains seven settings categories: Look and Feel, Site Actions, Site Collection Administration, Microsoft Search, Web Designer Galleries, Site Administration, and Search.

Look and Feel

The Look and Feel section of the Site Settings page includes links for managing things like the left navigation pane, known as the Quick Launch, navigational elements, and the look and feel of the site. You can easily change a number of things to customize your site and make it your own.

WARNING

The Look and Feel section of the Site Settings page is a perfect lesson in SharePoint frustration. The links that appear in this section depend on whether you have the SharePoint Server Publishing feature activated. Not knowing this could cause you frustration because you may read about a settings link, but when you look at your own SharePoint site, that link is nowhere to be found. To make matters worse, the links are different depending on whether SharePoint Server Publishing is activated at the site collection level or the site level. For example, you could have SharePoint Server Publishing activated at the site collection level but not activated at the site level. You will still see the Navigation Elements link in the Look and Feel section, as opposed to the Top Link bar and Quick Launch navigation links that appear if the publishing feature was deactivated at the site collection level. (We cover activating and deactivating SharePoint features later in this chapter.)

The Look and Feel section contains the following setting links (when the Share-Point Server Publishing feature is not active at the site collection or site level):

>> **Quick Launch** enables you to configure the navigation on the left side of the page. You can add headings, links, and change the order.

>> **Navigation Elements** enables you to turn the Quick Launch menu on and off and also the Tree View.

>> **Change the Look** is where you choose the colors and design of the site. There are some exciting and outrageous looks such as Sea Monster and Immerse. The looks available to choose from are in the Composed Looks gallery (see the later section, "Web Designer Galleries").

When you activate the SharePoint Server Publishing Infrastructure feature at the site collection and site level, the Tree View and Top Link bar setting links disappear and are replaced with a single Navigation Elements link. In addition, the following settings links appear in the Look and Feel section:

>> **Design Manager** is a web-based tool that you can use to create your own SharePoint site designs. The tool is wizard based and walks you through uploading design files, editing your master page, changing page layouts, and publishing and packaging your design.

>> **Device Channels** enables you to specify certain characteristics of your site based on the device used to view the site. A channel can be optimized for the device to display the site in a specific way. For example, you can set up a channel for smartphones (such as an iPhone or Android). You could set up a different channel for the iPad or Surface tablets. And finally, you can set up a channel for laptops and desktop browsers.

>> **Image Renditions** lets you set the default behavior for how images and videos render on the site. You can set the width and height for how images are displayed on a page.

>> **Import Design Package** enables you to import a design package developed by a third party or in-house designer.

>> **Navigation** enables you to manage navigation links and also change how the navigation behaves. You can configure global navigation (top of page) and also current navigation (left side of page). The Navigation settings page also enables you to change the sorting order of the navigational links and show and hide the ribbon.

>> **Master Page** is where you choose which master page the site uses and which master page the system uses. The system master page is for pages used by the system, such as when you view an app.

>> **Page Layouts and Site Templates** enables you to control which page layouts and site templates are available for users of the site. All the page layouts are contained in a gallery (see the later section, "Web Designer Galleries"). This settings page enables you to limit the page layouts and site templates that users of the site can use.

>> **Welcome Page** is the landing page for a publishing site. You can use this settings page to determine which page should be used for the landing page.

>> **Top Link bar** enables you to configure navigation at the top of the page.

>> **Tree View** is where you enable or disable the Quick Launch (left navigation) or turn on a special type of navigation on the left side that shows a tree of the site's content.

We cover changing the look and feel of your site later in this chapter and cover setting up navigation in Chapter 19.

The Look and Feel category, with the SharePoint Server Publishing feature activated, is shown in Figure 18-3.

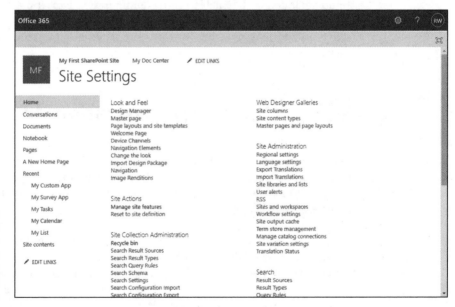

FIGURE 18-3:
The Site Settings page in SharePoint with the SharePoint Server Publishing feature activated.

WARNING

To activate the SharePoint Server Publishing feature in Site Collection Features, we first had to activate the SharePoint Server Enterprise Site Collection features (which also adds some links to the Site Settings page). This is a great example of how complicated SharePoint can quickly get once you leave the safety of the default behaviors. If you try to activate one feature that relies on another you might just receive an error that appears random, like we did. The only reason we knew to activate the Enterprise features first was based on experience and trial and error. This is why we claim that you never really *know* SharePoint. We still learn new things about it every day.

TIP

The term *feature* can be a bit confusing in SharePoint. You often hear people talk about functionality in terms of features. The term has a double meaning in SharePoint. The first meaning of feature is in the traditional sense, so you could say web-based administration is a feature of SharePoint. The second meaning is technical and specifically means a package of code that can be activated and deactivated (turned on and off).

Site Actions

The Site Actions section of the Site Settings page is where you manage the SharePoint features for the site. You can activate or deactivate particular features using the Manage Site Features link. This is important because some features show up only when certain features are active. For example, the Save Site as Template link and the Enable Search Configuration Export option show up when the SharePoint Server Publishing Feature is not active and disappear when it is active. In addition, you can reset the site to its original template definition or delete the site completely. (We cover activating and deactivating SharePoint features later in this chapter.)

Site Collection Administration

A *site collection* is a container for multiple sites. SharePoint allows organizations to delegate different levels of administration. For example, you might be a site collection administrator, and there might be an administrator for each site. This delegation of duty is important for offloading the work required to keep a large number of websites running smoothly.

The Site Collection Administration section of the Site Settings page is used to administer the overall site collection. The result is that any changes made to these settings pages affect all sites in the site collection. In addition, you can activate or deactivate a feature here to make it available or remove it from all the sites in the collection. The next step up in administration from site collection administrator is SharePoint farm administrator. A SharePoint farm administrator uses a tool called Central Administration, and the changes they make at the farm level affect all site collections in the SharePoint farm.

In order to see this section, you must be a site collection administrator.

There are a lot of links to settings pages in the Site Collection Administration section. Most of the links are similar in nature to the Site Administration section but affect all sites in the collection and not just the current site. Keep in mind that having a feature active or not causes links to appear or disappear. For example, activating the SharePoint Server Publishing Feature alters this settings page.

Microsoft Search

The Microsoft Search section includes a link to configure search settings. When you click the link you see a dashboard with the title Microsoft Search. This is a new feature and seems to still be in development. The dashboard shows things about search such as the query volume, impressions, and top queries.

Web Designer Galleries

A common theme throughout SharePoint is reusability. When you spend the time to develop something, you want to be able to use it over and over again. In SharePoint, reusability takes the form of things like data containers, templates, layouts, and solutions. The Web Designer Galleries section is where you manage all these reusable components. The components are stored in galleries and are designed to hold the pieces you use when designing your websites. With that in mind, Web Designer Galleries is such a perfect name. (What a nice break from other horribly named technology and acronyms like XSLT, HTML, and CSS.)

The Web Designer Galleries section of the Site Settings page includes the following links (note that the items you see may be different depending on which features you have active):

>> **Site Columns** is a gallery that contains columns you can use throughout the site. For example, you might create a column called Product Name that you could add to any app in the site. SharePoint ships with a number of existing site columns.

>> **Site Content Types** is a gallery that stores site content types (which are a collection of columns) so that you can use them throughout the site. For example, say you want to store all the information about a product. A product might contain many different data fields (called site columns) such as Product Name, Product Description, Product Bar Code, Product ID, and probably a lot more. You could create the site column for each data field and then group all of the data fields together into a content type. Now, rather than adding each data field to every app throughout the site, you can simply add the content

type when you want to work with a product, and all the columns come along with it. SharePoint ships with a number of content types out of the box. The content types are grouped into categories for easy reference.

» **Web Parts** is the gallery where all Web Parts (both out of the box and third-party) are stored. *Web Parts* are functional components that can be added to pages. (Web Parts are covered in Chapter 6.)

» **List Templates** is the gallery where an app saved as a template is stored. (List Templates is a bit of a naming snafu. In SharePoint, all lists and libraries are called apps, so this gallery would more aptly be named App Templates.) Each app based on a list has a link on the List Settings page. Under the Permissions and Management section is the Save List as Template link. When you save a list app as a template, it is then stored in the List Templates gallery. You can then take the template and upload it to this gallery on a different SharePoint site. After it's uploaded, you see a new app type on the Your Apps page, and you can then create apps based on the uploaded template. This is handy when you spend a lot of time building a list app just the way you want it and need to transfer it to another location.

» **Master Pages** is the gallery that contains all the master pages and page layouts. A *master page* is a template type page that provides a consistent look and feel throughout every page in the site. For example, notice how in every out-of-the-box SharePoint site, the navigation is on the left, there is a header at the top, and the pages are in the middle? That is all due to the master page that ships with SharePoint. (Creating custom master pages for your organization is best left to developers — master pages are a lot of work and can quickly turn into a nightmare project. SharePoint also requires the master page to contain certain things and behave in a certain way.) A page layout is a similar concept to a master page but is designed to be a template for a single page.

» **Themes** is the gallery that holds SharePoint themes. A *theme* is a collection of colors and fonts. When you apply a theme, your SharePoint site magically changes. A number of themes ship with SharePoint, and you can also have a web developer build your own custom themes.

» **Solutions** is a gallery that stores custom SharePoint solutions. A *SharePoint solution* is a bunch of custom-developed functionality all packaged together. The entire package is called a Web Solution Package (WSP). A SharePoint solution might be developed by your in-house developers or purchased from a third party. For example, the company Portal Integrators has developed a number of SharePoint solutions for clients all over the world. When they send the final product to a client, they send them the WSP. One of these solutions is geared towards Human Resources. If you purchase it, you get a WSP with all sorts of SharePoint functionality designed for Human Resources. Upload the WSP to this gallery, and your Human Resources department now loves SharePoint.

>> **Composed Looks** is a gallery that has to do with the look and feel of your site. A *composed look* is relatively new in SharePoint; it expands on the idea of themes and adds a background image and a master page. A number of composed looks ship with SharePoint. To give you a sneak peek, SharePoint ships with composed looks called Sea Monster, Breeze, and Immerse. You can look forward to spicing up your SharePoint site, if you so desire.

Site Administration

The Site Administration section of the Site Settings page is where you manage options that are specific to this individual site. The changes you make in this section won't affect other sites in the same site collection container. This is different than the Web Designer Galleries section of the Site Settings page, which includes components that are used throughout the site collection. So if you upload a solution, it will be available to other sites in the site collection.

REMEMBER

It's easy to get confused about which site the Site Administration page affects. This is especially true if you manage multiple sites or are a site collection administrator. When working with the Site Administration settings, make sure you are on the correct site.

The Site Administration section contains a large number of settings, so many that we can't cover them all in this book. We encourage you to explore these settings. Among the settings in the Site Administration section are Regional Settings, User Alerts, Workflow Settings, Term Store Management, Popularity Trends, and even Translation Status (which is only available when SharePoint Server Publishing Feature is active).

Refer to Figure 18-2 to see the Site Administration category without the Publishing Infrastructure activated and Figure 18-3 for the same section with the Publishing Infrastructure activated. This is an important concept in SharePoint. Like a magician, SharePoint often changes shape depending on the features you have activated.

Search

The Search section of the Site Settings page is where you manage all the search functionality for your site. Search can be an incredibly powerful productivity tool. It's worth spending the time to discover the capabilities of SharePoint search.

The Search section contains the following links:

>> **Result Sources** is a settings page where you define where SharePoint search should look for content. You can set sources to local SharePoint content, remote SharePoint content, Exchange, or any other external system that supports the OpenSearch protocol.

>> **Result Types** is where you define how a result will look based on the type of content displayed. For example, you might want the results of a person to look different from the results of an Excel or Word file. A number of prepackaged types ship with SharePoint, and you can also define your own. For example, you might want all your products to display in a search result in a particular way. You might want the picture on the left and a description and price on the bottom. You might then want a link to the product page and also a link to the product documentation. You define this with a custom search result that uses a custom template. Building these isn't simple, but it is possible with the right technical resources.

>> **Query Rules** is a place where you can promote important content into search results. This is valuable because most people are looking for common content. The search engine doesn't know the difference between an actual marketing template and a hundred other documents that might include the words *marketing template*. Using the query rules, you can let SharePoint know that the actual marketing template is what people are looking for when they search the term and that it should be displayed at the top. You can also show additional blocks of search results based on a search that you might think someone is trying to find. For example, if someone searches for *sales decks,* they might really mean *sales PowerPoint documents.* Query rules are very powerful, and it's worth taking the time to figure out the capabilities to provide the best search experience.

>> **Schema** is where you can manage properties and map the properties that the search engine uses when searching. A *property* is a piece of data about the thing that you search for. For example, if you search for a person, you might create a property to hold the person's department. The search engine can then reference that property when you look for a person in a particular department. Managing properties is only available to site collection administrators.

>> **Search Settings** is where you define the general search settings for the site. You can point the search results to a special site called a Search Center or a specific custom page you have developed to show search results. In addition, you can configure navigation for moving between search and the rest of the site.

>> **Searchable Columns** is a where you define which columns you want the search engine to reference when you search. You can use this settings page to let SharePoint know it should use a particular column of metadata when searching for content. The Searchable Columns link is available only when the SharePoint Server Publishing Feature is active.

>> **Search and Offline Availability** allows you to ban the site content from appearing in search results, set fine-grained search permissions, and even allow items from the site to be downloaded to offline clients.

>> **Configuration Import** lets you import a search configuration file. A search configuration file can contain all the settings and details that you have already spent the time to set up. You definitely wouldn't want to go through the entire exercise on every site, so you can use configuration files to move settings between sites.

>> **Configuration Export** is used to export a search configuration file after you have everything set up just how you want it. You can then use the Configuration Import setting to import on the new site.

SharePoint search is a very broad topic and it takes some time to get familiar with its capabilities. It is well worth the effort, however, because search can greatly improve your organization's productivity. (We discuss SharePoint search in more detail in Chapter 23.)

Getting a High-Level View of SharePoint Features

We have to admit that SharePoint features took us a long time to really understand. The reason is that a feature can do anything in SharePoint. A feature is just a collection of code that alters SharePoint in some manner. For example, say you want to write some code that adds a new item to the drop-down list that appears when you click the Settings gear icon. SharePoint lets you do this in code. Now, how do you deploy it to SharePoint? How do you let site administrators turn it on and off? The answer is that you package that code up in a SharePoint feature. When the feature is installed, an administrator can activate (turn on) or deactivate (turn off) the feature. The result is that your custom item appears in the Settings drop-down list when the feature is activated and disappears from the drop-down list when the feature is deactivated.

SharePoint ships with a number of features out of the box. In fact, features can be a major source of frustration. Take the earlier example of a feature that makes an item appear on a menu when the feature is activated. The way you reach navigation in SharePoint (covered in Chapter 19) depends on whether a particular SharePoint feature is activated. That feature is the SharePoint Server Publishing Infrastructure feature. This feature does a lot of things when you activate it, including altering the settings links for navigation. Before you activate the feature, the navigation links on the Site Settings page in the Look and Feel section are displayed as Quick Launch and Top Link bar. When you activate the SharePoint Server Publishing Infrastructure feature, it removes those two links and adds one called Navigation.

REMEMBER

You will find that the answer to a SharePoint question is often that it depends on which features are activated!

Turning Features On and Off

You turn features on and off by activating and deactivating them. Features are activated at two different levels. The first is a site collection; the second is a site. Features activated at the site collection level affect all sites contained within the site collection. Features activated at the site level only affect that particular site.

When a feature is active (turned on), a blue Active status indicator appears next to the feature on the right side of the page. See the Following Content row in Figure 18-4 and note the Active button in the status column. When a feature is inactive (turned off) the status column is empty, as shown in the second row (Getting Started) in Figure 18-4.

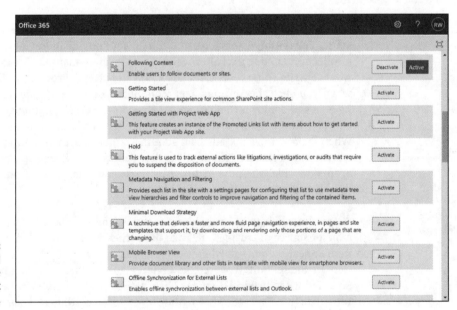

FIGURE 18-4:
Active and inactive SharePoint features.

To view a listing of all features for a particular site:

1. **Click the Settings gear icon, choose Site Contents, and then click the Site Settings button.**

   The Site Settings page appears.

2. **In the Site Actions section, click the Manage Site Features link.**

   A listing of all the features for this particular site is displayed. Each feature includes an icon, name, description, Activate/Deactivate button, and status column.

To view a listing of all features for a particular site collection:

1. **Click the Settings gear icon, choose Site Contents, and then click the Site Settings button.**

   The Site Settings page appears.

2. **In the Site Collection Administration section, click the Site Collection Features link.**

   A listing of all the features for this particular site collection is displayed. Each feature includes an icon, name, description, Activate/Deactivate button, and status column.

If you don't see the Site Collection Administration section on the Site Settings page, then you do not have Site Collection Administrator permissions.

WARNING

It's easy to get turned around when working with SharePoint features. For example, if you are in a subsite and go to the Site Settings page for that subsite, you don't see all the settings links in the Site Collection Administration section. You instead see a link that takes you to the settings page for the site collection. When you click that link, the Site Settings page reloads for the site collection, and you see all the Site Collection Settings links. (A site collection is also a site.) So if you then click the Manage Site Features link, you are actually managing the features scoped for only the site collection site and not the subsite where you originally started.

Exploring Common Features

Exploring all the features that ship with SharePoint could fill a book unto itself. Each feature on the settings page includes a name and description. We wish we could tell you that they are all straightforward, but they are not. Some features are massive and complicated and others are simple. For example, the

SharePoint Server Publishing Infrastructure feature can do a mind-boggling number of things. Conversely, the Site Feed feature simply enables the use of site feeds on a site.

A couple of the most common feature sets are the SharePoint Server Standard Site features and the SharePoint Server Enterprise Site features. These features include functionality for the different editions of SharePoint Server (Standard and Enterprise). The Standard Edition features include functionality such as user profiles and search, and the Enterprise Edition features include functionality such as Visio Services, Access Services, and Excel Services.

TIP

If you're looking for functionality such as Excel Services, and you can't find it, then check to make sure the SharePoint Server Enterprise Site features are activated for your site.

Extending SharePoint with Features

Microsoft ships a ton of features with SharePoint, but the product can always be extended further. If your organization has a dedicated development team, they can build features specific for your organization. For example, a company might use in-house developers to create custom SharePoint features for different groups within the company. For example, some features could provide functionality for the sales department, others for human resources, and still others for engineers. Each team in the company can then choose whether to activate or deactivate the features based on whether they need the specific features for their relevant workload on the SharePoint site.

Alternatively, third-party companies also develop features to extend SharePoint for a particular audience. After installing a third-party feature, it shows up right alongside the features that Microsoft ships with SharePoint.

Changing the Look and Feel of Your Site

Changing the look and feel of a site can be very powerful. The standard SharePoint colors work just fine, but perhaps you want to change the color palette for a holiday or to match your team's color scheme. SharePoint provides some very powerful features for changing the look and feel of your site. You don't need web designers or any specialized technical skills.

Usability experts have a lot to say about the look and feel of a site. After users are familiar with the look and feel of a site, it's best not to change it. Creating change when it isn't required causes a productivity loss. However, it can be a good idea to spice things up a bit by changing some of the colors for a holiday or special day. You just shouldn't go too crazy (unless you want your users to do the same).

A *composed look* in SharePoint is a collection of colors, fonts, and layouts that all come together to display your site with a certain look and feel. SharePoint comes with several predefined looks, and your organization may have added others to coordinate the look and feel of other sites.

To change the look of your site, follow these steps:

1. **Click the Settings gear icon, choose Site Contents, and then click the Site Settings button.**

2. **In the Look and Feel section of the Site Settings page, click the Change the Look link.**

    The Change the Look page appears, as shown in Figure 18-5, with a preview of many different site looks. Some examples include Sea Monster, Lime, Nature, City, Orbit, Immerse, and Wood. Each preview pane shows you a sample of the site look.

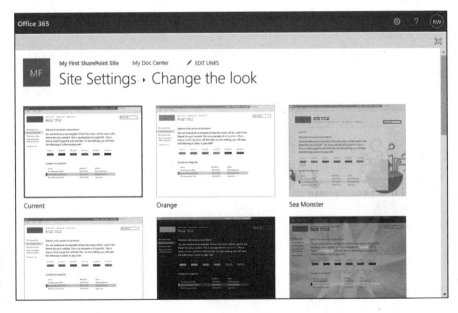

FIGURE 18-5:
The Change the Look settings page.

3. **To try out a look, simply click the preview image.**

The preview image is enlarged and settings are displayed so you can change the background image, the color palette, the site layout, and the font combinations used in the site, as shown in Figure 18-6.

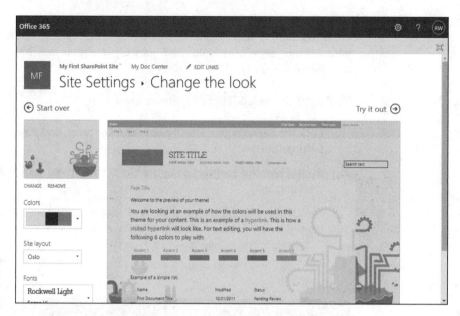

FIGURE 18-6:
Changing settings
on a particular
look.

4. **Click the Try It Out link in the top-right corner of the page to see what your actual site will look like.**

SharePoint does some work and shows your site with the new look in place. The top of the page lets you decide whether to keep the site (by clicking Yes, Keep It) or to revert to the original settings and make more changes (by clicking No, Not Quite There), as shown in Figure 18-7.

5. **When you're satisfied with the new look of your site, click Yes, Keep It.**

Your site loads with the new look and feel.

TIP

If you want to go back to the original look of a SharePoint site, you can always change back to the Office look.

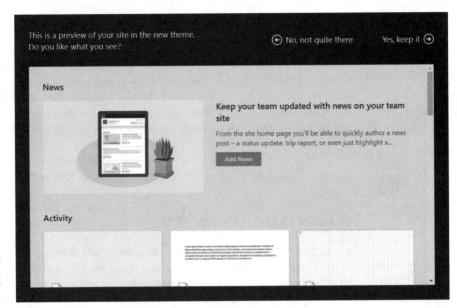

FIGURE 18-7:
Previewing a
particular look for
your site.

A note on fonts

The most common fonts used in web design used to be of two families — ones with *serifs* (the strokes that extend from letters), such as Times New Roman, and *sans-serif* (those without strokes from the letters), such as Arial and Verdana. You couldn't guarantee what fonts users had on their computers, so those fonts were a safe default. They're also recognized as fonts with good readability. (For those reading this book that can't wait to pick Gigi, Jokerman, or Curlz MT, and you know who you are, you may want to hold up and read the "A word on usability" section, later in this chapter.)

The best practice when we first learned to design websites was that serif fonts were good for paragraph text and sans-serif fonts were good for very large and very small text (like headings and footer notes). The trend today for many sites is to use only sans-serif fonts, or in the case of SharePoint, the Segoe UI Light and Segoe UI fonts.

Many companies have a large amount of font styles available on employee computers, especially as the options in Microsoft Office have grown. However, if your users don't have the font you selected, the browser will convert to a default font.

When you're customizing a look (as we describe earlier in this chapter in "Changing the Look and Feel of Your Site"), you can choose different font combinations. The font combinations have been matched for each packaged site look.

A trend in Microsoft technology is the use of Segoe UI fonts. The Segoe font family is used across all Microsoft products such as Windows 10, the new Surface tablet and Surface Book, and of course Office. In Windows 11, Microsoft stuck with the same font family but instead of the classic Segoe font, a new font called Segoe UI Variable is used. The variable font technology adjusts the look and feel of the font based on things like the device and high-definition displays. This improves readability by adjusting for small or large screens, taking into account screen resolution.

TIP

The default look of a SharePoint site uses the Segoe font family.

A word on usability

We suppose the reason you have a SharePoint site is that you and your team are *using* it, and a big part of using a site is being able to read it. The following common checkpoints for websites might apply to your site look choices or perhaps your content on the Team site pages as well:

>> **Make sure there is a strong contrast between the background colors and the text.** Dark text on a white background is generally considered the easiest to read. The second best is very light text on a very dark background.

One area of SharePoint that this has been a problem with in the past is the Quick Launch menu or left navigation area, where the contrast between the background and links isn't distinct enough. Be careful with your selections. Even if red and green are holiday colors, red text on a green background isn't very readable.

>> **Choose a font that's simple and easy to read.** No matter that the Chiller font looks cool at Halloween, a whole page of Chiller will have your users running for the door, or at the very least not reading your site.

>> **Use only a few colors.** Even though it seems like the theme palette has a lot of color options, many of them are similar in hue. Using the entire rainbow makes it hard for your users to focus on what's important.

>> **Make link colors obvious.** If the text is black and links are navy blue or brown, it becomes difficult to identify them.

>> **Make the *followed* (or visited) link color different enough from the unvisited link color.** A red hyperlink that changes to maroon when visited may not be enough of a visual cue to users that they've followed that link.

Microsoft took the liberty of helping you choose decent combinations when it created the out-of-the-box looks. Some of the looks are downright scary, though. Don't believe me? Try changing your site to the Sea Monster look and see how your users run away, or maybe run to you, screaming.

The benefits of composed looks

Composed looks are a big step up from previous versions of SharePoint. Composed looks allow you to change the background image, colors, site layout, and fonts. Best of all, composed looks can dramatically change the look and feel of your site with just a few clicks of the mouse. You don't need to worry about breaking SharePoint by fiddling with a master page.

Whenever a discussion of branding occurs, you should take note to pose a major question. Can you achieve what you need with an out-of-the-box composed look, or do you need to create a completely custom look? If you need a completely custom composed look, then be prepared to bring in web designers and developers. Depending on your needs, a custom look can be a considerable investment and involves creating custom master pages, CSS files, and themes.

The Composed Looks link is found on the Site Settings page in the Web Designer Galleries section.

Checking Out SharePoint Metrics

Once you have a site set up, the next thing you might want to keep an eye on is its usage. A new feature of SharePoint allows you to see statistics about the site such as when people are using the site by date and by time of the day.

To access Site Usage, click the Settings gear icon and then choose Site Usage. The metrics for the site appear and you can click around and find out all sorts of things about how people are using the SharePoint site.

Chapter **19**

Configuring Site Navigation

SharePoint automatically provides standard navigation. When you create a site based on a template, you already have navigational links to pages such as your Documents app, the home page, and the contents of the site. As you get more advanced with SharePoint, you may want to start modifying the default navigation and customizing it to fit your needs.

In this chapter, you see how to configure SharePoint navigation. You add your own links not only to SharePoint pages, but also to anywhere on the World Wide Web. You discover the differences between dynamic and static navigation and you delve into some of the options available when configuring navigation in your SharePoint site. In addition, you learn about navigation when the SharePoint Server Publishing Infrastructure feature is activated for the site collection. Without this feature, you can simply add, remove, and order links. With this feature activated, a whole world of SharePoint navigation is flung open.

Changing Team Site Navigation

Microsoft has done a good job of making navigation updates fairly simple for the Team site. You can add navigation to the Quick Launch menu on the left side of the page, and you can add navigation within any SharePoint page using a Web Part called Quick Links.

Later in the chapter we cover adding navigation when using a site that has the SharePoint Server Publishing Infrastructure feature enabled. If you don't have this feature enabled, navigation is much more straightforward.

TIP

You can also link sites together using hub sites. Hub sites lets you group SharePoint sites together into a hub. Hub sites are covered in Chapter 5.

Staying local with Quick Launch

SharePoint Team sites display a list of navigational links along the left side of the page in the Quick Launch menu. Quick Launch, also known as the Current Navigation, displays links to featured site content such as apps and pages. By default, the Team site Quick Launch includes the following links, though keep in mind that Microsoft is known to change these from time to time:

>> **Home:** A link back to the main start page for the Team site.

>> **Conversations:** A link to Microsoft Outlook, which includes a feature called Groups where you and others can have conversations, share files, and connect apps. In our opinion, this sounds a lot like Microsoft Teams and we expect Teams will take over this functionality in the future.

>> **Documents:** A direct link to the Documents app.

>> **Notebook:** A link to the OneNote notebook for the site.

>> **Pages:** A link to the pages for the site.

>> **Site Contents:** A link to the Site Contents page, which shows all the apps in the site.

>> **Recycle Bin:** A place to retrieve items that have been deleted.

TIP

The Quick Launch navigation takes up valuable space. If you are on a smaller screen, the menu is hidden for you by default. You can test this by dragging your web browser to be narrower and watch as the menu disappears. When the menu disappears, you access it by clicking the app launcher icon that appears in the top-left corner, as shown in Figure 19-1.

App launcher icon

FIGURE 19-1:
FIGURE 19-1:
Expand the left
navigation pane
on smaller
screens.

The items that appear in the Quick Launch are determined by the apps you add to the site and the links you manually add to the Quick Launch. Each app contained in a site can display a link to itself on the Quick Launch.

You can easily add or remove an app from the Quick Launch using the app's settings:

1. **Browse to the app you want to add or remove from the Quick Launch.**

   For example, click the Documents app on the Site Contents page.

2. **Click the Settings gear icon located in the top-right corner of the page and then click Library Settings (or List Settings if it is a List-based app).**

   The Library Settings page appears.

3. **In the General Settings section, click the List Name, Description, and Navigation link.**

   The General Settings page appears.

4. **In the Navigation section, indicate whether to include the list or library on the Quick Launch by selecting Yes or No.**

5. **Click the Save button.**

   The links in the Quick Launch update to reflect your changes.

You also can disable the Quick Launch entirely for a site. You can add a site hierarchy called a *Tree View* to the left navigation panel instead of the Quick Launch. If you leave the Quick Launch enabled, the Tree View appears below the Quick Launch. To perform either of these tasks, follow these steps:

1. **Click the Settings gear icon, choose Site Contents, and then click Site Settings for the site you want to manage.**

2. **In the Look and Feel section, click the Navigation Elements link.**

   The Tree View/Navigation Elements page appears. Figure 19-2 shows the Tree View/Navigation Elements page.

3. **Choose whether to enable the Quick Launch or the Tree View or both by selecting the Enable Quick Launch and/or Enable Tree View check boxes.**

4. **Click OK.**

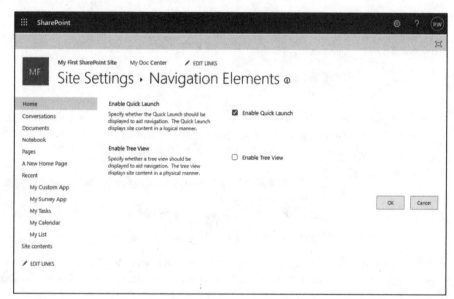

FIGURE 19-2: The Tree View/ Navigation Elements page is used to enable or disable the Quick Launch and the Tree View.

Adding quick links to a page

The Team site includes a section called Quick Links by default, as shown in Figure 19-3. You can add links to this section to make the site easier to use. For example, you might want to add a link out to a help article on `docs.microsoft.com` or you might want to add links for your partners. You can add any link to the Quick Links section.

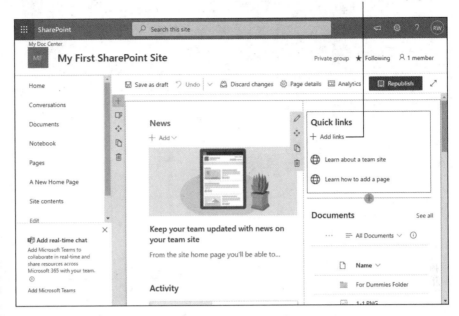

Click to add links to the page

FIGURE 19-3:
Adding links to
the Quick Links
Web Part.

TIP

The default Quick Links section is really just a Web Part that you can add to any page. We cover adding Web Parts to pages in Chapter 6.

To add links to the Quick Links Web Part, follow these steps:

1. **Navigate to the page that contains the Quick Links Web Part.**

2. **Click the Edit button in the upper-right corner to enter Edit mode for the page.**

3. **Click Add Links at the top of the Quick Links Web Part, as shown in Figure 19-3.**

4. **Choose a link to add.**

   You can add a link to any recent locations, to stock images, to a OneDrive document, to another SharePoint site, to a document you upload, or to an actual web link. In this example we will add a link to the docs.microsoft.com website, as shown in Figure 19-4.

5. **Once you have the link in place click Insert.**

   The link will be added to the Web Part and you will be presented with the details of the link (see Figure 19-5). Here you can change the title, the thumbnail, and provide alternative text.

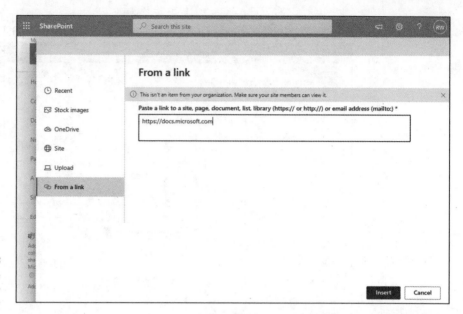

FIGURE 19-4:
Adding the docs.
microsoft.
com link.

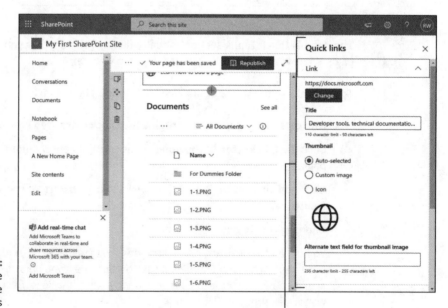

FIGURE 19-5:
The details pane
for a link in the
Quick Links
Web Part.

The link details

6. **Click the close button at the top right of the pane to close the details pane for the link.**

7. **Click the Republish button, which appears in the top-right corner of the page, to publish the page with the new link.**

The final result is shown in Figure 19-6. Now anyone that visits the site can click the link that was just added to open a new web browser tab that takes them to the Microsoft technical documentation site.

The newly added link

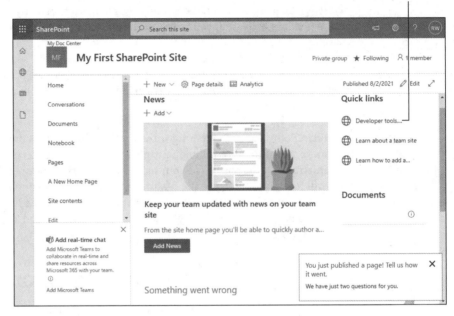

FIGURE 19-6:
The result of adding a link to the Quick Links Web Part on the home page of a Team site.

MICROSOFT 365 NAVIGATION

All SharePoint Online sites have a common navigational element that appears at the top of the site's page. The component is called the app launcher and it looks similar to a "waffle." The button is called a waffle button because it looks like a grilled waffle. When you click it, you see all of the Microsoft 365 apps you can use, such as Outlook, OneDrive, Word, and Excel, to name a few. (If you are using SharePoint On-Premises, you won't see the app launcher icon.)

The Microsoft 365 apps in the launcher menu are constantly changing and new apps are constantly being added to them. It is worth it to spend some time looking through these apps and getting a feel for all of the things you get with your Microsoft 365 subscription.

Taking on Advanced Navigation

SharePoint navigation is fairly straightforward until you turn on the SharePoint Server Publishing Infrastructure feature. This feature is activated and deactivated at the site collection level and also the site level. When the feature is not active for the site, you manage SharePoint navigation in a straightforward manner. When it is activated, you manage SharePoint navigation in a more advanced manner. In addition, the names of the navigation settings links on the Site Settings page change when the feature is activated. To see exactly how the SharePoint Server Publishing Infrastructure changes the names of the links, check out Chapter 18 where we turn it on and take a look at what changes it makes to Site Settings.

TIP

The SharePoint Server Publishing Infrastructure feature is activated for a site collection first and then for individual sites within the site collection. If you're a site administrator, it may be out of your hands whether this feature is available or not. You will know right away if the feature is activated by looking at the links in the Look and Feel section on the Site Settings page. If you see the Navigation link, the Feature is activated. If instead you see the Quick Launch and Top Link Bar links, the feature is not active.

Configuring SharePoint navigation

The navigation options in a publishing site adds additional configuration options for managing SharePoint navigation. There are two kinds of navigation that can be managed:

» **Global navigation** is the primary navigation your site visitors use to reach the main areas in your site, no matter where they are in your site. Global navigation is usually positioned somewhere at the top of the page and is consistent across every page in your site.

» **Current navigation** is contextual navigation that is usually found in the body of the page, usually on the left, and provides access to pages within each major area of your site. This navigation is considered contextual because the navigation items may change, depending on where the visitor is in the site.

SharePoint provides two navigation menus that correspond with global and current navigation. The Top Link Bar is the global navigation menu that's usually present at the top of publishing pages. The Quick Launch menu provides the current navigation that appears along the left side of most pages.

SharePoint's publishing site assumes that you want global and current navigation menus created dynamically based on site hierarchy. To that end, configuring navigation in a publishing site requires two things:

» **A site hierarchy that matches your navigation requirements.** In other words, you have subsites for the major items in your global navigation and pages for the items below. Any time you want to create a new grouping of pages in the navigation menu, you have to create a new subsite.

This often leads to extensive nesting of sites, which we recommend you avoid. This is one reason that people start looking for alternative approaches to navigation.

» **The ability to think in terms of the current site you're setting navigation options for, its parent site, its sibling sites, and any child sites that may exist.** This can be extremely confusing to people, which is one reason why we see many people abandon dynamic navigation. It's too hard to keep track of what's happening where.

Configuring global navigation

In most publishing sites, you want all pages and sites to display the same navigation settings. SharePoint can dynamically display all subsites and pages within a subsite in your global navigation. Pages display in a drop-down list.

Each site in your publishing site can have its own global configuration settings. So you need to perform the following steps for each site. The settings you make in a subsite, such as whether to display pages, impacts navigation for the entire site, not just what the visitor sees when they're on that site. Follow these steps:

1. Browse to the publishing site or subsite for which you want to configure global navigation.

2. Click the Settings gear icon, choose Site Contents, and then click Site Settings.

3. Click the Navigation link in the Look and Feel section.

   The Site Navigation Settings page appears.

4. In a parent site, such as the top-level site, use the Global Navigation section to indicate whether you want to display navigation items that are below the parent site.

   Select the Show Subsites options to display each subsite in the global navigation. To show the pages that have been created in the parent site, select Show Pages.

TIP

Scroll down to the Structural Navigation: Editing and Sorting section of the page to get a sneak peek at your global navigation hierarchy.

5. **In a child site, use the Global Settings section to determine whether the subsite will display the same global navigation items as its parent site.**

Select the Show Subsites and Show Pages options to display subsites and pages on the current site and any other site (parent or child) that opts to display navigation for the site you are configuring.

REMEMBER

A child site can be a parent site to another site. For example, you might create a subsite in your publishing site called MyPubSubSite. If you enable Show Subsites and Show Pages, the top-level home site will also display any pages and subsites of the MyPubSubSite navigation option.

6. **Click OK to save your global navigation settings.**

TIP

We usually have two browser windows open when we configure navigation. We use one browser window to configure the navigation and another to view the changes we made.

The subsite, MyPubSubSite, is configured to show pages. Table 19-1 summarizes typical global navigation settings.

TABLE 19-1

Typical Global Navigation Settings

When You Select This Option	This Appears in Global Navigation
Select the Show Subsites check box in each site in your hierarchy.	Subsites automatically appear in the global navigation as soon as they're created. If this option isn't selected in the parent site, no subsites appear in your global navigation.
Select the Show Pages check box in each site in the hierarchy.	Pages automatically appear in the global navigation as soon as they're approved. If this option is selected in the parent site, the parent's sites pages appear as siblings to any subsites in the global navigation.
Select the Display the Same Navigation Items as the Parent option.	All sites have the same global navigation. Make sure you select this option in each site's global navigation settings.

Configuring current navigation

Configuring current navigation settings for each site is similar to global navigation. You have the same options to automatically show pages and subsites. As shown in Figure 19-7, you have these options to determine what items appear in the site's current navigation:

- **Display the Same Navigation Items as the Parent Site:** This option displays the current navigation items using the settings of the parent site.

- **Managed Navigation:** This option enables you to manage navigation using a set of terms you define called Managed Metadata. When you select this option, your site will show sites and subsites based on the terms you have defined and not the subsites and pages in the site. When you select the Managed Navigation option, the option to show subsites and pages disappears.

- **Structural Navigation:** This option gives you the choice to display subsites and pages below the current site.

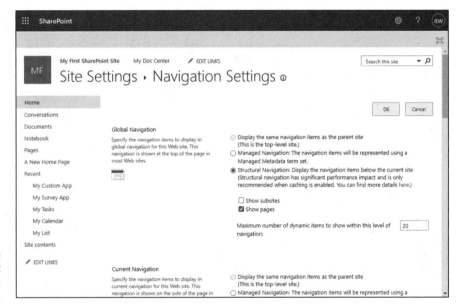

FIGURE 19-7:
Current navigation options.

REMEMBER

Choosing the Show Pages and Show Subsites options in the Global Navigation section makes navigation items appear for pages and subsites in the top navigation. Choosing the Show Pages and Show Subsites option in the Current Navigation section shows the navigational links in the left navigation.

Configuring Static Navigation

Most clients we work with don't want pages and subsites showing automatically in their navigation. They usually want a static menu that doesn't change when someone publishes an article page.

You can opt to use a static navigation menu by deselecting the Show Pages and Show Subsites options in the navigation settings for each site. You can then manually enter whatever navigation you want to appear in the global and current navigation for each site.

To manually configure your navigation items:

1. **Browse to the site you want to configure, choose the Settings drop-down (gear icon), select Site Settings, and then click the Navigation link in the Look and Feel section.**

2. **Scroll down to the Structural Navigation: Editing and Sorting section.**

   This section shows a hierarchy of your global and current navigation items, as shown in Figure 19-8. The items you see here depend on the settings you make in the global navigation and current navigation settings of the page. For example, if you select the Show Subsites option in the Global Navigation section, you see subsites listed in this section of the page.

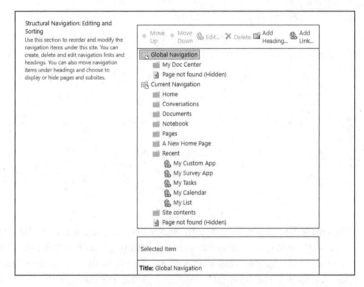

FIGURE 19-8:
View the navigation hierarchy.

3. **To add a new navigation to your global or current navigation, click the place in the hierarchy where you want to add the item.**

4. **Click the Add Heading button to add a new heading, or click the Add Link button to add a new link.**

   Figure 19-9 shows the Navigation Heading dialog box. The Add Link dialog box looks exactly the same. A heading doesn't require a web address or URL. That is, you can use a heading to contain links without requiring that the heading point to anything in the browser.

5. **Enter the details for the navigation item.**

   You have these options:

   - *Title:* The text you enter in this field appears in the navigation menu.

   - *URL:* Enter the page where the item links to. This is an optional field for headings.

   - *Open Link in New Window:* Select this check box to open the link in a new window.

   - *Description:* The text you enter in this field displays as a tooltip when someone hovers the cursor over the navigation item.

   - *Audience:* Use this text box to filter the navigation item so that only members of the selected audience can see the navigation item.

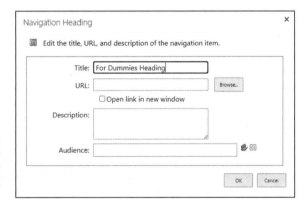

FIGURE 19-9:
Adding a new heading to your current navigation.

TIP

Get creative about adding navigation items. We often add static links to the current navigation for common tasks that people need to perform, such as managing a group's membership.

6. **Click OK to save your heading or link.**

   The heading appears in the site's navigation hierarchy, as shown in Figure 19-10. Use the Move Up or Move Down buttons to reposition the item in the hierarchy.

7. **Repeat Steps 3–6 to add more links and headings to your navigation hierarchy.**

8. **Use the Edit button to make additional changes to the hierarchy.**

   Click the Edit button to modify the Title, Description, URL, or Audience for a navigation item.

9. **Click OK to save your navigation settings.**

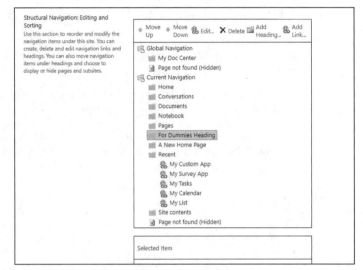

FIGURE 19-10:
Your item appears in the navigation hierarchy.

Navigating with Web Parts

It'd be naïve to expect that you only need to use two kinds of site navigation. In reality, webmasters and site visitors expect lots of ways to get to content. In Chapter 6, we discuss the Content Rollup Web Parts. These Web Parts are often used to provide the additional navigation options that you want to see inside your web pages, not just in the header and along the side.

One such Web Part, the Table of Contents Web Part, can be used to create a sitemap. A considered best practice is to provide a sitemap, and the Table of Contents Web Part dynamically generates it for you.

TECHNICAL STUFF

Advanced web developers can use a custom master page to control where the site's navigation menu appears on the page. For example, if you want the current navigation on the right instead of the left, you can have it moved there in the master page. Customizing master pages is not an easy task and should be left to SharePoint master page experts. SharePoint expects certain controls and behaviors from a master page, and if it is customized in the wrong way, SharePoint will throw errors.

Understanding Managed Navigation

In many cases, people want more control over the site navigation than SharePoint provides out of the box. Publishing sites provide great options for dynamically displaying the navigation based on the site's hierarchy, but what if you want to display navigation based on metadata?

SharePoint includes Managed Navigation. Managed Navigation allows you to drive SharePoint navigation based on managed metadata. Managed metadata is hierarchal in nature and is managed at the site collection level. When you tie navigation to this hierarchy, you can be sure that every site in the site collection will subscribe to the same structure. When you need to update the hierarchy, you update it for the entire site collection, and every site automatically updates navigation as well. The Managed Navigation option can be seen on the Navigation Settings page shown earlier in Figure 19-7.

If you still need more navigation control, you can always bring in developers. SharePoint is built on standard web technologies and allows developers to use special controls for modifying navigation. Because this involves writing code, it's best left to professional developers — but you should at least know it's possible.

Chapter **20**

Creating a Client or Partner Portal

Creating and using a client or partner portal based on SharePoint is now easier than ever. SharePoint takes away all of the difficulties in setting up the infrastructure, freeing you to work on the shared content with your clients and partners. In the first part of this chapter, you get such a portal set up in just a few minutes. You invite new users to the portal and figure out how to get them started. Finally, you explore options for creating a public-facing website.

Sharing a Site with External Guests

Microsoft has dramatically streamlined the process for sharing a SharePoint site with external guest users. For example, you might want to share a SharePoint site with clients or partners. In the past this required a significant amount of SharePoint knowledge and caused a tremendous amount of frustration for people.

The simplest way to create a client or partner portal is to create a site dedicated to those particular guests and then share the site with them. A more advanced way would be to fine-tune which users can see which areas of a site (which we cover in more depth in Chapter 21).

To create a guest portal you can use with clients or partners:

1. **Create a SharePoint site that you will dedicate to a client or partner (see Chapter 5).**

2. **Navigate to the site in your web browser.**

3. **Click the Settings gear icon in the upper-right corner of the screen and choose Site Permissions, as shown in Figure 20-1.**

   The Permissions pane opens.

Gear icon

FIGURE 20-1:
Selecting Site Permissions from the Settings menu.

Site permissions link

TIP

SharePoint changes the gear icon drop-down menu items depending on where you are in the SharePoint site. If you do not see Site Permissions in the drop-down menu, make sure you are on the Home page of the SharePoint site and that you are an administrator in order to see Site Permissions.

4. **Click the Invite People button and choose Share Site Only, as shown in Figure 20-2.**

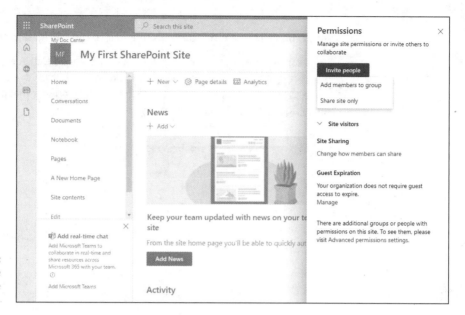

FIGURE 20-2:
Choosing the
option to invite
people to the site.

5. **Type the email address of the person you want to share the site with.**

When you enter a valid email address, the email will appear as a button under the text box, as shown in Figure 20-3.

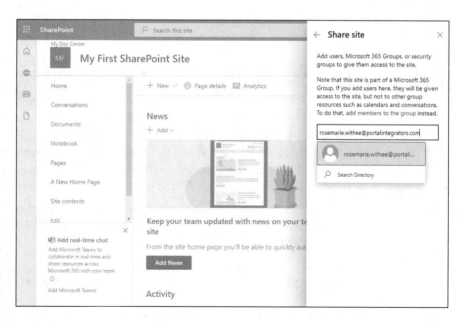

FIGURE 20-3:
Entering an email
address of the
person to invite
to the site.

6. **Click the validated email address to add it to the Permissions pane.**

Figure 20-4 shows the result. By default, a user is added with edit permissions with the assumption you want to use the site to collaborate. If you want to only allow the user to read and not edit the site, select Edit under that person's email address and change the setting to Read.

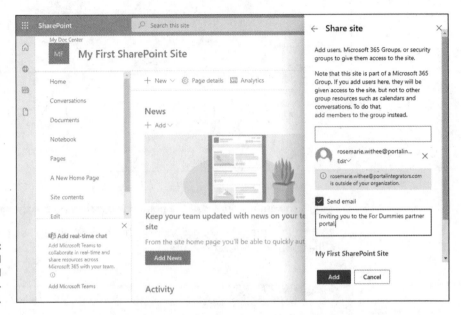

FIGURE 20-4:
The email address is added in the Permissions pane.

7. **Type a message to the person in the message box and then click Add.**

The person will be sent a message with a link to the site. Figure 20-5 shows the message received in a Microsoft Outlook email client.

When your guests click the link, they will be presented with a screen to sign into the SharePoint site. Your guests will need to use a Microsoft account or an existing Microsoft 365 account (which they might already have as part of their own organizations). Figure 20-6 shows the sign-in screen in a web browser.

Once your guests sign in with their existing Microsoft account or Microsoft 365 credentials, they will have access to the SharePoint site you have set up in your own Microsoft 365 tenant.

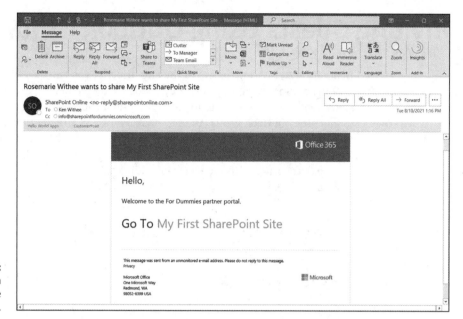

FIGURE 20-5:
Receiving a SharePoint invite in Gmail.

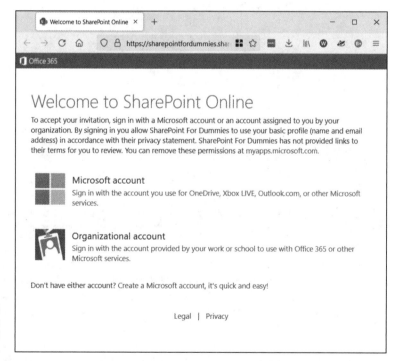

FIGURE 20-6:
Signing in to access a shared SharePoint site.

Inviting Guests Using Outlook Groups

In addition to inviting guests to the site directly, you can also invite people using Outlook groups. To do so you simply choose Add Members to Group in the Permissions pane (refer back to Figure 20-2) and then add the person just like you would to any other Outlook group. In fact, SharePoint has already automatically created an Outlook group for you to use, and you can add people by simply going to Outlook in your web browser (select it from the Apps menu that looks like a waffle in the top-left corner of the screen) and adding them to the Outlook group, as shown in Figure 20-7.

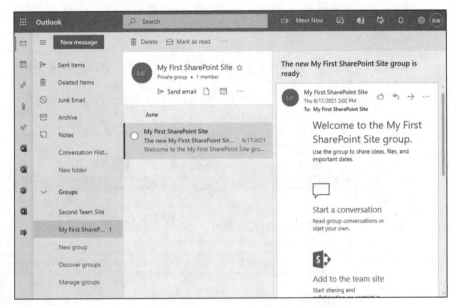

FIGURE 20-7:
Adding a user to the Outlook group for your SharePoint site.

Planning for Your Client or Guest Portal

In the previous section you invited guests to your SharePoint site in just a few minutes. This is great if you just want to get up and going and don't have time to put into a lot of planning. This section goes through some of the items you will want to consider when making a plan for your SharePoint site for your clients or partners.

Planning for a client portal is similar to planning for a regular SharePoint site in that you have to determine what the site will be used for and the types of activities that need to be supported in that environment. Here are a few items worth noting when planning your Microsoft 365 environment:

>> **The number of resources and the amount of storage space you have available in Microsoft 365 is limited.** Storage is easy to understand, but resources are not on the surface. Basically, a number of physical and virtual resources on the hardware and operating system are monitored daily by SharePoint Online. The types of items measured include counts, seconds, numbers, CPU cycles, bytes, threads, and Windows handles (which are technical data structures and that is probably already more than you wanted to know). Each of these items has a hard upper limit based on the hardware that is handling the requests, and so you're granted a set number of resources per Microsoft 365 subscription. You must allocate those resources based on what you think each site collection will need on a daily basis. You can change the allocation at any time, but remember that your total resource (and storage) allocations for your SharePoint subscription remain the same.

TIP

The SharePoint Online service administrator can set the storage limits for site collections and sites created by users. SharePoint storage limits depend on a number of different factors, but, in general, the storage is 1TB (terabyte) plus 10GB (gigabyte) per additional business or enterprise user license. You can find all of the specifics by searching for "SharePoint Online and OneDrive for Business software boundaries and limits" using your favorite search engine. Look for a link that is on docs.microsoft.com for official guidance. Also, keep in mind you can always buy more SharePoint storage if you need it.

REMEMBER

SharePoint Online is constantly being updated, and it's entirely possible that the limits will change. Make sure to check the Microsoft 365 website for the latest limits and pricing information.

>> **You don't have control over some of the configuration items in SharePoint Online that you have for SharePoint On-Premises.** Most of the differences are at the farm administration level, but it's something to keep in mind. If you're dead set on particular functionality, then you want to make sure it's available in SharePoint Online.

TIP

Keep in mind that SharePoint Online is a product in motion. Microsoft is constantly updating and tweaking the user interface and location of components. The concepts are usually the same, but if you see something a little different than we describe, you might have to hunt around because you are likely seeing a new change Microsoft has made.

In addition, you should consider a number of things when planning out your SharePoint Online environment. These include

>> Your DNS name, if you need to have a distinct URL to access your public-facing website. (We cover some more information about configuring the DNS name later in the chapter.)

» Whether you will allow external users to be able to edit the site and collaborate with you and others on the site or whether you want these users to have read-only access.

Launching Your Portal

If you are launching your client or partner relationships from scratch, then you are already done! Just invite them to the SharePoint site and start working. If, on the other hand, you have been working with your clients or partners using other tools, then you will need to think about how to get the site launched and usable. For example, you might need to migrate an immense amount of pre-existing documents and information in your network drives or on your local computer into the site so that your clients and partners can access it.

Here are a few approaches you can take to get your portal providing value as quickly as possible:

» **Have your users do the work.** This is a fairly low-maintenance version of migrating content from one SharePoint environment to the next because you put the burden of content on the users' shoulders. As long as your clients and partners can add content to the site, they can upload all of their content there going forward. Don't try to put a burden on yourself by having your clients email you documents and then you uploading them; instead, train your clients to upload the documents directly to the portal. It is easier on your clients and partners, and easy on you, too.

» **Help users devise a plan to migrate their content or at least identify content (and sites) that need to be migrated.** This approach takes a lot more time, but may be the most effective way to get users migrated completely and according to your timeline. It may also require some coercive tactics, such as the threat of turning off existing servers or making their content read-only, but at least it shouldn't be an outright scramble at the end. For example, if you have been using a shared folder system, such as Dropbox, then move that content to your new client or partner portal as part of your launch strategy.

TIP

Our recommendation is to start using your new portal as soon as possible. Send the invites to your clients and partners and get everyone used to making it the one stop shop for working with you on content.

Creating a Public-Facing Website

If you have Microsoft 365 and you need a public-facing website, you will need to work with a third-party website provider. Microsoft used to provide public-facing websites based on SharePoint, but it discontinued the option. For a transitional period Microsoft was offering a discount at GoDaddy and Wix, but that seems to have been discontinued as well.

The good news is that creating a public-facing website has almost become a commodity in this day and age. Personally, we like to use WordPress on a hosting site like SiteGround (`www.siteground.com`). SiteGround is not the only option, though. There are seemingly hundreds and hundreds of web hosting companies. We like WordPress because it provides a powerful platform. If you just need a basic website and want to get up and running quickly, then check out Wix.

Chapter **21**

Securing SharePoint

SharePoint is a great tool for storing documents and managing calendars and contacts. But how do you know your information is secure? Although Microsoft makes sure the actual servers and backend network and databases are secure, managing the security for your SharePoint content falls on you as the site administrator.

When securing your site, you need to perform three basic tasks. We list them here in the order of the frequency you perform these tasks, from most often to seldom:

» **Manage SharePoint group membership:** When it comes to that dreaded time to manage SharePoint security, what you really need to be thinking is, "To which SharePoint group do I need to add this person?" If you don't have an existing group and you find yourself descending into a morass of permission levels, inheritance, and other such incomprehensible stuff, back away from your browser. The reality is that assigning permissions — breaking inheritance and assigning groups — should be a rare event, if done right.

» **Assign permissions to sites, apps, or folders:** Deciding which groups get access to what is an important task, and one you only want to think about infrequently — most usually at the time (or ideally before) you create your site. In other words, granting Read Only, Edit, and Delete permissions to the content in your site should be a set-it-and-forget-it task if you make those assignments to SharePoint groups. When these permission assignments are granted to your SharePoint groups, you only have to manage who is in each group.

>> **Manage administrative access:** Even less frequently do you need to grant or revoke administrative access to your site.

In this chapter, we explain these three tasks.

Using SharePoint Groups

SharePoint uses groups to manage the process of granting someone access to the content in a site. Each *SharePoint group* maps to a set of permissions that define the tasks that a user can perform. Most users fall into one of SharePoint's three default groups:

>> **Site Visitors:** Grants read-only access to the site and allows users to create alerts. Users who need read access to a site but don't need to contribute content are visitors.

>> **Site Members:** Confers the Contribute permission level for users, which allows them to add, edit, and modify items and browse sites. Most end users fall into this category for a site.

>> **Site Owners:** Grants full control. A site owner may or may not use the site on a regular basis, but the site owner can delegate administrative and design tasks to others. Also, a site owner may or may not be a technical person.

REMEMBER

Access to your site and its content is managed through *group membership.* Adding and removing users from SharePoint groups is the most efficient way of granting and revoking permissions.

A top-level site has a single set of Site Visitors, Site Members, and Site Owners. These three groups are created and named when the top-level site is created. All the apps and subsites that are created below the top-level site use these groups and have the same set of people inside the groups. By default, all the content and subsites in your top-level site have the same permissions, dubbed *permissions inheritance.*

WARNING

Microsoft recently introduced the Microsoft 365 Groups service as a default for new sites. The groups in Microsoft 365 add another way for people to access your SharePoint sites. You manage the Microsoft 365 Groups in Microsoft Outlook. At the same time, the traditional SharePoint groups are still active, too. So be careful when reviewing access to your sites. Users can have access to a SharePoint site through the traditional SharePoint groups, the new Microsoft 365 Groups, or both! We have seen a common scenario where users are removed from Microsoft 365 Groups but not from the SharePoint groups and thus have unintended access to a site.

Adding users to a group

For people to access your site, you must share it with them by adding them to a group. This can be to one of the Microsoft 365 Groups or to a SharePoint group. In Chapter 5 you learn how to share a site with a user. This default method for sharing a site adds the person to the associated Microsoft 365 Group (which you manage in Outlook or on the web at `https://admin.microsoft.com`). You can also add a user to the SharePoint groups. For example, to add users to the *Site* Members group, follow these steps:

1. **Log in to the site as a Site Owner, and then click the Settings gear icon in the upper-right corner of the page and select Site Permissions.**

   The Permissions pane appears, as shown in Figure 21-1.

2. **Click Advanced Permission Settings and then click Grant Permissions on the Permissions tab in the ribbon to open the Share Site dialog box.**

   You can enter names or email addresses of users that SharePoint can add to the site. If you don't know the names of user accounts, you can type the email addresses. SharePoint tries to map the email address for the account.

3. **Include a personal message that will be included with the invitation.**

   This step is optional. If the field is left blank, users will be emailed a generic welcome message.

   If you don't see a field to enter a personal message, then email has not been configured for the SharePoint environment.

TIP

4. **Decide if you want to send the users a welcome email message by selecting or deselecting the Send an E-mail Invitation check box, which appears when you click Show Options.**

5. **Click the drop-down menu by the user's name and choose the permission level.**

   The full control option is the Site Owners group, the edit option is the Site Members group, and the read option is the Site Visitors group. By default, the dialog box adds users to the Site Members group.

6. **Click the Share button to add the users to the SharePoint group and thus share the site with them.**

With Microsoft 365, you have the ability to invite people to use your site who are outside your organization. We discuss using this functionality to create a client or partner portal in Chapter 20.

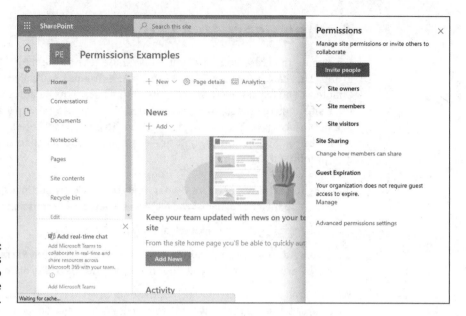

WARNING

You just gave a user access to your SharePoint site by adding that person to a SharePoint group. If someone else shares the site with the same user and uses the simpler way (discussed in Chapter 5) to share the site, the user will have access through both SharePoint groups and Microsoft 365 Groups. Another administrator might decide to remove the access and remove the user from one of the groups but not the other. It is critical to keep in mind that there are two different security mechanisms in SharePoint. Microsoft integrated SharePoint with Microsoft 365, which brings it into closer alignment with other cloud products like Microsoft Teams. However, the traditional SharePoint security mechanism is still in place. So make sure you understand both.

Understanding the permission structure

Members in the Site Owners SharePoint Group create the permission structure for a site. The Site Owner should have a pretty good understanding of which users need to access the site and what that access should be. This means that members of IT usually shouldn't be Site Owners. Instead, you want members of the business departments to take responsibility for site ownership.

Permissions are contained within a site collection. Therefore, all the people, groups, and permission levels defined for a site collection are available to every site and app within the collection. Permissions inheritance is in place by default, so all the content and subsites in SharePoint inherit permissions from their parents.

REMEMBER

Websites, apps, folders, and list items are all securable with permissions in SharePoint.

When a subsite is created, all the content structures within the site inherit permissions from the site collection. For example, when you create a new site using the Team Site template (see Chapter 1), all the apps in the site inherit permissions from the site collection. The default permissions configuration for a site collection is as follows:

>> The Site Owners, Site Visitors, and Site Members groups are created as SharePoint groups and a Microsoft 365 group is created.

>> The primary and secondary site collection administrators are added to the Site Owners group. These administrators are specified when the site collection is created.

The site collection administrator takes responsibility for planning the permissions. If desired, the site collection administrator can delegate the responsibility of implementing the permissions to the Hierarchy Managers group in Publishing sites. In Team sites, the owner has to create a new permission level that confers the Manage Permissions permission to those individuals and groups assigned to it.

A Team site includes the basic permission levels Full Control, Design, Edit, Contribute and Read. SharePoint also provides the following set of specialized administrative groups for sites based on publishing templates that enable the site's owner to delegate responsibility:

>> **Approvers:** Enables Approve permissions, which allow users to approve items and override document check-outs.

>> **Designers:** Grants permission to change the look and feel of sites with style sheets and themes.

>> **Translation Managers:** Grants permission to change the translated text of a page. This role works in conjunction with the translation features, which are part of the Publishing Infrastructure Feature.

>> **Hierarchy Managers:** Enables Manage Hierarchy permissions, which makes it possible to manipulate the site's hierarchy and customize lists and libraries.

In addition to providing several kinds of administrative roles, SharePoint provides the following groups for restricting access:

>> **Everyone:** Enables access for every SharePoint user.

>> **Excel Services Viewers:** Enables users to view Excel documents in a page. This is required so that the page they are viewing can read the Library app where the Excel document is located.

>> **Quick Deploy Users:** Moves content from one server to another, such as from a staging server to a production server. Available only when Publishing Infrastructure Feature is active.

>> **Restricted Readers:** Enables users to view only items and pages but doesn't show any item history.

>> **Style Resource Readers:** Enables users to read from the master page gallery and style library. Available only when Publishing Infrastructure Feature is active.

There are a number of other specialized groups to choose from in addition to the primary groups mentioned here. They become available when you activate certain features. You can view all of the groups in your site by clicking on the Advanced Permissions Settings link at the bottom of the Permissions pane. The result is the advanced permissions page, as shown in Figure 21-2. Note that we have activated the Publishing Infrastructure feature Enterprise features and thus are seeing different groups that you might see.

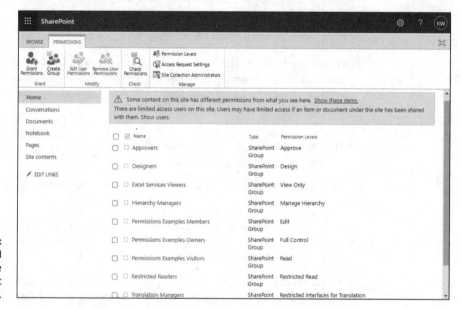

FIGURE 21-2:
The advanced permissions page for a SharePoint site.

Securing a site collection

After you know how to add new users to a SharePoint group, finish setting up security for a site collection by doing the following:

1. **Add user accounts to the *Site* Visitors group.**

   The *Site* Visitors group has Read permissions, which enables this group to view the site collection's content.

2. **Add user accounts or domain groups to the *Site* Members group.**

   Members of the *Site* Members group have Contribute permissions, which allow them to add content to the site collection.

3. **Add users to the Hierarchy Manager and Designers groups in Publishing sites.**

   You may want to create a separate permission level for consultants. SharePoint Team sites don't have these groups by default, but you can create similar groups if you need that kind of role.

4. **Configure unique permissions for content structures in and below the top-level site.**

   You have to stop inheriting permissions from the top-level site before you can create unique permissions for subsites and apps. See the section, "Creating unique permissions for a subsite," later in this chapter, for details.

5. **Add subsites to the main site collection site.**

   You can inherit permissions or use unique permissions when you create the site. Note that Microsoft is now recommending to avoid using subsites and stick with top level sites instead. The size of your organization has a lot to do with whether you really need subsites for administrative and organizational purposes or not. For smaller organizations, we agree with Microsoft that you should stick with only top level sites and perhaps even just a single default site to start with.

REMEMBER

Remember that everything *in* the site collection inherits *from* the site collection by default. Make sure your site collection permissions don't grant too many people access.

Securing Apps, Folders, Documents, and Items

In theory, you could set up security once for a site collection and allow everything to inherit. In reality, you may not want everyone to have the same access. In order to create unique permissions for a site, app, folder, or item, you have to stop inheriting permissions from the parent.

Creating unique permissions for a subsite

TIP

You must be in a subsite to create unique permissions; the following steps don't make sense otherwise.

To stop inheriting permissions in a subsite from a parent site, follow these steps:

1. **Browse to the Site Permissions page for a site by clicking the Settings gear icon and choosing Site Permissions and then clicking the Advanced Permissions Settings link at the bottom of the Permissions pane.**

   The Site Permissions page is displayed with a message reading `This website inherits permissions from its parent (<parent site name>)`. If you wish to change permissions for the entire site collection, click the <parent site name> link.

2. **Click the Stop Inheriting Permissions button in the Permissions tab on the ribbon.**

   A message window appears reading, in part, "You are about to create unique permissions for this website."

3. **Click OK.**

   The Set Up Groups for this page is displayed. Choose the groups you want to use in the site. By default, the page uses the groups from the site collection.

4. **If you need your own groups for this site, you should select the Create New Group radio button.**

5. **Set groups for Site Visitors, Site Members, and Site Owners by selecting an existing group from the drop-down list.**

6. **Click OK to create the new unique groups for the site.**

   The main home page for the site reloads, and your site now has unique permissions. Repeat Step 1 to return to the Site Permissions page. You see that there is now a `This website has unique permissions` message. Any permissions changes you make on this site are now unique to this site. No other sites in the site collection will be affected.

WARNING

Be careful about adding users to SharePoint groups at the site or app level. You're actually adding users to the entire site collection group. Individual subsites and apps don't have their own SharePoint groups. This behavior causes a great deal of confusion. To drive the point home, do the following. When you stop inheriting site permissions and are on the page for setting up groups (Step 4 in the preceding list), choose to create new groups for the site. After you have finished, go to the Site Permissions page for the site collection. You see the groups you created in the site are in the site collection. This is because all groups in SharePoint are located at the site collection level, even if they are only used by a subsite that is set to use unique permissions.

To reinherit permissions from the parent site, choose Inherit Permissions in Step 2. Any changes you've made are discarded, and the site inherits the parent's permissions.

TIP

After you stop inheriting permissions, the parent's permissions are copied to the site.

WARNING

Be extremely careful when deleting groups and permissions! If you are in a site that is inheriting permissions and you delete a group, you are actually taken to the site collection to delete the group. We have seen highly trained IT administrators make this mistake and wipe out the entire permission structure for the entire site collection. Before you delete a group, make certain that your site isn't inheriting permissions and you're not deleting all the permissions at the site collection level by deleting the group at the site level.

Removing existing permissions

Follow these steps to remove existing permission assignments:

1. **Browse to the Site Permissions page for a site by clicking the Settings gear icon, choosing Site Permissions, and then clicking the Advanced Permissions Settings link at the bottom of the Permissions pane.**

2. **Place check marks next to the permission assignments you want to remove.**

   Remember to leave yourself with permissions; otherwise, you won't be able to access the site.

3. **Click the Remove User Permissions button, and then click OK to confirm the deletions.**

   All the permissions are deleted for the selected permissions assignments.

Creating unique permissions for an app or document

Allowing a site's content structures to inherit permissions from the site is usually sufficient. Don't try to secure everything individually. But at times, you need to secure a folder in an app or limit access to an app. You may want to delegate ownership of an app, thus pushing administrative responsibilities for the app to an app administrator.

TIP

To manage permissions, the user must have the Manage Permissions permission. You must be a member of the Hierarchy Managers group to edit permissions.

To create unique permissions for an app, follow these steps:

1. **Browse to the app, click the Settings gear icon, and choose Library Settings or List Settings.**

2. **Click the Permissions for This Document Library link in the Permissions and Management section.**

   The Permissions page appears.

3. **Manage the permissions as you would for a subsite by breaking inheritance and managing the permissions uniquely for the list.**

   Managing permissions on apps is the same as managing permissions for subsites — see the earlier section, "Creating unique permissions for a subsite."

You can also give unique permissions for an individual document, folder, or list item. You do this by sharing the particular item with a person and selecting their level of permissions in the Share dialog box. Accessing the Share dialog box depends on the item you are sharing. For example, to share a document in the Documents app of a default Team site you select the document and then click the Share button that appears in the ribbon. We will do this in the next procedure.

TIP

With SharePoint, you can even share a document without requiring the other person to log into your SharePoint site.

Follow these steps to give permissions for a document, item, or folder in an app library:

1. **Browse to the app where the item, document, or folder is located.**

2. **Select the radio button next to a document and then click the Share button in the ribbon, as shown in Figure 21-3.**

   The Send Link dialog box appears.

3. **Enter the name, email address, or group, and then select the permission you wish to give, as shown in Figure 21-4.**

4. **Click the Send button to send the link and give permissions.**

TIP

You can manage the access to an individual document or item. To manage access, click the ellipsis next to the item and choose Manage Access.

FIGURE 21-3:
Click Share for a
document in a
Library app.

FIGURE 21-4:
Select the
permissions for
the link you will
send.

Managing permissions scenarios

Managing permissions is tricky, and the steps we outline in this section are our recommendations. These aren't the only ways to manage permissions. Try a scenario to help you better understand permissions. Assume you have a site with the SharePoint groups we outline here.

SharePoint groups	Members
Site Members	John, Bill, and Steve
Site Visitors	Mary, Sue, and Sally

Everything in the site inherits from the top-level site. In this scenario, those in the Site Members group have Contribute permissions, whereas those in the Site Visitors group have Read permissions.

Assume you create a new subsite, and you want only your Site Members to access it. You don't want Site Visitors to even know the subsite exists. In this case, you create unique permissions on the subsite and remove the Site Visitors group.

Assume you have an app for policy documents, and you want John and Sally to have Contribute permissions. We recommend creating a new Policy Reviewers SharePoint group at your top-level site and then adding John and Sally as members to the group. You aren't done here, however. You haven't actually granted the group permission to anything yet. You have to browse to the app, break inheritance from its parent, and then grant the Policy Reviewers SharePoint group the Contribute permission level.

Why not just add John and Sally to the app and grant them the Contribute permission level? That approach will certainly work, but it's hard to manage. That approach obscures that John and Sally have some permissions granted outside the context of a SharePoint group. We like to be able to look at our SharePoint groups and have a good idea of what the role of that group is, based on their names on the site. If you start adding users individually to subsites, apps, documents, folders, and items, it becomes difficult to get a big-picture view of how your permissions for the site are configured.

Viewing a group's permissions

You can easily check the permissions for a given group to see everything that group has been granted access to in your site. You must repeat these steps at each site in your site collection. To do so:

1. **Browse to the top-level site in your site collection.**

2. **Click the Settings gear icon and choose Site Permissions.**

3. **Click Advanced Permissions Settings at the bottom of the Permissions pane.**

4. **Click the name of the group for which you want to view permissions.**

5. **Choose Settings ⇨ View Group Permissions.**

   The View Site Collection Permissions window appears, as shown in Figure 21-5. All the sites, lists, and libraries that the group has permission to access appear in the list.

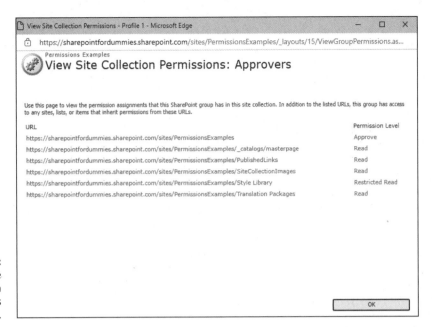

View Site Collection Permissions - Profile 1 - Microsoft Edge — ☐ ✕

https://sharepointfordummies.sharepoint.com/sites/PermissionsExamples/_layouts/15/ViewGroupPermissions.as…

Permissions Examples
View Site Collection Permissions: Approvers

Use this page to view the permission assignments that this SharePoint group has in this site collection. In addition to the listed URLs, this group has access to any sites, lists, or items that inherit permissions from these URLs.

URL	Permission Level
https://sharepointfordummies.sharepoint.com/sites/PermissionsExamples	Approve
https://sharepointfordummies.sharepoint.com/sites/PermissionsExamples/_catalogs/masterpage	Read
https://sharepointfordummies.sharepoint.com/sites/PermissionsExamples/PublishedLinks	Read
https://sharepointfordummies.sharepoint.com/sites/PermissionsExamples/SiteCollectionImages	Read
https://sharepointfordummies.sharepoint.com/sites/PermissionsExamples/Style Library	Restricted Read
https://sharepointfordummies.sharepoint.com/sites/PermissionsExamples/Translation Packages	Read

OK

FIGURE 21-5:
The View Site Collection Permissions window.

REMEMBER

Everyone who is a member of the group has the permissions shown on the View Site Collection Permissions window. Don't forget about the Microsoft 365 Groups though, too. You can view and manage the Microsoft 365 Groups using either Microsoft Outlook or using your web browser and navigating to the Microsoft 365 Admin Center at https://admin.microsoft.com.

Checking a user's permissions

Sometimes, you just want to know who has permission to do what in a given site. SharePoint provides just such a method:

1. **Browse to the site where you want to check a user's permissions.**

    This command only checks permissions within a single site and for SharePoint groups. You have to check each site manually. You have to check Microsoft 365 Groups either in Outlook or at https://admin.microsoft.com.

2. **Click the Settings gear icon and choose Site Permissions.**

3. **Click Advanced Permissions Settings at the bottom of the Permissions pane.**

4. **Click the Check Permissions button on the ribbon.**

5. **Enter the name of the user or group whose permissions you want to check for the current site in the User/Group field, and then click the Check Now button (see Figure 21-6).**

    The permissions appear in the bottom of the window.

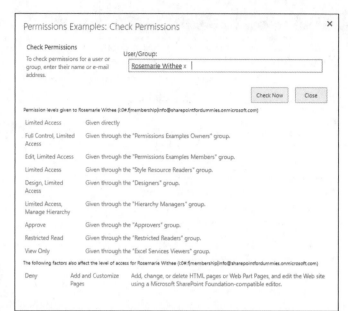

FIGURE 21-6:
View a user's permissions to the current site.

PUTTING IT ALL TOGETHER

If you are part of a smaller organization or just getting started with SharePoint, we recommend sticking with only the Microsoft 365 Groups and avoiding SharePoint groups altogether. If you are going to use the SharePoint groups, we often encourage site owners to create their own SharePoint groups instead of using the built-in Visitors and Members. There's something about naming your own groups that makes managing them more intuitive (maybe because you don't refer to your coworkers as *members*).

By creating your own groups, you can very easily add a new employee to a particular group when someone asks, "Hey, can you add the new employee to the Accounting Clerks group in the Team site?" Because you've already assigned proper permissions to the Accounting Clerks group throughout your site, the new employee is guaranteed to have all the access needed. When the not-so-new employee gets promoted a year later, you can change this employee's membership to the Accounting Supervisors group and get back to important stuff.

Granting Administrative Access

You'll find a number of different administrator levels in a SharePoint deployment. If your IT department is hosting and managing SharePoint then it is called an on-premises deployment and the administration levels include a level of power not seen if you are using SharePoint in Microsoft 365. Administrators usually have full access over the area they've been charged with administering. The levels of administrators in SharePoint are:

>> **Server administrators:** By virtue of having local administrator access to the physical server, a server administrator can do anything from the server console. Server administrators are usually members of the technical staff.

>> **Service administrators:** Administration of SharePoint's services, such as Search or User Profiles, can be delegated. This allows administrators to specialize.

>> **Site collection administrators:** These administrators can access everything within a site collection. SharePoint allows you to appoint a primary and secondary administrator for each site collection, who both receive email notifications when the site hits its storage quota or is slated for deletion due to lack of use. Site collection administrators also manage all the features that affect the entire site collection.

>> **Site administrators:** Members of the *Site* Owners SharePoint group are the site administrators. If subsites inherit permissions, a site administrator has full access to each site.

>> **App administrators:** Permissions can be unique for an app, which allows for the delegation administration. Depending on the size of your department or team, you might have different people administer different apps.

>> **Document/item administrators:** For extremely sensitive documents and items, you can use unique permissions that in effect enable someone to administer just that document or item.

In Microsoft 365, the server administrator role is replaced by the SharePoint Online administrator. Microsoft manages the entire infrastructure for you, so you just have to manage SharePoint Online. Keep in mind that Microsoft 365 has its own level of administration beyond SharePoint.

The primary and secondary site collection administrators are determined at the time the site collection is created. Additional site collection administrators can be added to the site collection itself.

To set the site collection administrators for a site:

1. **Browse to the top-level site in your site collection.**

2. **Click the Settings gear icon and choose Site Permissions.**

3. **Click Advanced Permissions Settings at the bottom of the Permissions pane.**

4. **Click Site Collection Administrators in the Manage section of the ribbon.**

   The Site Collection Administrators page appears.

5. **Add or remove users from the Site Collection Administrators box by typing in their names or deleting their names using the backspace key, and then click OK.**

   Users are separated by semicolons.

Viewing Site Permissions

A site can have all the elements of an *authorization model* — people, groups, and permissions, in other words — but still not be secure. The deciding factor in securing SharePoint's content lies with the permission assignments made on securable objects such as sites, apps, folders, documents, and items. A permission assignment consists of permissions, *principals* (users and groups), and securable objects.

Permissions are the smallest unit for managing security in SharePoint. Permissions confer rights a user may have, such as View Pages rights or Add Items rights. In SharePoint, you deal with following three permission types:

>> **App (List or Library):** Permissions related to accessing apps, folders, documents, and items.

>> **Site:** Permissions related to accessing sites, pages, and permissions.

>> **Personal:** Permissions related to creating personal views of web pages.

When permissions are managed properly, you never have to work with permissions on a case-by-case basis because permissions are never assigned directly to principals. Rather, they're assigned to *permission levels*, which are assigned to default SharePoint groups. You can also assign permission levels directly to user accounts or custom SharePoint groups you create.

Follow these steps to view a list of permission levels for a site:

1. **Browse to the site where you want to check a user's permissions.**

This command only checks permissions within a single site. You have to check each site manually.

2. **Click the Settings gear icon and choose Site Permissions.**

3. **Click Advanced Permissions Settings at the bottom of the Permissions pane.**

4. **Click the Permission Levels button on the ribbon.**

The Permission Levels page appears, as shown in Figure 21-7. You can use this page to create new permission levels or modify existing ones. You will only see the Permission Levels button in the ribbon if you have broken inheritance. Otherwise, the site inherits permissions from the parent, and to see the Permission Levels button you need to go to the parent where those permissions originate.

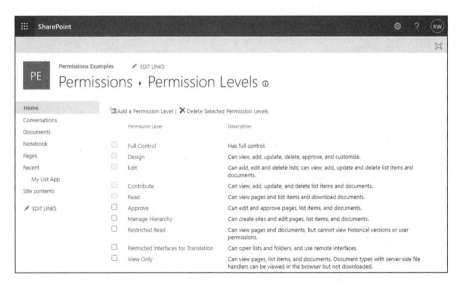

FIGURE 21-7: View the site's permission assignments.

5. **Click a permission level, such as Contribute, to view or modify the permissions in the permission level, as shown in Figure 21-8.**

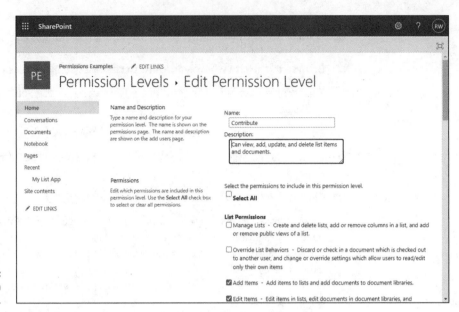

FIGURE 21-8:
View permission
levels.

Note: The permissions you see might not be the entire set of permissions available in SharePoint. The server administrator can limit the list of permissions available to a web application using Web Policies.

TIP

Keep in mind that the Permissions Levels page doesn't really show individual permissions. Instead, the page shows permission levels. The complexity in Share-Point security is one of the key reasons Microsoft has moved towards a simplified model with Microsoft 365 groups. If you don't need the fine grained control outlined here then stick with the very basic Microsoft 365 group and avoid SharePoint groups all together.

Table 21-1 lists the permission levels, the rights they grant, and the SharePoint group they're assigned to by default. Note that the last four permission levels are specific to sites with the Publishing Infrastructure Feature active.

TIP

SharePoint security can take some time to comprehend. Sometimes things just don't seem to work the way they should. Hang in there, though. The more you work with it the easier it is to get your head around what SharePoint is doing and why it behaves the way that it does.

TABLE 21-1

Permission Levels

Permission Level	Rights Granted	SharePoint Group Assigned to by Default
Full Control	Wield administrative access	Site Owners
Design	Change the site's look and feel	Designers
Edit	Add, edit, and delete apps as well as the items and documents contained within the apps	Site Members
Contribute	Add and modify content	Site Members
Read	View all content, including history	Site Visitors
Limited Access	Open (same as guest access)	Quick Deploy Users
View Only	View items and pages	Viewers
Approve	Approve content	Approvers
Manage Hierarchy	Manage the site's structure and permissions (this is only available in the site collection when the SharePoint Server Publishing Infrastructure feature is active)	Hierarchy Managers
Restricted Read	View and open	Restricted Readers
Restricted Interfaces for Translation	Open apps and use remote interfaces	Restricted Interfaces for Translation

Locking Down a Partner Portal

The biggest hurdle to locking down a partner portal is figuring out permissions. You need to determine which users have access and what they can do on the site. So you need to understand what SharePoint permissions are and how they are assigned, which we cover in this chapter. In Chapter 20, you learn about creating a partner portal, and that by default when creating a portal, you give users access to the site to edit and collaborate with you. This is generally fine, but be aware you can go much more granular for a partner portal should you choose.

Permissions in SharePoint Online versus SharePoint On-Premises

Working with users and groups in a SharePoint site has diverged depending on whether you use SharePoint On-Premises or SharePoint Online. Microsoft has started integrating SharePoint Online with the rest of the Microsoft 365 apps such as Teams. The primary difference is the use of Microsoft 365 Groups by default for most sites. As we mention earlier in the chapter, you manage Microsoft 365 Groups in either Outlook or in the Microsoft 365 Admin Center at `https://admin.microsoft.com`. Don't forget that users can have access to your SharePoint Online sites by being part of the Microsoft 365 Groups or SharePoint groups.

Going Further with Custom Permissions

After you realize how easy it is to create a new group, you may want to explore the types of permission levels you can assign to new groups. Earlier in the chapter we edited the Contribute permission, but you could just as easily have created a new permission instead of using the Contribute permission. To create a new permission level:

1. **Browse to the site where you want to check a user's permissions.**

2. **Click the Settings gear icon and choose Site Permissions.**

3. **Click Advanced Permissions Settings at the bottom of the Permissions pane.**

4. **Click the Permission Levels button in the ribbon.**

5. **Click the Add a Permission Level button at the top of the page that lists all the built-in permission levels.**

   The Edit Permission Level page allows you to create a new permission level that can be assigned to your group. The Add a Permission Level link only shows up if you are at the Site Collection level because that is where permission levels are located.

6. **Type a name and description in the Name and Description text boxes.**

7. **Select the check boxes for the permissions you want to assign to that level, as shown in Figure 21-9.**

8. **Click Submit.**

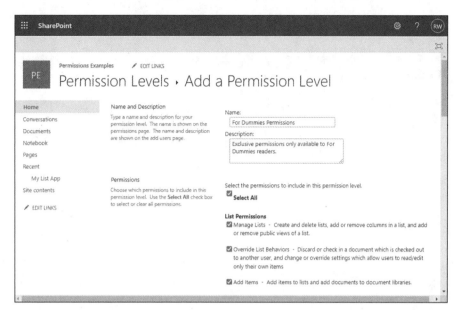

FIGURE 21-9:
Creating a new
permission level.

After you create a new permission level, you can use that level to assign your groups the correct permissions. After you do that, it's as easy as adding members to the particular group that gives them the appropriate access to your portal.

TIP

In some cases, you simply need to assign one or two people special permissions to the site, and you won't want to create a new permission level and a new group for them, and that's okay. You don't want to burden yourself with the rule that all users should be managed via a group with the right permissions, but you do want to be able to manage users effectively with little ongoing maintenance. A well-planned group and permission level structure will help you in the end.

TIP

You can also create a new permission level by starting with an existing permission level. To do this, click on a permission level, like we did with Contribute, and then scroll down to the bottom of the page and choose Copy Permission Level.

5

Managing Enterprise Content

IN THIS PART . . .

Explore records management in SharePoint, define terms, create information management policies, set up a Records Center site, and use the Content Organizer tool.

Find out how search works in SharePoint, refine search results, and create your own Search Center site.

Create data dashboards with Microsoft Power BI and learn how to integrate them in SharePoint.

Chapter **22**

Managing Content and the Content Lifecycle

SharePoint has always been an excellent platform for managing content. The good news is that Microsoft didn't make the mistake of taking a great thing and changing it. It left the content management systems in SharePoint mostly alone and fine-tuned them with bug fixes and smoother interfaces.

In this chapter, you learn about the basics of managing content, such as checking a file out and checking it back in, and get a feel for content approval workflows. You explore the records management functionality in SharePoint and discover how to define terms, create information management policies, and set up a site based on the Records Center template. Finally, this chapter covers some of the finer points of records management, such as using the Content Organizer tool and placing holds on content.

Starting Simple: Co-Authoring

One of the best practices we like to follow is to start simple and only use something that is more advanced and complicated when absolutely necessary. When it comes to working on content with multiple people, the simplest method is for everyone to work on the same document at the same time.

Modern versions of Office allow you to see who is working on a document or spreadsheet and what they are doing in real time. This scenario works fine for small groups of people, relatively simple documents and spreadsheets, or content where everyone isn't working in the same area at the same time. If you start conflicting with each other, then it is time to move to a more advanced model of checking out content to work on it and then checking it back in when you are done.

Checking a Document In and Out

A document library is just like any library — it holds a collection of artifacts (in this case, documents). Much like we check out books from a library and check them back in when we are done with them, checking out a document in SharePoint allows the user to make changes to the document without running the risk of someone else working on the document at the same time. When a user is done making changes, checking the document in allows others to do the same. The document check-in and check-out feature is a great way to keep track of and control how content is updated.

The ribbon displays many of the same document actions as the ellipsis menu next to each file. This is a common theme in SharePoint. There are often multiple ways to achieve the exact same outcome. To check out a document using the ribbon:

1. **In your app, select the circle (left-most column) next to the document you want to check out.**

   Alternatively, you can click the ellipsis next to the document itself and find a Check Out link in the More fly-out menu. This saves you from having to click to select the document first and then going up to the ribbon.

2. **Click the ellipsis in the ribbon and click the Check Out button (which might be on the More fly-out menu depending on your screen resolution and classic or new experience settings), as shown in Figure 22-1.**

   The document is checked out, and a small checked-out arrow appears to the right of the document name.

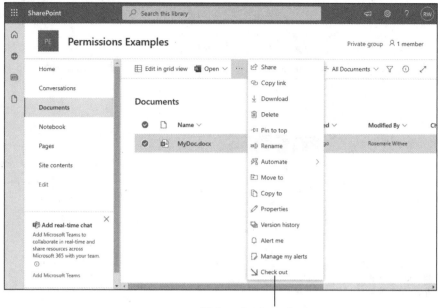

FIGURE 22-1:
Checking out a document in SharePoint.

Click to check out the document

TIP

You can check out multiple documents at the same time. We do this fairly often when we are working on multiple documents and we don't want others making changes as we get a cohesive content update in place across all the docs.

You may be thinking, "That's great, but why would I want to check out a document?" To us, checking out — and its counterpart, checking in — is just good document editing etiquette. What better way to let others know that you're making changes to a document than by checking it out? Checking out a document sets the Checked Out flag to Yes and stores the name of the person who checked out the document. Of course, always remember to check in documents when your edits are complete.

TIP

An app can be configured to force a person to check out a document before it can be edited. This is achieved on the Versioning Settings page located in the Library Settings.

Documents that are checked out show an arrow to the right of the document name. As shown in Figure 22-2, the Important Work.xlsx file is checked out (it has a check-out icon in the shape of an arrow next to it), whereas the rest of the files are not checked out.

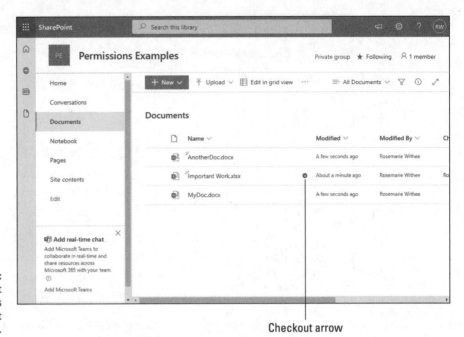

FIGURE 22-2:
A checked-out document shows a check-out arrow.

Checkout arrow

TIP

If you want to see who has a document checked out, you have to look at the Checked Out To column in the app view. This column is displayed by default. You can customize views and rearrange columns. (We discuss working with views in Chapter 14.)

To check in a document after you're done making your changes, repeat the steps you followed earlier in this section to check out the document, only in Step 2, choose the Check In option from the menu. Think of a check-in as a snapshot of the document at that state. You can use the ellipsis at the top of the library (shown in Figure 22-1) to check in documents as well.

If you change your mind and want to pretend that the check-out never happened, you can click the Discard Check Out option instead of the Check In option. This can be useful if you accidentally checked out the wrong document or made changes that you wish you wouldn't have made. When you discard the check out, the document reverts to the state it was in before you checked it out.

Configuring Content Approval

Trust, but verify: Sometimes you want to let folks add a document or create an item in an app but you don't want those items unleashed on an unsuspecting world before someone approves them. SharePoint has a few ways to help you enact and enforce content governance policies to define what gets published and under what conditions, how many revisions are retained, and how they're secured and tracked. Depending on the complexity of your approval process, you can use the standard content approval option, or you can create a more sophisticated — and custom — approval workflow. Using Power Automate to create custom workflows to approve documents and items is discussed in Chapter 15.

Content approval is approval-light; it's a publishing function that you turn on or off at the app level, and it has just a handful of configuration settings. Content approval — also called *moderation* — doesn't include item routing or notifications, and it doesn't facilitate reviews and commenting. Content approval just ensures that drafts and new uploaded content don't get published to your app until someone with some authority says it's okay. The content approval process controls who can see those documents until they're approved.

Content approval also can specify (in the case of documents) whether items must be checked out before they can be edited. And content approval can hide draft documents from everyone except the item author and those users with approve permissions on the app. (Contrast this with draft item security on apps without content approval enabled in which you can limit views only to users with app-level Read permissions or users with app-level Edit permissions.)

This is a subtle distinction, but specifying that only the item author and users with approve permissions can view items means that the author can check in an item without exposing it to the view of other readers or editors until it's formally published and approved. We find this useful in cases when we have multiple authorized contributors to an app and we want to keep them from seeing each other's work until someone (the approver) says it's okay. This also gives me a way to let authors work on drafts without readers looking over their shoulders. (Few things are more frustrating than editorial feedback on something you're still working on!)

Turning on content approval

By default, content approval is turned off and (usually) any user with Read access can see Draft items in most apps. Sites created with the publishing site template, however, already have content approval turned on in the Pages app.

To turn on and configure content approval, follow these steps:

1. **Navigate to your app's Settings page (Library Settings or List Settings) and click the Versioning Settings link.**

The Versioning Settings page appears. Remember, you can find your app's Library Settings or List Settings page by first navigating to the app and then clicking the Settings gear icon in the top-right corner of the screen and clicking List Settings or Library Settings.

2. **Select the Yes radio button below Require Content Approval for Submitted Items.**

You see options to retain versions, specify who can see drafts, and in library-based apps — document check-out options.

Notice that the options below Who Should See Draft Items in This Document Library switches to the Only Users Who Can Approve Items (And the Author of the Item) option as soon as you select the Yes radio button to require content approval for submitted items, as shown in Figure 22-3.

You need to decide whether readers, editors, or only authors and approvers can see drafts. We usually enable content approval partly because we don't want to expose items to just anyone before they meet some level of credibility or *done-ness*. So we select the Only Users Who Can Approve Items (And the Author of the Item) option.

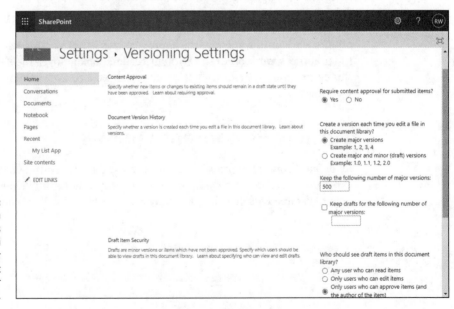

FIGURE 22-3:
The Draft Item Security settings change after you select Yes under Require Content Approval for Submitted Items.

3. **Verify the Document Version History settings in the Document Version History section.**

   You can specify versions *without* turning on content approval. A major version is created when you publish a document and a minor version is created when you save a document. You can configure which level of detail you want to set in versioning by choosing Create Major Versions or Create Major and Minor (draft) Versions.

4. **Click a Draft Item Security option in the Draft Item Security section.**

   TIP

   The security referred to by draft item security — Read, Edit, and Approve — maps to SharePoint's Visitors, Members, and Approvers groups. (See Chapter 21 for details on managing security groups.)

5. **Click a check-out option in the Require Check Out section.**

6. **Click OK to save your changes.**

   You return to the Library Settings or List Settings page whence you came. The items created in (or changed in) the app are subject to approval (unless you disable content approval later).

REMEMBER

If content approval is active, when users add an item to the app, they see a note that items require content approval in the item properties window. After the item is added, it appears in Pending status in the app view until it is approved.

Identifying approvers

You need to specify who the approvers include, generally by adding users to the created Approvers group. (See Chapter 21 for information about groups and permissions.)

Oh, and by the way, content approval isn't just about Big Brother checking someone else's work. You may want to ensure that documents can be checked in and versioned, but that they aren't displayed to readers until they're formally approved. In these cases, you set the same person or people both to create and to approve items. That way, all people in the group can see the item's current version, but the rest of the organization can't see it until it has been approved by someone in the group.

Casting an approving eye

In an app that has approval turned on, when a new document is created and a major version is published, the approval status is marked "Pending" (see Figure 22-4) and designated approvers can approve, mark as pending, or reject the item by clicking the ellipsis next to the document and choosing Approve/Reject from the More flyout menu, as shown in Figure 22-5.

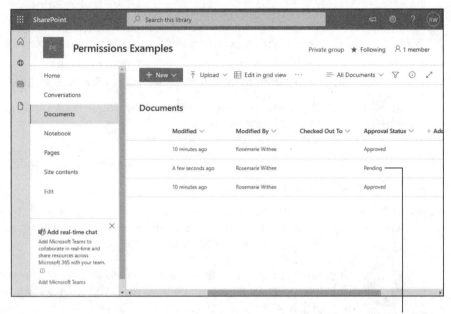

FIGURE 22-4:
The new document is in Pending status until approved.

Pending approval status

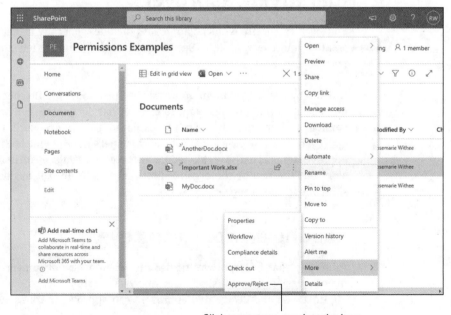

FIGURE 22-5:
Opening the dialog box to approve a new document.

Click to approve or reject the item

When you select Approve/Reject, you're presented with the aptly named Approve/Reject window, as shown in Figure 22-6, with the Pending option selected by default. At this point, you can leave a comment in the Comment text box but leave the item as Pending or you can select the Approved or the Rejected option to approve or reject the item with or without comment. (Rejecting without comment is pretty poor form, though.) The action, name of the person who took the action, and timestamp are recorded in the item's version history.

Approve/Reject Important Work.xlsx

Approval status

◉ **Approved** - This item will become visible to all users.

○ **Rejected** - This item will be returned to its creator and only be visible to its creator and all users who can see draft items.

○ **Pending** - This item will remain visible to its creator and all users who can see draft items.

Comment

Confirming the data you entered looks correct to me too.

[Ok] [Cancel]

FIGURE 22-6:
The Approve/
Reject window.

Unless alerts are enabled on the app or the item itself, the item originator won't know you've taken an action until the next time that person is in the app and checks the approval status on the item. We recommend using alerts with content approval unless you have some alternative process where approvers make it part of their daily routine to check for pending items.

Disapproving: Not just for stern parents

Everyone wants approval, but sometimes you don't get it. Sometimes an approver rejects an item. When this happens, the item is changed to Rejected status, and then it's visible only to the author and anyone with permission to manage the app.

When you first enable content approval on an app, all existing items are approved automatically.

REMEMBER

Getting alerts on approval/rejection status

When an item is marked Pending with content approval turned on (and no associated approval workflow), that item just sits there, marinating in its own pending status until someone notices and either approves or rejects it. When the app we're managing sees a lot of traffic, we rely on the approvers to check for pending items because they're working in the app all the time anyway. But another way to make sure approvers get the heads-up is to set alerts (see Chapter 10). In addition to alerts, you can create a workflow that periodically emails a person or group until an item is approved. We have found this constant nagging type behavior is actually very effective, and people appreciate it because they don't have to remember to do something. (Approving content with a Power Automate workflow is covered in Chapter 15.)

WARNING

If you turn off content approval, be aware that pending and rejected items, which were hidden from public view, are now viewable. We recommend resolving all draft, pending, and rejected items before disabling content approval; it's a dirty trick to reveal someone's draft to the world when the author isn't expecting it!

Digging into a SharePoint Records Center

In SharePoint, the Records Center is a useful and powerful tool for declaring holds and managing records. First, it's *metadata-driven,* which means that all policies for automatic declaration, retention, and disposition can be based on metadata. Second, it's capable of *hierarchical archiving,* meaning that each level or folder where documents are routed, based on their metadata, can inherit from its parent or have separate policies. Third, you can manage the entire lifecycle of the document in a single policy, from declaration through disposition. Fourth, administrators can allow users to declare records outside of the official Records Center, allowing records to be kept where they are actively being accessed and updated.

Defining the terms

SharePoint provides many records management features, including the Managed Metadata Service, Content Types, Content Organizer, Policies, Document Sets, and the Records Management site template. The following list is a quick guide to these terms and what functionality they provide:

>> **Managed Metadata** ensures a common vocabulary and a central place for terminology used in your company, which can be managed centrally or by departments.

- » **Content Types** scale across the enterprise with SharePoint and are not limited to each site collection. This means you have a much more scalable way of controlling and managing the types of content people can create, the metadata on those content types, and the information policies associated with them.

- » **Content Organizer** enables you to take routing documents and content beyond content types. You can create rules based on one or more pieces of metadata on the content. Essentially, this simplifies routing from the user's perspective, and content gets routed to the right place without too much forethought.

- » **Information Management Policies** can be applied to the content type or the location of the content, which can become part of the policy. You can expire record and non-record content in the same policy.

- » **Document Sets** allow you to group together multiple documents into a single set. This helps keep track of all the documents you might use for a particular idea or task. For example, you might want to group all of the documents for a proposal that multiple people are working on.

- » **Records Management Site Template** is a SharePoint site template that has most of the records management capabilities of SharePoint already included and ready to use. You can use this site template to get up and running with managing records in SharePoint with very little configuration overhead.

With these features, declaring records, holds, and policies is scalable and powerful in SharePoint.

Creating information management policies

Here are four different types of policies that you can set up in a single information management policy:

- » A **Retention** policy enables you to manage how items, documents, team mailboxes, and sites are stored on the server and what happens to them after the retention stage expires. A simple example of this would be that if a document has not been modified in one year, its version history is deleted.

- » An **Auditing** policy enables you to track what happens to an item at particular stages as the item is being moved or copied, opened, downloaded, viewed, checked in and out, and deleted and restored, so you have a full history of who has done what to an item.

» A **Barcodes** policy assigns a barcode to each item, allowing you to incorporate the barcode into your tracking of the item. You can optionally specify that you want users to insert a barcode before saving or printing.

» A **Labels** policy allows you to insert important and contextual information about the document when it is printed.

As shown in Figure 22-7, all these policies can be part of a single information management policy.

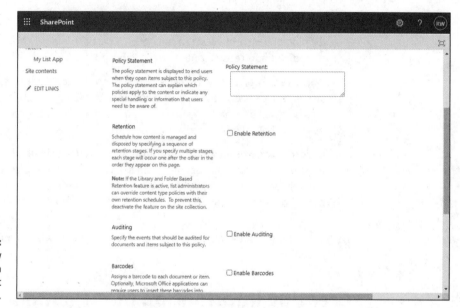

FIGURE 22-7:
Creating a new information management policy.

To create a new information management policy, you can start from an app or content type. Content type retention policies are the most powerful because they scale across the farm, but for the purposes of this example, we stick to a retention policy in a Library app. (If you want to follow along with a content type, simply browse to that content type in the site collection's Site Content Types gallery.)

TIP

Site collection administrators can turn off this feature of allowing app-based retention policies.

Follow these steps to create a new information management policy:

1. From the app settings page (Library Settings or List Settings), or from the content type's properties, click the Information Management Policy Settings link, as shown in Figure 22-8.

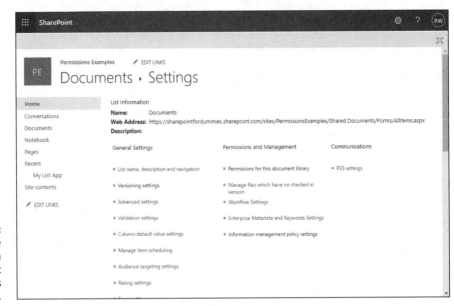

FIGURE 22-8:
Selecting the
Information
Management
Policy Settings
link.

2. **Click either the item or the folder; if you're on the content type, you don't have to do anything.**

For Document Library apps, you can have the policy inherit from the content type, or you can choose to create a new policy just for the app.

TIP

These policy pages look a bit different if you're using a List-based app or a list content type because you don't have as much to manage, but they have the same essential functionality.

3. **After you're on the policy settings page (refer to Figure 22-7), give the policy a description and a statement by typing in the Administrative Description and Policy Statement text boxes, respectively, and then select the Enable Retention check box.**

We just talk about retention here because it's the most interesting, and the other policy settings are straightforward.

After you select Enable Retention, you see some extra information, a link, and some options. For Document Library apps, you can treat non-records and records the same way if you choose, or different stages for handling records. Whichever you choose, you should define at least one retention stage for either records, non-records, or both.

TIP

If you don't define a stage, the retention policy will not do anything.

4. **Click the Add a Retention Stage link in the new section that appears after you enable retention.**

   A dialog box appears, shown in Figure 22-9, that has a few different options.

5. **Choose the event that triggers the retention by selecting the This Stage Is Based Off a Date Property on the Item radio button, select an option from the Time Period drop-down list, and enter a number and select Years, Months, or Days from the drop-down list.**

   From the Time Period drop-down list, you can select Created, Modified, or Declared Record. This determines the amount of time the stage lasts.

6. **In the Action section, select an option from the When This Stage Is Triggered, Perform the Following Action drop-down list.**

   You can choose from a variety of actions:

   - Move to Recycle Bin
   - Permanently Delete
   - Transfer to Another Location
   - Start a Workflow
   - Skip to Next Stage

- Declare Record

- Delete Previous Drafts

- Delete All Previous Versions

You can also set the action to recur, but this depends on the action you've specified previously. You can't, for example, keep deleting the same document over and over again, but you can keep purging previous drafts or all previous versions until the next stage is active.

7. Click OK to close the dialog box, and then click OK again to save the policy.

So what does this all have to do with archiving and records management, you may wonder? Retention policies (and the other types of information management policies you can create in SharePoint) provide a direct way of managing records and non-records alike and give you a lot more control over the who, what, when, why, and how of documents, items, and content types stored in your SharePoint site. In fact, one of those retention policy actions is Transfer to Another Location, and that location can be a Records Center.

Setting Up a Records Center

A *Records Center* is a special type of SharePoint site template. Using a site based on the Records Center template, you can

>> Have more than one Records Center in your farm

>> Move a document to the Records Center instead of creating a copy, and put a link in the old location that points to the new location in the Records Center

>> Route more intelligently based on content or item properties

>> Have better control over the naming of the folders when items are routed to the Records Center

>> Allow users to create records in place and not have to use the Records Center at all

With all these improvements, it's time to create a Records Center and start setting it up. Because a Records Center is a site template, you simply create a new site based on that template.

TIP

Microsoft has been on a mission to simplify SharePoint so you will need to do a little digging to create a site based on the Records Center template. First, log into the SharePoint Admin Center in Microsoft 365 (see Chapter 21 on how to do it). Select Create and choose Other Options. In the Site Template selection drop-down menu, choose Other Templates. You will then see all of the traditional SharePoint templates that Microsoft would rather you didn't use.

After you have created a Records Center, your home page will look similar to Figure 22-10.

FIGURE 22-10:
The Records Center home page.

Click the Settings gear icon and choose Manage Records Center. On this new page, you see a lot of information to help you set up your Records Center. Read the steps about tasks and file plans because those are much like standard SharePoint functionality, such as creating Library apps, looking at and/or creating content types, and designing the home page. We talk about Content Organizer rules in the next section.

TIP

You can set up Send To links in Central Administration for users to send documents to a Records Center. In the Action section of the Stage Properties dialog box, you specify three options: Copy, Move, and Move and Leave a Link.

Using the Content Organizer

The Content Organizer, and specifically the rules that it manages, is where all the intelligence happens in the Records Center. Rules allow you to control where records go after they are submitted to the Records Center and what properties those items have. The absolute best thing about the Content Organizer is that it allows users not to have to think about their own content — they just declare it a record and their job is done.

Figure 22-11 shows the Content Organizer new rule page. You navigate to this page by clicking the Settings gear icon and choosing Manage Records Center and then Add New Item in the Content Organizer Rules section.

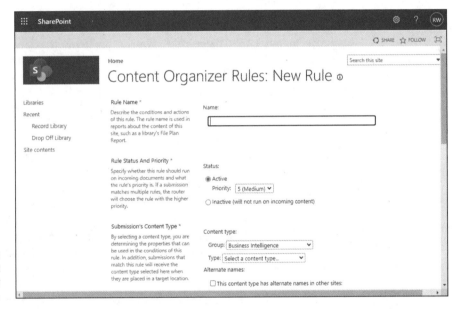

FIGURE 22-11: The Content Organizer new rule page.

A rule has five different categories — Rule Name, Rule Status and Priority, Submission's Content Type, Conditions, and Target Location. Rule Name and Rule Status and Priority are self-explanatory, so we focus on explaining the other categories.

Submission's Content Type may seem simple, but it has the ability to make matches across multiple content type names, so you can check the This Content Type Has Alternate Names in Other Sites check box and add those names to the list. What's really powerful here is that you can specify the catch-all asterisk (*) and sweep up all the content types based on the base content type for this rule. For example, you might want to include the rule for all legal-based content types that might have multiple names. You might have content types called Legal Documents, Briefs, and Cases. All of these are legal-based content types and should be included.

Conditions allow you to devise some logic based on the properties of the item submitted. Take the Picture content type, for example. You can choose from one of the properties of the content type, such as Date Picture Taken, and set the condition to a date at the end of last year, so all pictures can be moved to a location based on when they were taken.

Also notice you can have multiple conditions by clicking the Add Another Condition link. So you could have a rule that routes pictures taken during the 2021 or 2022 calendar year.

Target Location, the last item for your new rule, is where you want to send these items. Remember that these rules are run on items that are submitted to the Records Center. So items are held in the Drop Off Library until the Content Organizer has a chance to evaluate the content based on the rules set up for the Records Center. That's a long-winded way of asking, where do you want these documents to go?

You can specify another site that has a Content Organizer configured, or you can route the items that meet the conditions to a Library app in the Records Center itself. You can also have the Content Organizer group items with the same properties together in the same folder, and you have control over the name of that folder. Based on a property of the content type, the folder name includes, by default, the name of the property and its value. So if, for example, you had a custom picture content type that included the employee's department name, and the column on the content type was called Dept, your folder would be named Dept — Claims Adjusters if the user worked in the Claims Adjusters department.

REMEMBER

Having (or creating) the right columns on the content types that you want to manage is critical for getting the rules to function the way you need them to. So spend some extra effort to identify and get the right content types in place for your important documents and files. Not only will it help you maintain some sort of control over how content is created, but it also helps you establish good policies for organizing your records.

Managing Records in Place

In the effort to make records management more flexible, SharePoint supports managing records outside the Records Center, on any document and on any site. As we mention earlier, Microsoft would rather you just create a basic Team site and activate the features you want instead of creating a site, like a Records Center, that is already pre-built for you. We have been using the Records Center site template for years and we like it so we are sticking with it. If you are brand new to SharePoint then perhaps it is better to follow Microsoft's guidance and stick with a simple Team site and activate the In Place Records Management feature on the site you want to use for records. When you use a Records Center template, the features you need are already activated for you.

TIP

The In Place Records Management feature must be activated at the site collection level. After it is, each list-based or library-based app gets a Record Declaration Settings link on the app settings page. As shown in Figure 22-12, the settings on this page enable you to control whether and how records are declared, and you can even declare records automatically as items are added to the Document Library app (not that this feature is used very often).

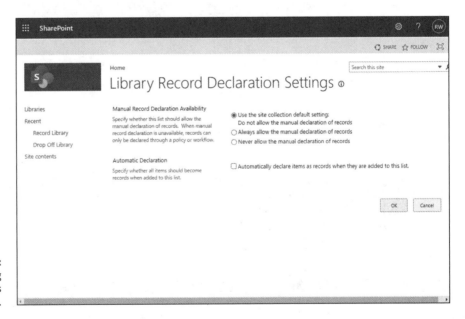

FIGURE 22-12:
Controlling
in-place records
declaration.

TIP

The Automatically Declare Items as Records When They Are Added to This List check box is selected by default. This causes the Manual Record Declaration Activity options to be disabled until you deselect the check box.

If records are allowed to be declared in the Library app, you click the ellipsis for the document, click the second ellipsis, and then select Compliance Details from the Advanced menu, as shown in Figure 22-13. The Compliance Details dialog box includes a link to declare the document as a record if records are allowed to be declared in the app. Clicking it shows a warning about locking down the item for editing. After you click OK, SharePoint makes the document a record. Users can revert a record to a document from this same dialog box, and if anyone tries to edit the document while it's a record, they receive an error message saying that it's checked out by the system account.

TIP

The powerful feature of in-place records management is that it keeps the documents available for users to reference without taking them out of the context of the app and site where they were originally created. But the record still shows up on records reports and can be managed centrally.

Placing Records on Litigation Hold

After you have all these retention policies and records being managed based on rules, you may have to temporarily suspend these policies. This is typically due to pending litigation where records matching certain criteria must be preserved until the litigation or court matter is settled.

The first thing you have to do is create the hold. You can do this in the Records Center, or you can do it at the site collection level. Figure 22-14 shows the Hold section of the Site Settings page for a Records Center site. Holds are easy to create and need a title, description, and an owner. Make sure to create at least one of these for each litigation or court matter that is required.

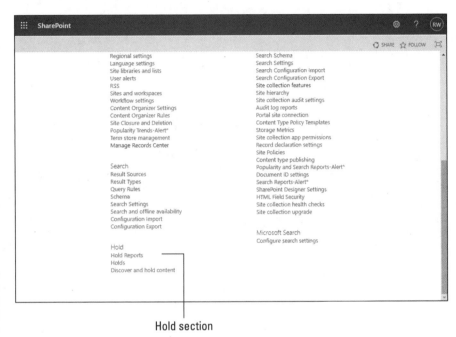

Regional settings
Language settings
Site libraries and lists
User alerts
RSS
Sites and workspaces
Workflow settings
Content Organizer Settings
Content Organizer Rules
Site Closure and Deletion
Popularity Trends-Alert*
Term store management
Manage Records Center

Search
Result Sources
Result Types
Query Rules
Schema
Search Settings
Search and offline availability
Configuration Import
Configuration Export

Hold
Hold Reports
Holds
Discover and hold content

Search Schema
Search Settings
Search Configuration Import
Search Configuration Export
Site collection features
Site hierarchy
Site collection audit settings
Audit log reports
Portal site connection
Content Type Policy Templates
Storage Metrics
Site collection app permissions
Record declaration settings
Site Policies
Content type publishing
Popularity and Search Reports-Alert*
Document ID settings
Search Reports-Alert*
SharePoint Designer Settings
HTML Field Security
Site collection health checks
Site collection upgrade

Microsoft Search
Configure search settings

FIGURE 22-14:
Managing holds and eDiscovery at the site collection level.

Hold section

The more interesting part is the Discover and Hold Content link. As shown in Figure 22-15, there are a few different parts to discovering content to put on hold. The first one, Search Criteria, allows you to select a site and enter search terms much the same way that you regularly search for content in SharePoint. Click Preview Results after typing in one or more terms to see the results in a new window.

After you have your search terms down, you can choose whether you want the items that come back in the search results to be kept in place and added to a local hold or copied to another location. If you choose another location, most likely that will be the Records Center site, which might be the best way to put items on hold without alerting users.

The last thing you need to specify is the hold you're going to apply to the records. This ensures that the documents do not expire or do not otherwise get altered due to an information management policy, and it also ensures that users can't "accidentally" delete the items.

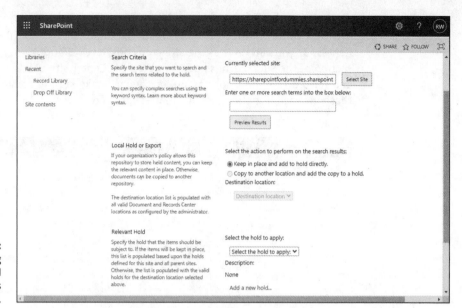

FIGURE 22-15: Configuring eDiscovery and placing items on hold.

Chapter **23**

Finding What You Need with Search

SharePoint search provides a powerful and intuitive mechanism for finding content. Right out of the box, SharePoint lets users search for content and narrow down results. SharePoint search can be configured and fine-tuned to meet the needs of your organization. In this manner, you can think of search as a platform instead of a feature that is either on or off.

In this chapter, we walk you through how search works in SharePoint. You find out how to search for content and refine results. You then explore some of the configuration options available for search and discover how to create your own Search Center site.

Understanding How SharePoint Search Works

Search is an often-misunderstood feature in SharePoint. Many users simply think that search is either on or off. In fact, search can be configured and is very robust. For example, the results of a SharePoint search can be tweaked using query rules in order to provide the best possible results for users. Maybe a user searches for *marketing*, but what the user is really looking for is the Marketing app, which contains all the official marketing documents for the organization. Using query rules, you can make the Marketing app show up at the top of the search results.

TECHNICAL STUFF

One of the biggest improvements in search in SharePoint is the integration of FAST search. FAST was an Oslo, Norway–based company that Microsoft acquired. In previous versions of SharePoint, FAST search was a separate product. In modern SharePoint, the FAST technology is baked right into SharePoint. So when you search in SharePoint, you're using FAST technology even if you don't realize it.

Under the covers, SharePoint search is provided through a Search service. The Search service crawls through content and creates an index. The index is then used to provide results for a search query.

When a user types a term in the Search text box and presses Enter, the Search service consults the index and returns the results in a web page.

If you add a new document or item but can't find it in a search result, then the Search service has not yet crawled and indexed the content. If your organization uses SharePoint On-Premises, the timing can be set by your administrator. If you organization uses SharePoint Online as part of your Microsoft 365 subscription, Microsoft handles the Search service for you automatically. We have found that new items generally appear in the search results within an hour or so after we create them.

Searching for Content

Searching for content in SharePoint is straightforward. Every site contains a Search text box at the top of the page, as shown in Figure 23-1.

To search for content, you simply type your term in the text box and click the magnifying glass to the right of the Search text box. The SharePoint search engine performs a query using your terms and displays the results. You will also notice that as you type, the search engine provides real-time recommendations.

Aside from simply typing in search terms, you can instruct the search engine to do special things in a number of ways when it performs the query. For example, you can use special characters and limit the search results based on properties in SharePoint.

Search text box

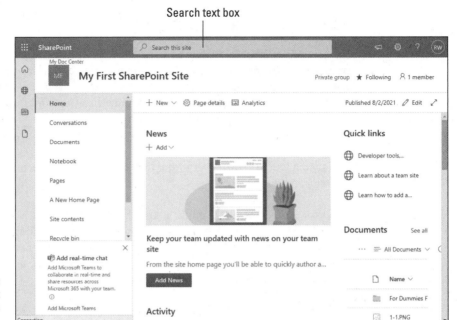

FIGURE 23-1:
The Search text
box on a
SharePoint site.

Searching for a string using quotation marks

When you enter multiple terms in the Search text box, the SharePoint search engine looks through the content and returns instances that contain any of those words. If you want a phrase of two or more words (called a *string*), then you need to surround the phrase in quotation marks. For example, the following search query returns any content that contains either the word *Annual* or the word *Report*.

```
Annual Report
```

If you're looking for content where the words are found together, then you would type the search string in quotation marks.

```
"Annual Report"
```

The search engine takes anything within the quotation marks and looks for that entire string in the content.

Wildcard searches

The asterisk character (*) can be used to represent a wildcard in a search. For example, maybe you need to find a document that you know begins with *Quarter*, but you can't remember if it is *Quarters* or *Quarterly*. You could use the wildcard character to search for everything that begins with the word *Quarter* as follows:

```
Quarter*
```

This search would return everything that begins with the term *Quarter*, including *Quarterly* and *Quarters*.

Along the same lines, you might know that the first word is *Quarterly*, but you don't know if the second word is *Reports* or *Results*. You would then use the quotation marks along with the wildcard character to tell the search engine that you want all content that contains the word *Quarterly* followed by any word that starts with the letter *R*. The query would be as follows:

```
"Quarterly R*"
```

The wildcard character is a very powerful way to expand your search results when you know only a piece of the puzzle instead of an exact term.

Including and excluding terms

You can instruct the search engine to only return results that include a certain word by using the + symbol. For example, you could write your search as:

```
Annual Reports +Marketing
```

The plus symbol says that any content that is returned must have the word *Marketing* in it, in addition to either the word *Annual* or the word *Reports*.

One problem with search is that you often get many more results than you can sift through. You can also exclude specific words to trim your search results. For example, you might be searching for product marketing content, but want to exclude any content that contains the word *internal*. You could write your search as follows:

```
"Product Marketing" -internal
```

The search engine then returns all content that contains either the words *Product* or *Marketing* and removes any content that also contains the word *internal*.

Building compound search queries using Boolean operators

Building compound search queries involves multiple search expressions. You use the Boolean operators to string expressions together into compound queries.

The Boolean operators consist of the following:

>> **AND:** Only returns content when both statements are true.

>> **NOT:** Only returns content where the statement is not true. This is the same thing as using the minus sign, as described in the previous section.

>> **OR:** Returns content when one or more of the statements are true.

TIP

Typing two words in the Search text box is the same thing as typing the first word followed by OR and then typing the second word. Where Boolean operators become valuable is when they are used with parentheses. Boolean operators are often used in combination with parentheses in order to let the search engine know how to group the query statements, as described in the next section.

Getting fancy with the parentheses

The parentheses characters, (and), are used to build compound search queries that use multiple expressions. For example, you might want to search for two key words and narrow the results down by one type of property or another. How would you write all this together in a search term? Wouldn't the search engine get confused? Well, you use parentheses to tell the search engine exactly what you want it to do and when. For example, say you want to search for any content that has the string *For Dummies* or contains the word *Reports*. You would write this query as:

```
"For Dummies" OR Reports
```

Now say you also want the query to also only show content where the location property of the content is *Pacific Northwest* or the author is *Rosemarie Withee*. You use parentheses to combine these two aspects:

```
("For Dummies" OR Reports) AND (location:"Pacific
Northwest" OR author:"Rosemarie Withee")
```

TIP

Note that when you actually type a long query, it will all be on one line in the Search text box. (The margins in this book required a line break.) When you enter a query into the Search text box, don't press Enter until you're ready to execute your search. Hitting the Enter key is the same as clicking the magnifying glass.

Finding terms in proximity

You sometimes may need to find content where you know two words are near each other but not necessarily right next to each other. For example, take a look at the following sentence:

> The sales figures for China are excellent.

This sentence contains the words *sales* and *China* in close proximity. If you were just to type *sales China* in the Search text box, you would surely get this content, but you also might get a ton of other, irrelevant content. You could find the result you're looking for using the NEAR operator as follows:

```
"sales" NEAR(5) "China"
```

The number in the parentheses lets the NEAR operator know that you want to only turn results where the words are within five words of each other. The number is not required, however. You could just as easily write the query:

```
"sales" NEAR "China"
```

When you do not specify the number of words, the search engine uses eight words as a default. That is, the words are considered near if they are within eight words of each other.

You might come across a scenario where it isn't enough if two terms are near each other, but they should also appear in a particular order. For example, you might want to only return results were the word *sales* is followed by the word *China* within a certain number of words. The Boolean operator that makes this possible is ONEAR.

The ONEAR operator works just like the NEAR operator; however, it assumes an order. The following query tells the search engine to only return content where the word *sales* is followed by the word *China* within five words.

```
"sales" ONEAR(5) "China"
```

Same meaning, different terms

Did you watch the TV, telly, or television? Did you go to the theater or theatre? Well, you could watch or attend either and it would all mean the same thing. Synonyms are easy for humans to understand. So easy, in fact, that we don't pay many of the obvious ones much thought. Have you ever heard people answer the question by saying they don't watch television but watch TV? If only computers could be so smart.

The WORDS operator is used to let the search engine know when two words mean the same thing. For example, if you're looking for all content that references *California*, you could write the query as follows:

```
WORDS(CA, California)
```

The result is that the search engine knows *CA* and *California* mean the same thing and returns the results accordingly. This begs the question, why not just type the two words in the Search text box? The answer is in the ranking of the results. If the search engine knows these words mean the same thing, then it will return results accordingly. If it doesn't know this, then it might return content that contains both terms *California* and *CA* at the top of the list but have more relevant content that only contains the word *CA* farther down the list. If you use the WORDS operator, the search engine knows that these words mean the same and will provide you the best matches in the results.

Viewing and Refining Search Results

After a query is run, you are presented with the results page, as shown in Figure 23-2.

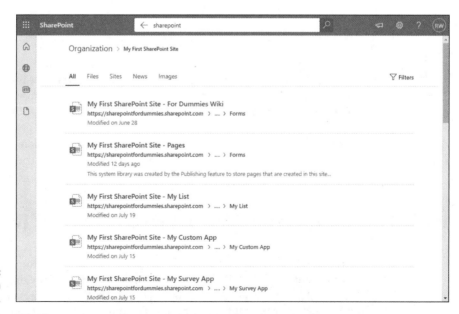

FIGURE 23-2:
The search
results page.

The results page has a lot going on, but it's mostly intuitive. If a result is an Office document, such as Word or Excel, or some other type of document that has a preview option, you will see a thumbnail preview to the right of the search result. In Figure 23-2, you can see that the first result is a SharePoint site, while in Figure 23-3 the first result is an Office Word document and there is a preview of the document contents to the right of the result.

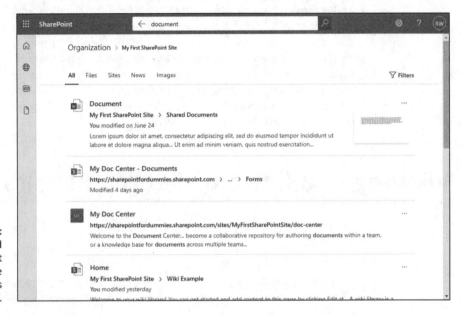

FIGURE 23-3:
An Office Word document preview in the search results page.

Buttons at the top of the page include filters that you can use for narrowing down the results. You can click a particular type of content or narrow the results based on the date the content was modified.

TIP

We find narrowing down content based on the last modified date to be an extremely useful feature because stale content can be a real problem in search results.

Making Search Your Users' Best Friend

Finding the right content can be an exercise in frustration. Companies like Google were founded on the basis of indexing the Internet and providing access through search. Before Google, the Internet was organized into pockets of content on services such as AOL. After Google roared onto the scene, you could just browse to www.google.com and type in what you were looking for in the Search text box, and presto, it was usually right there in the first few pages of results. How did Google do it? It used specialized algorithms to index all the content on the Internet.

Search has come a long way since the early days of Google (though Google still dominates). SharePoint search is a platform designed to let your users find content in, and outside, of your SharePoint environment. Right out of the box, SharePoint indexes content in your SharePoint sites and returns the results. Many organizations don't take search any further than the out-of-box experience, but they should.

As a site administrator, you can tweak the SharePoint search results based on the nuances of your company. For example, maybe you have a site for call center representatives. You know they're always searching for product documentation, so you don't want the official product documentation sites to appear mixed down in with the rest of the content that just happens to mention the products. You can configure SharePoint search to promote the official pages above other pages. You can even create related searches that will show up right next to the search results that users see. All of this is made possible using query rules.

A *query rule* is a rule that SharePoint search uses when processing a search query. In other words, a query rule allows you, as a site administrator, the ability to instruct the search engine how to respond to certain queries.

TIP

The search query functionality provides the same result as the Best Bets functionality of previous SharePoint versions. The Best Bets functionality has been extended to include related search blocks and result ranking. The entire feature set is now made possible in search queries.

Here's an example to help you understand how a query rule works. This example consists of two parts. The first is that you want an Employee Onboarding app to show up whenever someone searches for the word *onboarding* or the phrase *new employee.* In this example, the Onboarding app is a list that contains all the onboarding steps for new employees of the organization. The second part is that you want a result block added to the results whenever someone searches for onboarding or new employee. A *results block* is just a parallel query of your choosing that will show up in the search results.

To promote the Onboarding app whenever a person searches for the words onboarding or new employee, follow these steps:

1. **Navigate to the Site Settings page by the Settings gear icon in the top right of the screen and selecting Site Contents, and then click the Site Settings button.**

   The Site Settings page appears.

2. **In the Search section, click the Query Rules link.**

The Manage Query Rules page appears.

If you're a site collection administrator, you also see the Search Query Rules link in the Site Collection Administration section of the Site Settings page. The difference between these two Query Rules settings is that one affects only the site, and the other affects every site in the entire site collection. Because in this example, you only want to build the query for your particular site, click the Query Rules link in the Search section of the Site Settings page.

3. **Click the Result Source drop-down list and select Local SharePoint Results (System), as shown in Figure 23-4.**

The Query Rules load for the Local SharePoint Results source.

The Result Source drop-down list enables you to set the context of the query rule you're creating. Notice that there are many different result source options. These allow you to create finely tuned query rules. For example, you might want to create a rule for people search or conversations. In this example, you want only results for the local SharePoint site, so you choose Local SharePoint Results (System).

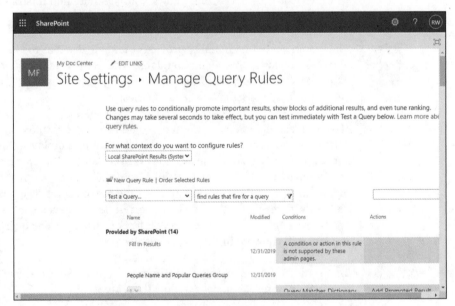

FIGURE 23-4:
Selecting Local SharePoint Results from the Manage Query Rules page.

4. **Click the New Query Rule button.**

The Add Query Rule page is displayed.

5. **Enter a name for the rule in the Rule Name text box, and then provide the search terms *new employee* and *onboarding* with a semicolon as a separator in the Search Term text box.**

   The exact text you should type is

   new employee; onboarding

6. **Click the Add Promoted Result link.**

   The Add Promoted Result dialog box is displayed, as shown in Figure 23-5.

   A *promoted result* is the same as a Best Bet in previous versions of SharePoint. When someone searches for the exact words *new employee* or *onboarding*, the promoted result appears at the top of the results page.

Add Promoted Result   ×

Title
Promoted Result for Employee Onboarding app
URL
https://sharepointfordummies.sharepoint.com/sites/MyFirstSharePointSite/
☐ Render the URL as a banner instead of as a hyperlink
Description
Whenever someone types "new employee" or "onboarding" in the search, this app will show up at the top of the search results.

                                   Save   Cancel

FIGURE 23-5:
The Add Promoted Result dialog box.

7. **Enter a title for your promoted result in the Title text box, provide the URL to the desired content in the URL text box, and type a description of the promoted result in the Description text box.**

   In this example, we typed Promoted Result for Employee Onboarding app in the Title text box. The Onboarding app is an app created from the Employee Onboarding template with the name Employee Onboarding.

8. **Click Save to save the promoted result to the query rule.**

9. **Click the Add Result Block link to add a related search to the results of a search that uses the specified words (*new employee* or *onboarding* in this example).**

   The Add Result Block dialog box is displayed, as shown in Figure 23-6. A results block lets you perform another search based on the terms you want to include and shows the results in its own block of search results. This is valuable when you want to help people's search terms based on your knowledge of the content. For example, if people are searching for "data" but in your organization your terminology is referenced as "statistics," you can add a search block to show "statistics" results even when someone searches for "data."

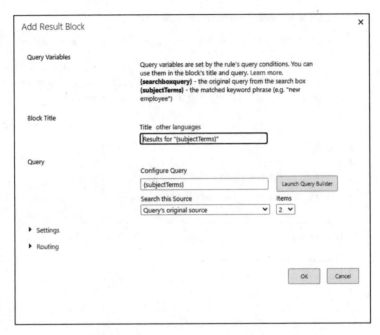

Add Result Block   ✕

Query Variables

Query variables are set by the rule's query conditions. You can use them in the block's title and query. Learn more.
{searchboxquery} - the original query from the search box
{subjectTerms} - the matched keyword phrase (e.g. "new employee")

Block Title

Title   other languages

Results for "{subjectTerms}"

Query

Configure Query

{subjectTerms}   [Launch Query Builder]

Search this Source   Items

Query's original source ⌄   2 ⌄

▶ Settings

▶ Routing

[OK]   [Cancel]

FIGURE 23-6:
The Add Result Block dialog box.

10. **In the Title text box, enter the title for the result block.**

The default is to show the search terms that were used for the result block.

11. **In the Configure Query text box, enter the search terms you want to use for the result block.**

Think of these terms as if you were searching the SharePoint site and want to include this second search in a search for *new employee* or *onboarding*. In this example, we use the default, which is the subject terms, to return all content with the exact string *new employee* or *onboarding*.

12. **Click OK to save the result block, and then click Save to save the query rule.**

TIP

On the Manage Query Rules page you can test queries to see which rules will be triggered. For example, while writing this chapter, we would select Promoted Results Contains and then enter the words *new employee* or *onboarding* and see which of the rules would be triggered.

Now when a user types the search term *new employee* or *onboarding* into the Search text box for the site, the user sees a promoted Employee Onboarding app at the top of the page and the result block for a parallel search on the same words. Figure 23-7 shows the result. We don't have a lot of content in our site so we only get one result but you can imagine how powerful this behavior can be as your content continues to grow.

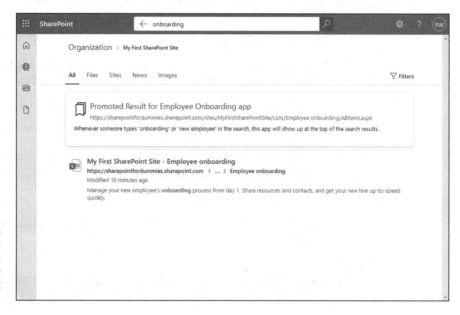

FIGURE 23-7:
The search results page with our Employee Onboarding query rule.

TIP

The example only covers a small portion of the possibilities with query rules. We recommend playing around with them and tweaking them to provide just the right results for your users. As users begin to search on the site, you can see what terms they type in the Search text box and adapt the query rules to suit their needs. From your users' perspectives, the search will get better and better as time progresses, even if you're the wizard behind the curtain pulling the strings to make it happen.

TIP

Search results don't appear immediately after you make a change. In order to see the change, you need to wait for the search engine to reindex the content in the site. *Indexing* just means looking through all the content and prepping it for search results accordingly. You can force the site to start reindexing by going to Site Settings, opening the Search and Offline Availability page, and then clicking the Reindex Site button.

Removing Content from Search Results

By default, items and documents in apps appear in search results. You may not want these items to appear in search results. To keep items and documents in apps out of search results, follow these steps:

1. **Navigate to the app that you want to remove from search by clicking the Settings gear icon and choosing Site Contents.**

You see a list of all apps.

2. **Click the app to open it and then open the app settings page by clicking the gear icon again and clicking List Settings or Library Settings.**

The App Settings page appears.

3. **Click the Advanced Settings link in the General Settings section.**

The Advanced Settings page appears.

4. **In the Search section, select the No radio button, as shown in Figure 23-8.**

5. **Click OK to save the settings.**

The content of the app will not be indexed the next time the search engine indexes content.

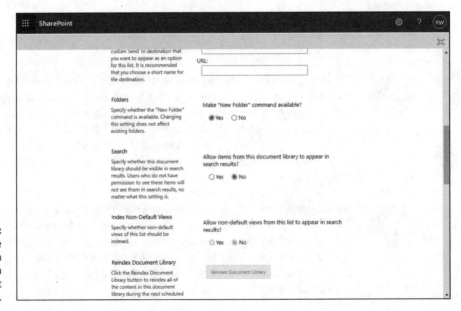

FIGURE 23-8: Removing the contents of an app from SharePoint search results.

You can view which properties are searched by clicking the Schema link in the Search section of the Site Settings page. The Search column shows whether the property is used in building the search index.

The administrator can also remove specific URLs from the current index so that they don't appear before the next crawl has time to happen. This is accomplished in the SharePoint Admin Center (see Chapter 21). In the SharePoint Admin Center, select More Features from the navigation menu in the upper-left corner of the screen and then Search Settings. Select Remove Search Results, enter the URLs you want to remove, and then click Remove Now. If you are using SharePoint On-Premises, the administrator can find the same functionality in the Search Service Application Management page. Click the Crawl Log, find the result to remove, click the ellipsis button for the item, and choose Remove the Item from the Index.

Likewise, a URL can be removed from the results by clicking the Search Result Removal page in the Queries and Results section of the Search Service Application management page in Central Administration and entering the URL that should be removed from the search result. You can find the result to remove by clicking the URL view and then clicking the arrow to choose the Remove the Item from the Index link.

Reviewing Search Analytics

SharePoint provides a number of usage reports for search. These include reports such as Number of Queries, Top Queries, Abandoned Queries, No Result Queries, and Query Rule Usage. The good news is that the reports are based in Excel, so you can download them, open them in Excel, and use the data to present in nice graphs for executives. The reports can be found in the SharePoint Admin Center (see Chapter 21). In the SharePoint Admin Center, select More Features from the navigation menu in the upper-left corner of the screen and then Search Settings. Select the View Usage Reports link to view the report.

Adding a Search Center Site

You can configure search for your site and settings at the site collection level and point results to a specific Search Center site. A *Search Center site* is a SharePoint site that has been created using a search template. By creating a Search Center site, you have the ability to customize it for your particular needs.

SharePoint provides two site templates that are built for delivering search results. You can use these templates to create a branded search experience or to customize how results appear. The Search Center site templates are:

>> **Basic Search Center:** This template delivers a stripped-down search experience in one page. This site template uses Web Part pages and is essentially a Team site specialized for search.

>> **Enterprise Search Center:** This template provides multiple pages for displaying search results. This site template uses publishing pages, which makes it easier to brand and customize than a page based on the Basic Search Center template.

Microsoft has been trying to simplify the SharePoint experience, so you have to dig a little bit to find the search site templates. Follow the steps in Chapter 22, where you create a site based on the Records Center template, and instead choose one of the Search Center templates. You will find them on the Enterprise tab, as shown in Figure 23-9.

FIGURE 23-9:
Selecting a Search Center template when creating a new site.

To configure your site collection to use your Search Center site:

1. **Click the Settings gear icon and choose Site Contents and then click the Site Settings button that appears in the ribbon.**

   The Site Settings page appears.

2. **In the Site Collection Administration section, click the Search Settings link.**

   The Search Settings page appears, as shown in Figure 23-10.

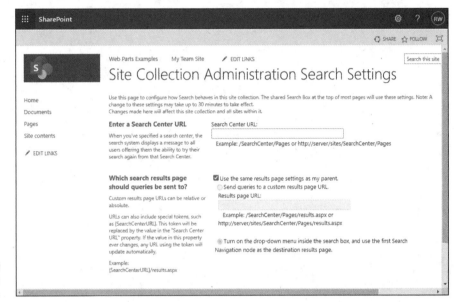

FIGURE 23-10:
Configure search
settings.

3. **Enter the URL of the Search Center site in the Search Center URL text box.**

   Your search center doesn't have to be in the same site collection as the sites that are using it for search. You can create a new site collection using one of the Search Center templates and configure multiple site collections to use that same search center.

4. **Click OK to save the settings.**

   After making the change, you need to wait up to 30 minutes before the change is reflected in search.

After the Search Center site is in place and configured in Search Settings, all results are directed to the search site. It takes some time for the changes to take effect, however, because a SharePoint scheduled process has to update the configuration for the site. If you don't see your changes right away, check back an hour later. You can then develop the search site to meet the specific needs of your organization.

REMEMBER

The settings we describe in this section set the default experience for all Search text boxes in your site. Individual Search text boxes found on the master page, in page layouts, or placed directly on web pages can be configured to use the default settings or have their own custom settings.

TIP

You aren't restricted to using the Search Web Parts in the search center. You can create your own search results page and add the Search Web Parts to the page.

Chapter **24**

Integrating with Power BI

M icrosoft Power BI (pronounced "bee-eye" as an acronym for *Business Intelligence*) is a cloud-based business analytics service. It can be found at https://powerbi.microsoft.com. You don't need to have a Microsoft 365 subscription in order to use Power BI; there is a free version available to get you started, and a more advanced version (called Power BI Pro) for which you pay a small monthly subscription fee (around $10 a month). If you purchase a Microsoft 365 E5 subscription, you get the Pro version of Power BI included.

In this chapter, we focus on how you can integrate SharePoint with Power BI. You learn how to build a report with Power BI and how to connect your reports to SharePoint so that people can use them without ever needing to leave a SharePoint site.

Signing into Power BI

You can sign into Power BI with your existing Microsoft 365 credentials (that you create in Chapter 1 with your Microsoft 365 trial subscription, if you are following along). When you first log into Power BI at https://powerbi.microsoft.com, (and then click the Power BI Service button at the top of the page) you are notified that your Power BI account will be linked to your Microsoft 365 account.

TIP

The terms of service notification that appears when you first sign in also notifies you that the administrator of your version of Microsoft 365 (such as your organization) will also have control over your Power BI data. If you know any compliance officers, this would be a good thing to bring up to them to win brownie points.

Once you complete the sign-in process, you are presented with your Power BI workspace, as shown in Figure 24-1. Think of this as your one-stop shop for all your Power BI information. This is where you will create connections to pull data into your reports and upload the reports themselves. To build reports you will use a tool called the Power BI Desktop, which we take a look at next.

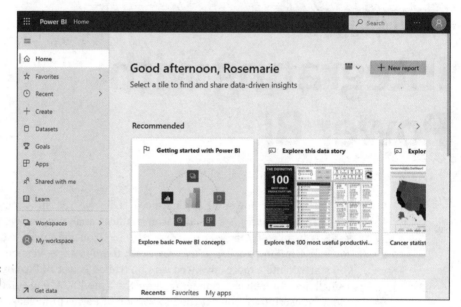

FIGURE 24-1:
The Power BI workspace.

Installing the Power BI Desktop

You build Power BI reports using a tool called the Power BI Desktop. You install this tool onto your computer, and then use it to build reports. If you are familiar with building documents with Microsoft Word, you are already familiar with the concept. Just like you can install Microsoft Word on your computer and create Word documents, you can install Power BI Desktop on your computer and create reports. After you build a report in Power BI Desktop, you can then upload it to your online Power BI workspace and view it using a web browser.

To install the Power BI Desktop tool:

1. **Open a web browser and log into your Power BI workspace.**

2. **Click the ellipsis that appears in the upper-right corner of the screen and choose Download and then Power BI Desktop, as shown in Figure 24-2.**

The download page appears and you can download the installer. You can choose to download either 32-bit or 64-bit depending on your computer (you can check by right-clicking the Start menu and then selecting System). We are using a 32-bit computer so we choose the standard setup option.

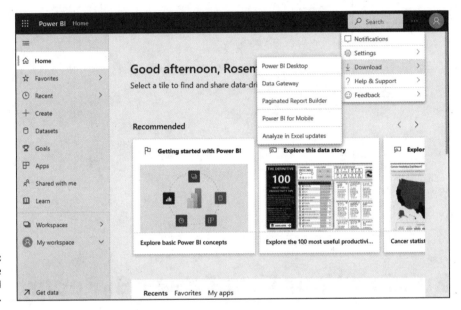

FIGURE 24-2:
Downloading the
Power BI
Desktop app.

WARNING

If you choose the wrong option, and we did this at first, then the installer starts and then just disappears. It took us some time to realize we chose the 64-bit option even though we are using a 32-bit computer. Once we went back and downloaded the 32-bit option, the installer completed successfully.

3. **Click Run in the installation window and follow the installation process.**

Once installed, you will find Power BI Desktop in your Apps menu on your computer.

When you open the Power BI Desktop for the first time, you are presented with a screen to sign up for a new Power BI account. At the bottom of this dialog box you will see a link to use an existing account to sign in.

4. **Click the Get Started button and enter your Microsoft 365 credentials, as shown in Figure 24-3.**

   Your Power BI Desktop app is now connected to your Power BI account, which is in turn connected to your Microsoft 365 account, and you are presented with some videos to watch to get started.

   You are now ready to build a report!

FIGURE 24-3:
Signing into the
Power BI Desktop
app with your
Microsoft 365
credentials.

Building Your First Power BI Report

Using Power BI Desktop to build reports is a topic for an entire book unto itself. The Power BI Desktop app is a very powerful tool, and you can pull data from almost any source. In a nutshell, you build queries to pull data into Power BI and then use various visualizations to display that data in a report. In Figure 24-4, notice the Get Data drop-down menu in the top-left part of the screen and the components for adding visualizations on the right side of the screen. These tools are all you really need to build your first report.

For your first report, click the Enter Data button in the Data group on the Home tab of the ribbon and type in some data. In this example, we will enter dates in the first column and values in the second column, as shown in Figure 24-5. Click the Load button to load the data.

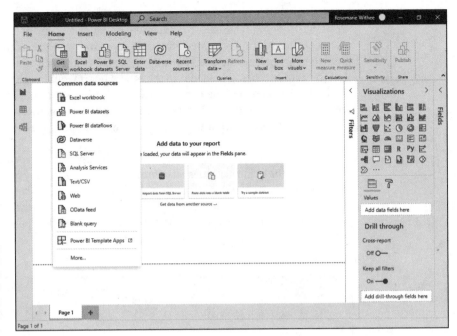

FIGURE 24-4:
Getting data and finding the visualizations components in the Power BI Desktop.

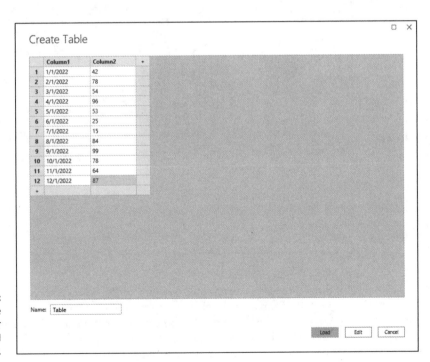

FIGURE 24-5:
Adding simple test data for our first Power BI report.

While writing this chapter, we experienced an issue where our Microsoft 365 account was not properly synced with the computer we were using. The result was that when we clicked the Load button, the dialog box would stall with the message that the data was being loaded into the model but it would never finish. To resolve the issue, we rebooted the computer and fixed the sync issue that appeared on reboot. The root cause was that we had to revalidate our password and authentication code. Once we did that the data loaded without an issue into Power BI.

Once the data is loaded, you will see it just to the right of the visualizations. In this case, we left the column names as Column1 and Column2. Play around with adding visualizations onto the design canvas (the middle part of the desktop) and clicking to select data columns. In this example we added a bar chart and then displayed the month for each bar and the sum for each bar height, as shown in Figure 24-6.

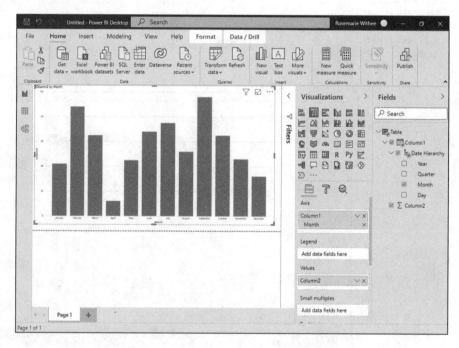

FIGURE 24-6:
A simple Power BI report using months and sums.

Building a report is very cool, but you can't expect everyone to download the Power BI Desktop in order to open and view your report. Therefore, to ensure others can see it, you can publish it to the Power BI website by clicking the Publish button in the Share group on the Home tab of the ribbon.

Make sure to save your Power BI file regularly. A Power BI file has the .pbix extension. If you ever want to send your "source" file to others, you can send them the .pbix file to open in the Power BI Desktop on their own computers.

Once your report is published, you will see it in your Power BI workspace. You can share links to this file so anyone in the world can view your report by just clicking on a link in their web browsers. The report we created is shown in our Edge web browser in our Power BI workspace in Figure 24-7.

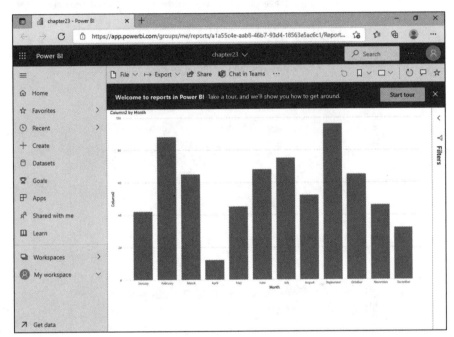

FIGURE 24-7:
Viewing a Power BI report using a web browser.

Pulling Data into Power BI from SharePoint

You can use countless data sources for your Power BI reports. One option is to pull data directly from SharePoint's Library app and List app. (SharePoint apps are covered in Chapter 11.)

SharePoint Library app

A SharePoint Library app includes content and also metadata about that content in the form of columns. You can pull this data into Power BI so that you can include it in your reports.

To pull SharePoint Library app data into your Power BI report:

1. **In the Power BI Desktop app, click the Get Data drop-down menu located in the Data group on the Home tab of the ribbon and select More.**

   The Get Data dialog box appears.

2. **Scroll down, or search for the word "sharepoint," and choose SharePoint Folder, as shown in Figure 24-8.**

FIGURE 24-8:
Choosing a data
source in the
Power BI
Desktop.

3. **Click Connect.**

4. **Enter the URL for your SharePoint site.**

   In this example we enter `https://sharepointfordummies.sharepoint.com/sites/MyFirstSharePointSite`.

5. **Click OK to connect.**

6. **Enter the credentials the report will use to allow access to the SharePoint site.**

In this example we choose Microsoft Account, and we click Sign In so that we can use our Microsoft 365 credentials.

7. **Click Connect to connect the Power BI Desktop with your SharePoint site.**

Data from your SharePoint site will be displayed so you can preview it, as shown in Figure 24-9.

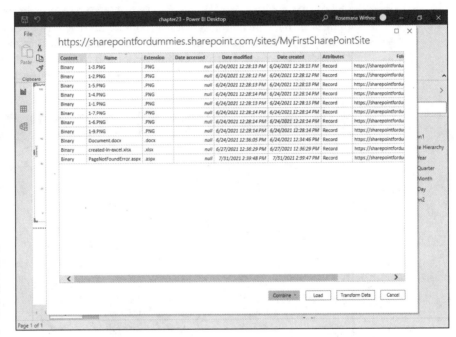

FIGURE 24-9:
Loading data from a SharePoint Library app into the Power BI Desktop.

8. **Click Load to load the data into the Power BI Desktop.**

Once your SharePoint data has finished loading, you can use it to build a report with Power BI. Some of the types of data you can include for content include Date Accessed, Date Created, Date Modified, File Extension, Folder Path, and Name.

SharePoint List app

A SharePoint List app is similar to a spreadsheet. Your app contains columns and rows of data. These apps are central to SharePoint and you can import the data in them into your Power BI reports.

Importing SharePoint List app data is the same process previously outlined for importing SharePoint Library app data; however, instead of selecting SharePoint Folder as a data source, select SharePoint Online List or SharePoint List.

TIP

The Get Data dialog box (shown earlier in Figure 24-8) includes many different sources of data including all of the popular third-party sites such as GitHub, Google Analytics, Adobe, Facebook, Mailchimp, QuickBooks, Stripe, Twilio, Zendesk, Webtrends, and SurveyMonkey, just to name a few. If you have data you want to report on, chances are you can use Power BI to connect and report on it.

FIGURE 24-10: Choosing the Power BI Web Part to add to a SharePoint page.

Displaying a Power BI Report on a SharePoint Page

Earlier in the chapter you learned how to publish your Power BI report to the Power BI workspace website. People can view that report by opening their web browsers and entering a shareable link you provide to them. You can also embed a report directly into a SharePoint page on a SharePoint site.

To embed a report on a SharePoint page, you must use a special Web Part for Power BI. (Refer back to Chapter 6 for information on adding Web Parts to a SharePoint page.) To add a Power BI report, choose the Power BI Web Part, as shown in Figure 24-10.

Once you add the Web Part to a page, you need to configure it. The configuration is very simple. You just provide the link to the Power BI report (the web URL of the report you viewed in Figure 24-7) and SharePoint takes care of rendering it for you right inside the SharePoint page, as shown in Figure 24-11.

FIGURE 24-11:
Rendering a
Power BI report
in SharePoint.

People using SharePoint can now view your Power BI reports without ever realizing it. All a regular user knows is that a report shows up on the SharePoint page.

In order to share reports directly from your Power BI workspace, you will need the Power BI Pro license. This license comes with a Microsoft 365 E5 subscription. You can also obtain a license for a stand-alone fee of approximately $10 per month.

REMEMBER

6

The Part of Tens

IN THIS PART . . .

Explore the Microsoft websites for the inside scoop on SharePoint.

Learn where to find help with the Office support site.

Maintain control with SharePoint governance.

Become a SharePoint guru.

Chapter **25**

Ten Hot SharePoint Topics

Microsoft has a number of websites on which it posts all of its detailed product information. This chapter outlines some of these sites, including those geared for IT professionals, administrators, and end users of SharePoint.

Getting Up to Speed with SharePoint

Using SharePoint is fairly straightforward. At the base level, it's simply a website that users navigate to using their web browser. In this sense, SharePoint is no different than any other website. A number of resources go deeper into the intricacies of SharePoint from a user level.

Microsoft maintains an excellent resource for help at https://support.office.com. This site contains all sorts of help topics for Office apps, including SharePoint Online. To find the SharePoint content, navigate to the site and click the SharePoint icon.

SharePoint Online Videos

https://channel9.msdn.com/Tags/sharepoint

Channel 9 is a Microsoft-focused video-content site. It includes a ton of resources for SharePoint and is worth checking out. Whether you are an administrator, power user, or end user you will find something worth watching on Microsoft's Channel 9.

SharePoint Online Official Documentation

https://docs.microsoft.com/en-us/sharepoint/sharepoint-online

Nothing beats the official, Microsoft created, documentation and you can find it on the docs.microsoft.com website. You will find all sorts of details for just about every feature in SharePoint. The documentation is technical in nature and not always the most interesting but it is a great resource when you want to dive deeper.

SharePoint Development

https://developer.microsoft.com/en-us/microsoft-365

When you need to bring in the developers, or if you are a developer yourself, you will find the Microsoft 365 Dev Center as a great place to point your browser. The Dev Center provides resources for Office development of all types, including SharePoint development. Just look for the SharePoint icon under the list of Office applications on the main landing page.

TIP

The term *developer* has an ever-changing meaning. In the past, a developer was a hard-core computer programmer. A modern SharePoint developer may have never taken a single computer class. Just because you don't dream in code doesn't mean you won't find the Office Dev Center very useful.

SharePoint Power Automate

`https://flow.microsoft.com`

Workflow is a critical business component to many organizations and Microsoft realizes that stability is incredibly important to business process.

Every organization accumulates processes. Processes are critical to every organization, whether you realize it or not. Maybe a new account has to be opened, or a new property has to be managed or transitioned: A process will be in place to help you get the job done. When you get down to it, the amount of processes that happen in and around any organization is staggering. We could produce a binder full of processes in a few hours.

In the SharePoint world, the orchestrator of processes is workflow. Using workflow, you can integrate not only technical processes, such as approving documents, but also human-based processes, such as giving a property tour.

Microsoft has introduced Power Automate, which we cover in Chapter 15, in order to accommodate workflow across many products, including non-Microsoft products. Using Power Automate you can build a workflow for just about anything.

TIP

If you are using SharePoint Server you might also check out workflow development platforms from Nintex (`www.nintex.com`) and K2 (`https://www.k2.com`).

Taking SharePoint for a Spin

In Chapter 1, we walk through setting up a SharePoint environment so you can get started in a few minutes. If you are looking to give SharePoint Server (On-Premises) a try you can download it at:

`https://docs.microsoft.com/en-us/sharepoint/install/install`

We recommend you start with Chapter 1, though, and stick with SharePoint Online as much as possible. Microsoft has made it very clear that the future is SharePoint Online and SharePoint Server is only for extremely large organizations with dedicated departments for installing and managing it.

Staying Current: The SharePoint Blog

https://www.microsoft.com/en-us/microsoft-365/blog/sharepoint/

The SharePoint product team maintains a blog where they keep the community informed about what is coming and what is changing. If you want to stay current with SharePoint, be sure to add this blog to your list.

TIP

The lines have blurred between Office products recently and you will find SharePoint along with all of the other products discussed on the SharePoint Blog site. We view this blurring of product boundaries as a good thing as it means SharePoint is becoming more and more integrated with the rest of the Office products. We picture a day when most people (who haven't read this book) won't even realize when they are using some aspect of SharePoint. To the uninformed world, the product will just be Microsoft Office even when they are actually using SharePoint under the covers.

New On-Premises Features in SharePoint Server

https://docs.microsoft.com/en-us/sharepoint/what-s-new/new-and-improved-features-in-sharepoint-server-2019

We have been working with SharePoint for years and years, and we still learn something new almost daily. SharePoint is a product with such depth that we doubt any one person can be a true expert on everything. Maybe a SharePoint master is out there somewhere who has explored every nook and cranny, but we have yet to meet that person.

When you're ready to dig deeper, the official SharePoint website excavates the SharePoint product in depth.

Plan for SharePoint

https://docs.microsoft.com/en-us/sharepoint/planning-guide

One of the primary reasons an organization will hire a consulting firm to deploy SharePoint is because of their experience and expertise. Remember the old saying that hindsight is 20/20? Well, it couldn't be truer with SharePoint. We remember our first few implementations back in the mid-2000s. We cringe when we recall how painful those first few installations were. Having worked with SharePoint for years and years at hundreds of organizations, we have finally built up an expertise to get implementing SharePoint right the first time.

Not everyone has the time, or desire, to dedicate so much time to SharePoint. And not everyone wants to hire a consultant. Microsoft has captured much of the knowledge it takes to plan for a SharePoint implementation and posted it to the `docs.microsoft.com` website.

SharePoint from the Leader

`https://twitter.com/jeffteper`

The de facto leader of the SharePoint team at Microsoft is Jeff Teper. He is a force of nature and regularly travels the world talking about SharePoint and learning from customers. If you want to know what is happening with SharePoint and you want to hear it directly from the SharePoint leader at Microsoft, following Jeff on Twitter is a must.

Chapter **26**

Ten Ways to Maintain Control with Governance

G overnance has gotten kind of a bad rap, in part because of its association with the banking scandals of past years. People hear the word and get all squirrely and anxious, especially when someone proposes governance that affects them. But a well-crafted website governance plan isn't about restricting people; in fact, it contains just enough detail to ensure a certain level of consistency and oversight. Website governance is about the people, policies, and processes that craft your site. *Your* governance helps you figure out how to apply all the best new SharePoint features you can read about in this book.

In this chapter, we show you ten things that influence how you think about your SharePoint governance.

Failure Is Not an Option (Neither Is Looking Away and Whistling)

One of Microsoft's key SharePoint product drivers was the goal to put more control and configuration in the hands of the users; SharePoint was designed to be The Platform of the People.

And people, as you've probably noticed, tend to be unpredictable. So SharePoint + Human Nature = Chaos. Sooner or later, an uncontrolled proliferation of sites and subsites, ways of doing things, ways of tagging and applying metadata, and ways of managing documents will produce a very unwieldy SharePoint installation indeed. Trying to identify and implement governance at that point can be an exercise in frustration.

This is a long way of saying that you'll have to address governance sooner or later. Take our advice: Make SharePoint governance a high priority and start now.

Getting Executive Buy-In and Support

Successful governance plans usually have a high-visibility advocate to support and communicate them. So find an executive to buy in. You won't have too hard a time making the case to leadership; they've already invested in a powerful SharePoint platform, and it's probably supporting functions that are crucial to the success of your organization. Line up executive support and enlist that support to drive the formation of and participation in governance committee activities.

Building an Effective Governance Group

The IT team commonly dominates governance committees; they have to manage server space, deal with security groups, and implement new functionality. These challenges provide ample motivation to formalize much of what the IT team does. But a governance committee comprised entirely or even largely of IT resources won't get you where you need to be.

We recommend that in addition to your executive sponsor, your governance group represent a diverse mix:

>> **Include representatives from the business.** The information workers who use SharePoint all the time often are in the best position to produce realistic governance policies and to identify governance gaps, too.

>> **Include representatives from any compliance areas.** They can advocate for governance that promotes adherence to regulations that affect your business.

>> **Recruit folks from corporate communications and training.** These people are well placed not only to address governance in areas such as branding but also can help craft a plan to publicize governance decisions and provide organizational change management to support those decisions.

Finding the Right Level

Don't try to identify and address everything that someone might do with SharePoint; provide guardrails to steer your users in the appropriate things to do or to avoid. Those things vary by organization; there's no magic list of what to address. (Larger organizations tend to need more governance than smaller organizations.)

Over time, your governance group will uncover areas that need governance, and this will be helped along if you already have a clear process in place to propose, evaluate, and implement governance when and where the need arises.

Yours, Mine, Ours: Deciding Who Owns What

Kick-start a governance effort by thinking about who: Who can do what? Who owns what? For example, you might start with identifying who can provision top-level sites and who can provision subsites. Or who should determine where certain types of documents belong. Or who decides what merits a new content type (and who owns the changes to it).

If you have global navigation, identify who decides what goes there. And so on. The who will suggest the how, so you can consider that next.

One of our favorite governance exercises is to project the home page on the screen for your governance group. Then ask who has the authority to update the page. Because the home page usually links to so many other pages, it naturally leads the discussion into other areas of the portal that need ownership.

(Re)Visiting Social Networking Policies

If you have a social media governance plan in place, it may have been developed to govern external social networking tools; if this is the case, you need to revisit it in the context of SharePoint.

When social media, such as instant messaging, started to become pervasive, a lot of companies responded by locking Internet access to those applications out of fear about what employees would say and how much time they'd waste using them. Likewise, Internet discussion boards and wikis were treated with suspicion, and all kinds of corporate rules and regulations rose around them, making a lot of corporate intranets more like schools. Over time, some companies evolved governance around when and how employees used external social networking on company time or using the company name. The goal was to keep everyone focused on documents and data and to minimize interpersonal exchanges.

Eventually, forward-thinking organizations recognized that actively facilitating informal interactions between individuals could benefit the organization by making the exchange of information more efficient, uncovering hidden pools of expertise, and (oh, by the way) recognizing that people are social creatures who need a certain degree of human contact to feel happy at work.

SharePoint integrates components of the social media used in the real world into the workplace. And the ability for employees not only to connect with their peers but also use a corporate-sanctioned tool (SharePoint) to follow coworkers' activities (via live feeds and Twitter-like microblogging status updates), exchange opinions with peers (via social tagging and ratings), and pool information (wikis) represents a significant change from external social media. So if you have a specific governance policy around social media, revisit it in the context of internal communications. You'll probably find that you need a whole new strategy.

Applying Consistent Design and Branding

Whether your SharePoint is an internal portal or a public-facing website, the interface should reflect your corporate image, present a certain level of design integrity, and provide users with a consistent navigation scheme that helps them find their way around.

Your governance plan should address look and feel and how things such as global navigation persist across your site. (To find out more about the look and feel capabilities of SharePoint, check out Chapter 18.)

Implementing Effective Content Management

Metadata, content types, and taxonomies (oh my!) can help reduce the plague of redundant-but-slightly-different information.

To leverage the content management of your SharePoint installation, encourage consistency around metadata and how things are tagged. Content types are a great way to ensure that a core set of tags are consistently applied to similar content, making the content easier to find, easier to reuse, and easier to filter. So identify key metadata that needs to be formalized via content types and applied across SharePoint sites, and then develop governance around them.

Reusing Web Parts

One great feature of SharePoint is the fact that someone can create a really useful Web Part and then export and import it for use somewhere else. Plenty of third-party Web Parts are available for download on the web. Unfortunately, some Web Parts contain malicious code that can pose security problems or just simply don't work as advertised. Likewise, even some internally developed Web Parts can present problems if they allow users to configure them. When you're ready to use a third-party Web Part, make sure you look at a reputable company with plenty of SharePoint expertise.

Web Parts need to be subjected to controls before they're added to your SharePoint sites. Develop governance around how they're tested and approved, what the change control process looks like, and how they're released and made available.

Keeping Things Current: Web Operations Management

Web Operations Management is the care and feeding of your SharePoint sites. You may find it's easy to think about SharePoint sites as projects with defined beginnings, middles, and ends. But in reality, they're more organic than that. Websites are like living entities, which grow and change over time. Like decorative hedges, they require pruning and maintenance or they get out of control pretty fast.

The more traffic your site sees, the more important it is to stay on top of that maintenance. Web Operations Managers wield the pruning shears that shape SharePoint to reflect the strategic vision and technical goals of the company while ensuring that things like verifying that links still work or identifying and deleting irrelevant or outdated content get done. You need to designate someone with a green thumb to prune and water your SharePoint site.

Chapter **27**

Ten Ways to Become a SharePoint Server Guru

As a SharePoint expert, you can add value to key SharePoint projects and your organization in general. By understanding the capabilities of SharePoint and understanding what is and isn't possible, you can steer a project and achieve efficiencies. By developing an encyclopedic knowledge of SharePoint, you avoid wasting the time of an army of people trying to figure out SharePoint for the first time. You will quickly become the go-to person for SharePoint in your organization. And because SharePoint is central to most processes, you will by default become a valuable asset. Don't believe us? Just put your resume up on a job board after you're a SharePoint expert and see how many organizations come calling.

In this chapter, we share with you some of the resources and approaches we've used to master SharePoint. Even if your goal isn't mastery, these suggestions help you get up to speed and become a SharePoint expert in no time.

Getting Information from the Horse's Mouth

If you use SharePoint, chances are you have used Microsoft's websites. In fact, you probably spend a lot of time on the support.office.com site because it comes up at the top of most search results.

If you're an IT professional, chances are you've used Microsoft's TechNet site, which is dedicated to the technical aspects of its products. On TechNet, you find technical libraries and administrator guides for IT administrators for SharePoint (and every other Microsoft product). The library includes loads of information on planning and deploying your SharePoint implementation. You also find dozens of worksheets you can use to assist in your planning. You can use TechNet to find all sorts of salient information.

Microsoft's site dedicated to developers — the Microsoft Developer Network (MSDN) — features portals showcasing development-related articles and resources. You can find a Developer Center for SharePoint along with all the other Microsoft products. The home page for MSDN is http://msdn.microsoft.com. You can find the SharePoint Developer Center at http://msdn.microsoft.com/en-us/sharepoint/dev.

TIP

Be sure to check out the latest edition of *MSDN Magazine,* the Microsoft Journal for Developers, while you're on MSDN. You'll find lots of detailed articles explaining how stuff works. Access *MSDN Magazine* at http://msdn.microsoft.com/en-us/magazine.

Software development kits (SDKs) are excellent resources for finding out how to develop custom SharePoint applications. Even if you never plan on writing one line of code, SDKs provide extensive documentation on product architecture. If you want to get your mind around what makes SharePoint work, poke your head into the SDK.

You can access the SharePoint SDKs online via the Developer Centers on MSDN. You can also find links that download the SDKs on the MSDN Developer Centers. When you download an SDK, it usually includes sample applications to demonstrate developer opportunities. The SharePoint Developer Center is located at https://docs.microsoft.com/en-us/sharepoint/dev.

One of the best resources for accessing end-user documentation is Office Online. You'll find walkthroughs of all sorts of tasks and resources for use with SharePoint clients and servers. You can find Office Online at https://office.

`microsoft.com/sharepoint`. Click the Solutions tab to see a list of all the products you can peruse on the site.

You can also find discussion groups for all the products in the Office suite, including SharePoint, at `https://techcommunity.microsoft.com/t5/SharePoint/ct-p/SharePoint`.

The Microsoft Download Center is an excellent resource for finding all sorts of downloads. By conducting an advanced search, you can choose SharePoint from a list of products to see all relevant downloads. Sort by release date to see the most recent downloads first. Visit the Download Center at `www.microsoft.com/downloads`.

TIP

Any time you download a file from Microsoft's website, be sure to scroll to the bottom of the page to see a list of related downloads.

Reading SharePoint Blogs

Now that SharePoint has been around for a while, you can easily find lots of good resources online. Plenty of websites are dedicated to SharePoint. And the blogosphere is chock-full of people blogging about SharePoint. Generally speaking, most of what you find about previous versions of SharePoint still applies to SharePoint. However, we recommend avoiding content related to SharePoint 2003, 2007, 2010, and 2013. Most content for SharePoint Server 2016 is still relevant for SharePoint Server.

Microsoft encourages its product teams and employees to blog about the products they're working on. These blogs give you an insider's track on announcements and tutorials that you can't get anywhere else:

>> **SharePoint Team Blog:** This is the official blog of Microsoft's SharePoint Product Group. You can find SharePoint-related announcements at `https://blogs.office.com/sharepoint`.

>> **Microsoft Cloud Blog:** Read everything you ever wanted to know about Office 365, including SharePoint Online, at `www.microsoft.com/en-us/microsoft-365/blog`.

Finding Local User Groups

Most major cities have a user group (or two) dedicated to SharePoint. If your city or town doesn't, look for a .NET or Windows group and ask about SharePoint. User groups are a great place to connect with other SharePoint junkies (or newbies). Groups in larger towns often have SharePoint celebrities visit from time to time.

Many user groups also have an online presence. If you can't find a group in your immediate area, go online and find the one closest to you. These groups often use SharePoint and post articles and content from their meetings. Maybe they'd be willing to use Skype so you can connect online.

We also recommend keeping an eye on the Microsoft Events and Webcasts page (www.microsoft.com/events). You might find an event in your area or one worth traveling to.

Building a Virtual Lab

Sometimes, you just need a place to play. That's the role of a virtual lab. (And not the role of your personal My Site, we might add.) Running a virtual lab is easier than you think.

TIP

Another option is to set up a Site Collection in your Office 365 tenant that you use as a playground. Then you can log into the site from anywhere and work with SharePoint. This is great for end users learning SharePoint and exploring SharePoint Online. If you are looking to learn more about SharePoint On-Premises, then you can leverage some of the other options we outline in this section.

In the old days, you had to use dedicated hardware to run a lab. Now, you can use software in a virtual machine — a kind of machine inside a machine. We use a dedicated server to host lots of virtual machines, but we also run virtual machines on our laptops all the time.

Popular virtualization platforms include Microsoft's Hyper-V, VMWare's Workstation, and Oracle's VirtualBox. If you use virtual machines on your own hardware, it takes some time to get up to speed.

If you want to have a company host your virtual machine in the cloud, you can check out Microsoft's Azure services and Amazon's Web Services. Lately, we have been using the Azure service and have been very happy.

You don't even have to build your own virtual machine. Microsoft has made available a prebuilt virtual machine in Azure so all you have to do to create a new virtual machine is log into Azure and choose the SharePoint Server template.

This has really saved strain on our backs because we no longer have to lug around a beefy laptop with all our virtual machines stored on external drives. We carry a light laptop and connect to our virtual machines (hosted in Azure) over the Internet.

Starting with a Good Foundation

If you really want to master SharePoint, you need a good foundation. SharePoint is built on the .NET Framework, which is a good starting place, but it also helps to know these skills:

>> Web developer skills, such as XHTML, CSS, and JavaScript for creating visually interesting user experiences

>> XML, XSLT, and XPath for manipulating content into the format you need to drive great user experiences

>> ASP.NET for understanding how to get the most out of the SharePoint toolkit

>> HTML and .NET development for creating next-generation visual presentation of content and building desktop SharePoint applications

Depending on what you're trying to master in SharePoint, you may need other domain-specific foundations.

Borrowing from Others

The code-sharing site GitHub is a great place to find utilities and add-ons that help you get the most out of SharePoint. Not only can you find useful tools, but you can also download the source code. Even if you aren't a coder, sometimes just reading through the help text and the code can give you insights as to how things work in SharePoint.

You can find GitHub at `https://github.com` and a SharePoint specific repository at `https://github.com/SharePoint`.

Getting Certified

Microsoft offers certifications for their products. You can find specifics at

`www.microsoft.com/en-us/learning`

Pursuing certification is a great way to really dig into any technology; it forces you to get familiar with all the dark corners of the software that you might otherwise ignore.

Taking a Peek under the Covers

One way to really get acquainted with SharePoint is to review the source of the web pages rendered by SharePoint. We like to use Chrome and Firefox because they both color-code the text. You can look at different kinds of pages — publishing pages and Web Part pages — to see the differences. Or you can create a new Web Part page using SharePoint Designer 2013 and then review the code after you methodically add and remove things from the page. Watching the source code change in the browser, you start to see the naming conventions and figure out how things work.

We also like to use a tool such as the Firefox Developer Tools to view the hierarchical structure of the page. This tool gives you lots of good information about whatever site you're viewing.

Digging Deeper under the Covers

When we're trying to figure out how to do something in SharePoint, we always ask: How did the Microsoft developers do it? All the site templates, pages, and Web Parts that come with SharePoint can be reviewed to see how they're implemented.

All these elements are stored in the Hive, which is located at `C:\Program Files\ Common Files\microsoft shared\Web Server Extensions\<version number>`. Most of what you want to review is in the Templates folder. This is where you find everything from the Publishing Portal template to the templates used to display menus on the web page.

WARNING

This is a look-but-don't-touch exercise. Don't change these files because they're used by the system. If you want to open them and check them out, make sure to copy them to a location such as your desktop or Documents folder. Never edit the files SharePoint is actually using.

Deconstructing a SharePoint Site

Visual Studio also provides some great new tools for deconstructing SharePoint sites. With Visual Studio, you can explore a site and copy items, such as columns and content types, for reuse. One of our favorite features is the ability to import a site template into Visual Studio. That means you can create a site with the browser, save it as a site template, and then import the template into Visual Studio. Then you can see the underlying XML that SharePoint uses to define the site.

Index

A

accessing
  administrative access, 314
  administrator's Recycle Bin, 209–211
  app settings, 160–163
  SharePoint, 28
  SharePoint files in Microsoft Teams, 116–118
  SharePoint SDKs, 404
  SharePoint sites in Microsoft 365, 61–64
activity feeds, 102–103
Ad Hoc views, 226–227
Add a Document dialog box, 212
Add Column button, 106
Add Link dialog box, 298
Add Promoted Result dialog box, 369
Add Result Block dialog box, 369–370
adding
  apps to Quick Launch, 289
  apps to your site, 159–160
  columns to apps, 177–184
  content to SharePoint, 101–111
  documents to OneDrive, 196–197
  links to Quick Links, 291–293
  pages to wikis, 146–147
  Search Center sites, 373–376
  SharePoint pages/lists to Microsoft Teams, 119–121
  tags to Wiki pages, 98
  users to groups, 315–316
  Web Parts to pages, 85–89
Adding Custom List dialog box, 177
Adding Survey dialog box, 159
adjusting
  Advanced settings, 169–171
  description, 164
  look and feel, 280–285
  navigation, 164
  site icons, 280–285
  Team Site navigation, 288–293
  title, 164

  Versioning settings, 165–166
  views, 229
  Web Part properties, 92–95
administration, 268–269
administrative access, managing, 314
Advanced (Web Parts), 93
advanced settings, 167–171
AI Builder link (Power Apps), 255
AI Builder option, 236
AJAX Options (Web Parts), 93
Alert Me button, 139
alerts
  on approval/rejection status, 346
  managing, 142–143
Amazon's Web Services, 406
analyzing form data, 247–248
AND operator, 363
Android, installing SharePoint Mobile App on, 50–51
anonymous visitor, as SharePoint user, 16
Appearance (Web Parts), 93
applying
  Advanced settings, 169–171
  versioning settings, 165–166
approvers, 317, 343
apps (applications)
  about, 39–40, 157–158
  accessing settings, 160–163
  adding columns to, 177–184
  adding to Quick Launch, 289
  adding to your site, 159–160
  assigning permissions to, 313
  configuring General Settings, 163–173
  creating permissions for, 321–323
  custom, creating, 175–192
  discussion board, 149–150
  downloading from SharePoint Store, 191–192
  editing data with Quick Edit, 223–224
  filtering with views, 221–222
  importing spreadsheets as, 186–188
  managing data in Datasheet view, 225–226

S

About the Authors

Rosemarie Withee is president of Portal Integrators (www.portalintegrators.com) and founder of Scrum Now (www.scrumnow.com) in Seattle, Washington. Portal Integrators is a Scrum-based software and services firm. She is the lead author of *Office 365 For Dummies* and *Microsoft SharePoint For Dummies*.

Rosemarie earned a Master of Science degree in Economics at San Francisco State University and an Executive Master of Business Administration degree at Smartly. In addition, Rosemarie also studied Marketing at UC Berkeley-Extension and holds a Bachelor of Arts degree in Economics and a Bachelor of Science degree in Marketing from De La Salle University, Philippines.

Ken Withee is the author and coauthor of several books on Microsoft technologies and currently writes articles on Azure for Microsoft. He earned a Master of Science degree in Computer Science at San Francisco State University and is currently completing a Master of Science degree in Computer Science at the University of Washington.

Dedication

We would like to dedicate this book to our families both in the Philippines and here in the United States, and especially to our nephews and niece, Lucas, Miguel, and Victoria.

Authors' Acknowledgments

We would like to acknowledge our families in both the United States and Philippines. An extraordinary amount of special thanks to Steven Hayes, Kelsey Baird, Kristie Pyles, Katharine Dvorak, Guy Hart-Davis, and the rest of the For Dummies team for providing more support than we ever thought possible. It is truly amazing how much work goes into creating a single book.

Publisher's Acknowledgments

Acquisitions Editor: Kelsey Baird

Project Editor: Katharine Dvorak

Technical Editor: Guy Hart-Davis

Production Editor: Tamilmani Varadharaj

Cover Image: © Joe Techapanupreeda/ Shutterstock

Dummies is the global leader in the reference category and one of the most trusted and highly regarded brands in the world. No longer just focused on books, customers now have access to the dummies content they need in the format they want. Together we'll craft a solution that engages your customers, stands out from the competition, and helps you meet your goals.

Advertising & Sponsorships

Connect with an engaged audience on a powerful multimedia site, and position your message alongside expert how-to content. Dummies.com is a one-stop shop for free, online information and know-how curated by a team of experts.

- Targeted ads
- Video
- Email Marketing

- Microsites
- Sweepstakes sponsorship

20 MILLION PAGE VIEWS EVERY SINGLE MONTH

15 MILLION UNIQUE VISITORS PER MONTH

43% OF ALL VISITORS ACCESS THE SITE VIA THEIR MOBILE DEVICES

700,000 NEWSLETTER SUBSCRIPTIONS TO THE INBOXES OF

300,000 UNIQUE INDIVIDUALS EVERY WEEK

PERSONAL ENRICHMENT

 **Staying Sharp**
9781119187790
USA $26.00
CAN $31.99
UK £19.99

 **Facebook**
9781119179030
USA $21.99
CAN $25.99
UK £16.99

 **Guitar**
9781119293354
USA $24.99
CAN $29.99
UK £17.99

 **Investing**
9781119293347
USA $22.99
CAN $27.99
UK £16.99

 **Beekeeping**
9781119310068
USA $22.99
CAN $27.99
UK £16.99

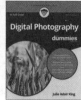 **Digital Photography**
9781119235606
USA $24.99
CAN $29.99
UK £17.99

 **Meditation**
9781119251163
USA $24.99
CAN $29.99
UK £17.99

 **Pregnancy**
9781119235491
USA $26.99
CAN $31.99
UK £19.99

 **Samsung Galaxy S7**
9781119279952
USA $24.99
CAN $29.99
UK £17.99

 **iPhone**
9781119283133
USA $24.99
CAN $29.99
UK £17.99

 **Crocheting**
9781119287117
USA $24.99
CAN $29.99
UK £16.99

 **Nutrition**
9781119130246
USA $22.99
CAN $27.99
UK £16.99

PROFESSIONAL DEVELOPMENT

 **Windows 10**
9781119311041
USA $24.99
CAN $29.99
UK £17.99

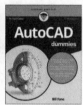 **AutoCAD**
9781119255796
USA $39.99
CAN $47.99
UK £27.99

 **Excel 2016**
9781119293439
USA $26.99
CAN $31.99
UK £19.99

 **QuickBooks 2017**
9781119281467
USA $26.99
CAN $31.99
UK £19.99

 macOS Sierra
9781119280651
USA $29.99
CAN $35.99
UK £21.99

 **LinkedIn**
9781119251132
USA $24.99
CAN $29.99
UK £17.99

 **Windows 10 All-in-One**
9781119310563
USA $34.00
CAN $41.99
UK £24.99

 **SharePoint 2016**
9781119181705
USA $29.99
CAN $35.99
UK £21.99

 **Fundamental Analysis**
9781119263593
USA $26.99
CAN $31.99
UK £19.99

 **Networking**
9781119257769
USA $29.99
CAN $35.99
UK £21.99

 Office 2016
9781119293477
USA $26.99
CAN $31.99
UK £19.99

 Office 365
9781119265313
USA $24.99
CAN $29.99
UK £17.99

 Salesforce.com
9781119239314
USA $29.99
CAN $35.99
UK £21.99

 **Coding**
9781119293323
USA $29.99
CAN $35.99
UK £21.99

dummies.com

dummies®
A Wiley Brand

Learning Made Easy

ACADEMIC

9781119293576
USA $19.99
CAN $23.99
UK £15.99

9781119293637
USA $19.99
CAN $23.99
UK £15.99

9781119293491
USA $19.99
CAN $23.99
UK £15.99

9781119293460
USA $19.99
CAN $23.99
UK £15.99

9781119293590
USA $19.99
CAN $23.99
UK £15.99

9781119215844
USA $26.99
CAN $31.99
UK £19.99

9781119293378
USA $22.99
CAN $27.99
UK £16.99

9781119293521
USA $19.99
CAN $23.99
UK £15.99

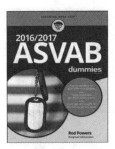

9781119239178
USA $18.99
CAN $22.99
UK £14.99

9781119263883
USA $26.99
CAN $31.99
UK £19.99

Available Everywhere Books Are Sold

Small books for big imaginations

GETTING STARTED WITH **Coding**
Get Creative with Code!
Camille McCue, PhD

9781119177173
USA $9.99
CAN $9.99
UK £8.99

MODDING **Minecraft™**
Build Your Own Minecraft Mods!
Sarah Guthals, PhD
Stephen Foster, PhD
Lindsey Handley, PhD

9781119177272
USA $9.99
CAN $9.99
UK £8.99

MAKING **YouTube** VIDEOS
Star in Your Own Video!
Nick Willoughby

9781119177241
USA $9.99
CAN $9.99
UK £8.99

DESIGNING **Digital Games**
Create Games with Scratch™!
Derek Breen

9781119177210
USA $9.99
CAN $9.99
UK £8.99

GETTING STARTED WITH **Raspberry Pi™**
Program Your Raspberry Pi!
Richard Wentk

9781119262657
USA $9.99
CAN $9.99
UK £6.99

EXPERIMENTING WITH **Science**
Think, Test, and Learn!
Chris J. Mullins, PhD

9781119291336
USA $9.99
CAN $9.99
UK £6.99

CREATING **Digital Animations**
Animate Stories with Scratch™!
Derek Breen

9781119233527
USA $9.99
CAN $9.99
UK £6.99

GETTING STARTED WITH **Engineering**
Think Like an Engineer!
Camille McCue, PhD

9781119291220
USA $9.99
CAN $9.99
UK £6.99

WRITING **Computer Code**
Learn the Language of Computers!
Chris Minnick and Eva Holland

9781119177302
USA $9.99
CAN $9.99
UK £8.99

Unleash Their Creativity

dummies.com

dummies®
A Wiley Brand